Jung and Spinoza

This volume presents the first major study of C.G. Jung's curious relationship with the philosophy of Baruch Spinoza.

Although Jung scarcely mentions Spinoza in his work, there is an unmistakable accord between the core ideas of both thinkers, most notably regarding Spinoza's theory of God and the monism found in Jung's writings. Exploring why Jung shows ambivalence toward Spinoza despite their affinity, Robert H. Langan argues that Spinoza offers Jung a radical solution to problems in his psychology. What results is a new interpretation of Jung's metaphysics, the evidence for which has gone unheeded in Jungian studies to date. Ultimately for both Jung and Spinoza, knowledge of the self leads to knowledge of the Divine, and it is this championing of a 'transcendental immanence' that makes Jung an unlikely yet consummate Spinozist.

Jung and *Spinoza* will be of interest to continental philosophers and depth psychologists who wish to bridge their respective fields, as well as general audiences curious about the ideas of both thinkers.

Robert H. Langan holds a doctorate in Psychoanalytic Studies from the University of Essex. A scholar of Jung and Spinoza, he also specializes in speculative metaphysics and psychological types. He lives in southern New Jersey.

PHILOSOPHY & PSYCHOANALYSIS BOOK SERIES
JON MILLS
Series Editor

Philosophy & Psychoanalysis is dedicated to current developments and cutting-edge research in the philosophical sciences, phenomenology, hermeneutics, existentialism, logic, semiotics, cultural studies, social criticism, and the humanities that engage and enrich psychoanalytic thought through philosophical rigor. With the philosophical turn in psychoanalysis comes a new era of theoretical research that revisits past paradigms while invigorating new approaches to theoretical, historical, contemporary, and applied psychoanalysis. No subject or discipline is immune from psychoanalytic reflection within a philosophical context including psychology, sociology, anthropology, politics, the arts, religion, science, culture, physics, and the nature of morality. Philosophical approaches to psychoanalysis may stimulate new areas of knowledge that have conceptual and applied value beyond the consulting room reflective of greater society at large. In the spirit of pluralism, *Philosophy & Psychoanalysis* is open to any theoretical school in philosophy and psychoanalysis that offers novel, scholarly, and important insights in the way we come to understand our world.

Titles in this series:

Jung and Spinoza

Passage Through the Blessed Self

Robert H. Langan

 Routledge
Taylor & Francis Group

LONDON AND NEW YORK

Designed cover image: Getty Images

First published 2025
by Routledge
4 Park Square, Milton Park, Abingdon, Oxon OX14 4RN

and by Routledge
605 Third Avenue, New York, NY 10158

Routledge is an imprint of the Taylor and Francis Group, an informa business

© 2025 Robert H. Langan

The right of Robert H. Langan to be identified as author of this work has been asserted in accordance with sections 77 and 78 of the Copyright, Designs and Patents Act 1988.

British Library Cataloguing-in-Publication Data
A catalogue record for this book is available from the British Library

ISBN: 978-1-032-85186-0 (hbk)
ISBN: 978-1-032-85185-3 (pbk)
ISBN: 978-1-003-51699-6 (ebk)

DOI: 10.4324/9781003516996

Typeset in Times New Roman
by Newgen Publishing UK

In memory of
Robert Harrison Langan III
(1944–2024)

Contents

Acknowledgments

This book is based on the thesis I submitted for my PhD. I am indebted to my former supervisor, Professor Roderick Main, who demonstrated inexplicable patience and trust over ten years as I went from being a student to no longer being a student to again being a student. Roderick provided me with the latitude to get this project done in my own way and in my own time, a leap of faith on his part that I had no right to expect, nor do I believe is commonplace in the academy. Furthermore, his editorial suggestions made my prose more comprehensible, and his thoughtful questions about my work were something of a compass, gently prodding me to acknowledge where I had left the flank of my argument open to attack or where improvements could be made. Calmly and steadfastly, Roderick pushed my writing to a level it would not have reached otherwise.

Many thanks to Dr. Bobby Emmons and Dr. Allen Woll, who ran the Honors College at Rutgers University-Camden when I attended as an undergrad many years ago. My academic career has always been circuitous—I certainly did not end up studying what I first thought I would study, nor did I feel (and still don't!) that I truly belong. The Honors College was something of an oasis within the uncompromising obstacle course of being a student, most notably for seminar-style courses where one had access to experts in all sorts of interesting fields. Among those seminars I took was one on the philosophy of mind and body by Dr. Charles Jarrett. Not only did this class first pique my interest in philosophy, but Dr. Jarrett was also a scholar of Spinoza, and this is how I was first introduced to Spinoza's ideas. For the first time, I found a subject that seemed to transcend and connect all my disparate interests. Without the Honors College, I am not sure I would find Spinoza, and without Spinoza, I have trouble imagining who I'd even be at this point.

Of course, Spinoza is just one of the two figures mentioned in this book's title. The other is Carl Jung. I have my father to thank for my discovery of Jung. A businessman with a passion for organizational psychology, my father's office shelves were crammed with books about gestalt psychology, emotional intelligence, and the words of Wayne Dyer. Often when I was looking for something to read I would peruse his library, and among the books I 'borrowed' was *Psychological Types*. While most of that text was frankly inscrutable to me, the definitions in the back are what first introduced me to Jung's key ideas. My journey down the rabbit hole began in my father's study.

While I've had some great teachers and have attended invaluable classes in my years at university, it always seems that the people I chat with after the bell rings, so to speak, matter the most and have the greatest impact upon me. That is certainly true at University of Essex, where I met many people who changed my life forever, but none more than Christian McMillan. It was Christian who took my fledgling interest in philosophy and made it a devotion, who introduced me to the works of Deleuze and others, who demonstrated to me not just what philosophy is but rather what it can do. Those countless hours we spent talking after class, either at the SU Bar or in the bowels of square four, invariably with pints in hand, are some of the fondest memories of my life. Christian also has the distinction of telling me one of the most important things I ever needed to hear, which happened after I had given a presentation at a conference. I felt I had bombed. As I stood there beating myself up, Christian said to me, not unkindly but in a way that quickly made me get over myself: "It's *supposed* to be hard."

One of the themes of this book is that one is never really alone—one's understanding of things is a reflection of their relationships with others and the world at large. I am fortunate then to have enjoyed such a cadre of loyal and caring friends devoted to similar or parallel causes. Besides Christian, I must mention Tom, Henry, and Mike, all who have, in different but equally invaluable ways, listened to, encouraged, and supported my writing and research for many years. Thanks also to Hector for being there the entire way (and, for a time, literally at uni!).

Also thanks to Russ, for his enthusiasm and support, and Rob, who helped furbish the illustrations used in Chapter 4.

Thanks to my older brother, Nick, for showing by example that a university career could, in fact, be extremely rewarding. Love to our dog, Judith, for being a most welcome distraction during the most unpleasant bouts of writing. Finally, thanks most of all to my parents. Far more important than that fateful discovery of *Psychological Types* on my father's bookshelf, I owe him for much of my intellectual curiosity to begin with. Any interest of mine, no matter how seemingly ephemeral (and, certainly by any conventional standard, impractical) was always fiercely encouraged and supported (even when my choices surely seemed baffling to my mother and him). For my mother, I am indebted for having inherited from her the preference of communicating through written word, and for having the twin gift and burden of only feeling accomplished when something is, at last, put to page.

Robert H. Langan

September 2024

Abbreviations

The following abbreviations are used for the work of Spinoza that appears in this text:

CM   Metaphysical Thoughts, an appendix to 'Principles of Philosophy'

E   *Ethics*

PP   *Descartes'* Principles of Philosophy

TIE   Treatise on the Emendation of the Intellect

TP   Political Treatise

TTP Theological–Political Treatise

All references to Spinoza's writings follow the precedent established by Spinoza scholar Edwin Curley in his two volumes of The Collected Works of Spinoza (CWS). These are also the editions of Spinoza's texts used for citations in this text. Citations of the CWS can be read as such: first, an abbreviation of Spinoza's text being cited is given, and then the location within that text. Then, the actual page number within Curley's CWS is also provided. Endnotes will explain further details when texts are first introduced, or when otherwise deemed necessary.

A Note About the Ethics:
The *Ethics* consists of five parts, I–V, and each part is broken down into an array of geometrical propositions: axioms (A) and definitions (D) typically are the starting points for each part, followed by propositions (P) that build on what has been established so far. The propositions contain demonstrations of the point Spinoza is trying to make, and the propositions often

feature supplemental arguments called corollary (C) and scholia (S) that Spinoza uses to bolster and clarify his exposition. So, for instance, E ID6 refers to part I of the *Ethics*, definition 6; whereas IIP1–2 refers to the first two propositions of part II. Spinoza at times uses other terms as well; these will be called out in the text when necessary.

Introduction

Writing this book did not always seem to be in my destiny. After completing my Masters in Jungian and Post-Jungian Studies in 2012 at the University of Essex, I commenced my doctorate at the same institution. Following a series of fits and starts where I shuttled back and forth between campus in Colchester, UK, and my home in southern New Jersey—a sort of transatlantic procrastination—I dropped out of school in 2014. I intended to never return.

I had multiple reasons for quitting, all of which seemed perfectly rational to me. One, I was leery of the money I had to spend to continue studying abroad. Second, I was determined to prioritize an independent career in writing, and had convinced myself that a more traditional route in higher education would somehow endanger or taint that goal. Third, I was skeptical that I was really suited for university life anyway—so, frankly, why bother?

In hindsight all those reasons don't seem as implacable to me as I once thought, or pretended, they were. In truth there was a fourth reason I dropped out of school, one I was loath to admit, even to myself: I was afraid. I was afraid because I did not believe I had what it took to write a text that I would be proud to put my name on—much less one that would be any good. In fairness to myself, I think that evaluation was, at the time, correct.

Why, after so many years, I decided to go back and finish the thesis that ultimately became this book is fittingly (and conveniently) inseparable from my topic of research: the curious relationship between the Swiss psychiatrist C.G. Jung (1875–1961) and the ideas of the seventeenth-century Dutch philosopher Baruch Spinoza (1632–1677). This is a problem that has long interested me, but the more I investigated it, the more I found it insurmountable—or at the very least, I feared I was poorly equipped to

DOI: 10.4324/9781003516996-1

tackle it. Hence my exodus from the academy. Yet it seems inevitable now that my departure would prove to be only temporary. One of the key ideas of this text, and something that I argue Jung and Spinoza strongly agree with, is that within falsehood there is always a kernel of truth to be discovered; moreover our knowledge is entirely inseparable from our emotions— or more properly, from our *affects*. Because of this, within diminishing emotions such as fear or worry, or what Spinoza calls the passions, one can uncover a powerful kind of happiness, an active joy that transforms and subsumes the original sorrow. And this active joy *must* be coupled with a better understanding of something.

This is all merely to say, in a bit of authorial meta-analysis I find far too cute but also not at all inaccurate, that after a long delay I began at last to grasp the lineaments between Jung and Spinoza, and from then on the problem was, in fact, no longer unassailable—nor was it a cause for despair. It did, however, remain a daunting subject to write about. The following is my attempt at that.

Jung's (Implicit) Metaphysics

What draws people to Jung's work more than his willingness to restore meaning and sacredness to the world, his psychology's acknowledgment of the fundamental nature of reality and the Divine—in other words, his metaphysics? Such lofty considerations, the adamance that the psyche cannot be reduced to biological instinct alone, that the individual is also influenced by a spiritual, numinous pole that runs counter to the biological, instinctual pole, are what intellectually led to Jung's break with Sigmund Freud (1856–1939), and so helped discredit Jung within the academy via the oft-repeated canard that he was a 'mystic' (1963/1989, pp. 167–169). Yet Jung's aim to restore numinosity to the world, to undermine what he judged as the shallow rationalism that dominated the twentieth century and helped perpetuate both historical atrocities and cultural disaffection alike, never comes at the cost of practical psychotherapy. His desire to give equal valence between the realms of both matter and spirit demonstrates not just an aversion toward eliminative materialism but also a sensitivity against grandiose cosmogony. For those who seek refuge from scientific reductionism and religious orthodoxy alike, Jung offers a potential antidote, a sophisticated pathway for 'reenchantment' with the world (Main, 2022).

Yet anyone who, for these very reasons, chooses to study Jung seriously and in depth may be surprised to discover that there has been at times a reluctance to articulate the metaphysical underpinnings of his work. One may even be taken aback to discover that Jung labeled himself an empiricist, not a philosopher, and that he claimed to hold no metaphysical views whatsoever (1977, p. 419). This reticence to explore the philosophy behind Jung's psychology has been upheld by at least some of his followers. But as Jungian therapist and scholar Jon Mills notes, this choice has become untenable, not just because it robs us of the opportunity to enrich Jung's theories by engaging with them philosophically—but also because, quite plainly, Jung *did* take philosophical positions within his work (Mills, 2019). This is true whether Jung was consciously aware of it or not. In any event, the mission of his psychotherapy to explore the deeper and universal meaning behind personal, everyday life inevitably grapples with the deepest questions of philosophy, and of metaphysics in particular (ibid.; Nagy, 1991; Bishop, 2007, 2008; Colacicchi, 2021, Mills & Goodwyn, 2023). Ultimately, Jung's protestations that he was merely a positivist, or that he dared not cross the Kantian distinction between what we perceive and what really is, do not hold up upon close inspection of his writing (Main, 2007, pp. 32–36).

Consequently, Jungians and non-Jungians alike have begun to recognize not only Jung's implicit ontological commitments but also his contributions to our understanding of being and existence. For example, Jung's influence on the radical ontology of the French philosopher Gilles Deleuze (1925–1995) has been explored at length; conversely, a Deleuzian critique has highlighted ways in which a philosophical engagement with Jung's work can be better refined (Kerslake, 2007; McMillan, 2015). The philosopher Grant Maxwell places Jung among a lineage of philosophers that includes Deleuze, Henri Bergson (1859–1941), Friedrich Nietzsche (1844–1900), Friedrich Schelling (1775–1854), Georg W. F. Hegel (1770–1831), Gottfried Wilhelm Leibniz (1646–1716), and Spinoza, among others, all of whom were dedicated to the problem of the "opposed, incompatible, paradoxical, or otherwise incommensurable truths, modes of thought, values, judgments, inclinations and affects" that continually bombard our finite existence, and who find answers not in hidden, transcendent realms but rather on a plane of existence that is immanent to us, yet always exceeds us as well. This is what Maxwell calls "transcendental immanence" (2022, pp. 2, 34, 75, 182,

184). In Maxwell's account, it is Spinoza who introduces this notion of virtual potencies beyond an ever-receding horizon, a concept that Maxwell argues Jung applies to his theory of universal, dominant unconscious patterns, or archetypes, in his late works such as *Mysterium Coniunctionis* (2022, pp. 34–35, 182–184). No discussion of Jung's ontology can indeed exclude his mature writing, where he explicitly took his theories beyond the realm of psychology *proper* (Atmanspacher & Fach, 2013, p. 226; Maxwell, 2022, pp. 175–176). In *Mysterium Coniunctionis* Jung posits that the psyche and matter might be two aspects of one and the same world, or a *unus mundus* (CW. 14, 1963/1970, par. 766, 776–789). In his work on synchronicity, he argues that archetypes manifest not just as images in the psyche, but in corresponding occurrences in the outer world as well—an admission of 'potencies' that envelop both inner and outer and are indeed transcendental yet immanent to us (CW. 8, 1952/1969a).

One factor that forced Jung to work out the metaphysical implications of his ideas was his dialogue with the quantum physicist Wolfgang Pauli (1900–1958). In a correspondence that lasted from 1932 until 1958, Jung and Pauli sketched out the notion that Jungian archetypes are ordering factors of both psyche and matter, hence their role in synchronicity (Meier, 2001; Gieser, 2005; Lindorff, 2013). The speculation between these two thinkers remained largely exploratory and was mostly confined to their exchange of letters. This has changed in recent years, as a formal articulation of Jung's and Pauli's ideas has been explicated at length by the theoretical physicist and Jungian scholar Harald Atmanspacher. In his writing on what he calls the 'Pauli–Jung conjecture', Atmanspacher argues that Jung and Pauli cast mind and matter as complementary, 'epistemic' aspects that originate from an underlying, psychophysically neutral whole, a metaphysics known as *dual-aspect monism* (Atmanspacher & Kronz, 1999; Atmanspacher, 2012, 2018; Atmanspacher & Fach, 2013, 2014, 2019; Atmanspacher & Rickles, 2022). This approach rejects a strictly materialist explanation of existence, where everything can be reduced to components of matter, just as it runs counter to an idealist metaphysics where all that exists is a manifestation of the mind or ideas. Dual-aspect monism also differs from other types of monism, a neutral or what Atmasnpacher calls a 'compositional' monism, where how neutral components assemble determines whether they are 'mental' or 'physical'; rather, Atmanspacher describes dual-aspect monism as 'decompositional', where the underlying whole decomposes into mental and physical states, both of which correspond yet do not interact directly with the other, thus abolishing any causal link between mind and matter. It is our awareness that mind and matter are 'emanations' of a neutral middle that is heightened during synchronistic experiences, and it is the Jungian archetypes that are, indeed, organizing patterns that spring from that middle. The archetypes become tantamount to psychophysical laws, where they are universal patterns of the psyche on the one hand and the laws of nature on the other (Atmanspacher & Rickles, 2022, p. xi, Ch. 3).

A monist ontology is the direction that Pauli urged Jung to go in, and it is the pathway Jung himself opens up in his essay *On the Nature of the Psyche* when he describes the 'psychoid' spectrum of the archetypes, or where they are no longer strictly psychic (CW. 8, 1946/1969a, pars. 420, 439; Meier, 2001, pp. 80–81). Atmanspacher's work has paved this road further, allowing Jungian psychology to have a sophisticated relationship with problems in ontology.

Spinoza

In his treatment of the historical precursors to Pauli and Jung, Atmanspacher credits Spinoza as the originator, "role model" and "protagonist" of dual-aspect theories (Atmanspacher & Rickles, 2022, pp. 5, 8). On some level, Spinoza's monism can be seen as a counter to his philosophical predecessor, René Descartes (1596–1650), who argued for a dualism that casts mind and matter as truly separate entities that nonetheless causally affect one another. Spinoza rejects dualism as a solution to the mind–body problem; at the same time, Spinoza's explanation does not fall back to either strict materialism or idealism. Instead, Spinoza's monism "provides an elegant and robust sense in which mind and matter are related to" the same ontological unity (Atmanspacher & Fach, 2013, p. 219). It is this idea of an epistemological dualism bound to an ontological union that Jung and Pauli are indebted to Spinoza (Atmanspacher & Fach, 2019, p. 42).

If in a sense Jung's implicit metaphysics is what cost him credibility among orthodox academia, then the price that Spinoza would pay for his *explicit* philosophical beliefs would be far more severe. Exiled from the Sephardic Jewish community in 1600s Amsterdam for his 'wicked' views about the nature of both God and man, Spinoza allegedly survived an assassination attempt, would earn the ire of the conservative Calvinists who held great power in the Dutch Republic and worked to restore the kind of authoritarian government that he despised; he would be forced to either publish almost all of his work anonymously or to forego publication entirely until after his death in 1677. By then it was known that Spinoza had held dangerous, heretical views about God that defied religious orthodoxy and all traditional notions of salvation and life after death (Deleuze, 1970/ 1988, Ch. 1; Nadler, 1999/2018). Beyond his quarrels with the Cartesians or even the dogmatists of his day, Spinoza's driving motivation—at least when viewed from the history of philosophy—was to confront a problem he was uniquely placed within the history of thought to solve. The philosopher Clare Carlisle suggests that Spinoza's philosophy is the answer to a millennia-old question, one that was formally posed by Saint Anselm at the dawn of scholasticism: how does one conceive God philosophically (2021, pp. 71–78)? Yet at the same, Spinoza helped usher in the scientific revolution and unmooring of religion that followed him (Stewart, 2006). Crediting Spinoza with both a celebration of the Divine and a critical blow against religion's hegemony is not as contradictory as it first seems. In Spinoza's estimate, the modern age must not forfeit divinity's *immanence to the world* (Deleuze, 1968/1990, Ch. 11; Carlisle, 2021, pp. 60–61). Spinoza's version of God was meant to secure this immanence. This theory is given in his most famous work, the *Ethics*, which was released posthumously; and it is this definition of God from which the monism of Pauli and Jung draws inspiration.

In the *Ethics*, Spinoza explains that God is an absolutely infinite and eternal being, expressed by not just two, but in fact an infinity of attributes; however, the two attributes we humans know of, as they pertain to our own nature, are thought and extension (E ID6, CWS I, p. 409; IIP1–2, pp. 448–449). The attribute of thought pertains to all minds and ideas, ranging from the mind of God down to the human mind, or even just the idea of a particular thing, like of a book or a chair (E IP21–22, CWS I, pp. 429–430). Similarly, extension contains all material bodies, from the human body to the actual book or chair, and to the cosmos itself (E IIEP13L7, CWS I, pp. 461–462).[1] So all finite things are expressed by the attributes, which are also direct expressions of God. Thought and extension are equal expressions of God's power; neither can affect the other, but both are expressions of the same thing, or essence, whether that be God or finite things such as ourselves (E IIP7, CWS I, pp. 451–452). Thus at first glance it appears that Spinoza's theory of God, with its attributes of thought and extension, accords well with the Pauli–Jung conjecture's dual-aspect monism and the twin aspects of mind and matter.

The full implications of Spinoza's God, this infinite substance in which all finite things inhere, were debated, derided, and rediscovered in the centuries after his death. Many accused Spinoza of concocting a stark sort of pantheism where all individuals are swallowed up by a faceless substance. This was the worry stirred up in the pantheist controversy in the 1780s, when interest in Spinoza was rekindled during the dawn of German Idealism, and where it was alleged that the end result of Spinozism was to submerge all of existence into soulless mechanism (Förster, 2012). This would be the depiction of Spinoza devised and propagated by Hegel, a portrayal that would govern the conventional understanding of Spinoza well into the twentieth century (Peden, 2014, p. 82). As we shall see in Chapter 2, Jung himself appears to hold this negative view of Spinoza—at least, so it seems.

Throughout this entire time there was always an undercurrent of thinkers who contended that Spinoza was seeking far more nuance than the caricature of the One Substance gives him credit for. Other German Idealists and Romantics sought and found within Spinoza a space for vibrancy and holism which they sought as a buffer against the very same mechanism and reductionism that Spinoza was accused of; such writers who found sanctuary in Spinoza's philosophy include Johann Wolfgang von Goethe (1749—1832) and Schelling, whose influence on Jung is well-documented (Bishop, 2007, 2008). During and after the Second World War, French philosophers would turn to Spinoza to find resources to counter both phenomenology and Cartesian idealism, which they saw as severely deficient and intellectually culpable for the atrocities of the day (Peden, 2014). The Spinozists that followed from this era articulated with detail the parts of Spinoza's philosophy that are often ignored, yet no less important than his grand vision of the God: the life of finite individuals, or what Spinoza calls modes, and how they all inhere, interact, and affect one another upon the same Divine plane. As French philosopher Étienne Balibar writes, what Spinoza really seeks is a network of reciprocal compositions; the individual, society, the state, and planet all compounding one another within the same tapestry (2018/2020). The individual is guaranteed existence within this immanent plane, a plane that always exceeds the individual, and yet it is also that same excessiveness that compounds the individual, that makes them aware that they are 'moving within' the Divine. This is the 'transcendental immanence' that Maxwell refers to. The experience of this transcendental immanence is what Carlisle argues is the central aim of Spinoza's philosophy: to know of our very 'Being-in-God' (2021, Ch. 3).

The exact implications of what Spinoza means to 'move within' divinity will be explored throughout this text. For now it suffices to say that this view is crucial for what it means to be a Spinozist (Deleuze, 1970/1988, Ch. 6); Spinozism is the philosophical foundation for the transcendental immanence sought by Jung. Whether or not Jung recognizes this affinity is, of course, an entirely different matter.

Jung and Spinoza

Jung cites Spinoza by name just seven times throughout his *Collected Works* (CW. 20, 1979, pp. 630–631). In their correspondence, Jung or Pauli never reference Spinoza as a precursor to their ideas (Meier, 2001). Instead, they draw upon the work of Spinoza's contemporary, Leibniz, who describes existence as an ensemble of mental and physical monads that express the same comprehensible world. Jung goes out of his way to praise Leibniz when he surveys historical precursors to the theory of synchronicity (CW. 8, 1952/1969a, par. 837). Yet as Atmanspacher observes, Leibniz's monadology does not align as closely with Pauli and Jung's monism as Spinoza's God does (Atmanspacher & Rickles, 2022, Ch. 1, 3). In the scant references that Jung makes to Spinoza throughout his writing, there are none at all about a metaphysics that Jung might approve of. Instead, Spinoza is treated either as merely one of the myriad historical figures Jung deploys throughout his writing, with no ostensible significance; or, Spinoza is actually propped up as an enemy, an overt rationalist contrary to Jung's project (CW. 8, 1919/1969a, par. 276; CW. 9i, 1948/1969b, pars. 385, 390). In this latter take, Jung plays up the image of Spinoza's monism as a lifeless, faceless machine, an exemplar of abstract, 'heady' philosophy taken too far and therefore unable to account for the emotional, visceral nature of life. This is even though those German Idealists and Romantics that influenced Jung, such as Goethe, were in turn inspired by Spinoza, and found that vibrancy and mystery in Spinoza's philosophy which Jung appraises as absent.

Jung and Spinoza agree on more than just metaphysics. The Jungian scholar and therapist Joseph Cambray has analyzed each of Jung's scant references to Spinoza, and he points out that these passages illuminate how both thinkers have similar theories of how desire plays a huge role in behavior and even knowledge—for Jung, this is articulated in his account of psychic energy; for Spinoza, this is via his theory of affects (Cambray, 2014, p. 47).[2] This accordance has even been applied to the therapy room by

Jungian therapist and scholar Giles Clark, who devised a 'Neo-Spinozan' approach to his practice, particularly in elucidating relations between mind and body (2006). Elsewhere, Jung directly references Spinoza when defining the psychological function of intuition, drawing upon Spinoza's third kind of knowledge, the intellectual intuition (CW. 6, 1921/1971, par. 770). According to Spinoza, intuitive knowledge enables one to see things *sub specie aeternitatis*, or as they appear in eternity (E IIP44C2, CWS I, p. 481). As will be discussed in Chapter 3, the 'view of eternity' is a concept Jung associates numerous times with the archetypes.

Could this convergence be due simply to Jung being influenced by thinkers who were more receptive of Spinoza? This is what scholar Christopher Myers suggests, that since Jung was directly influenced by Freud and Nietzsche, and Freud and Nietzsche are two thinkers who held Spinoza in esteem, that any resemblance of Spinozism in Jung is probably best explained as a passive inheritance of ideas. If so, it is strange that this 'accidental' influence was so pervasive throughout all of Jung's thought that Myers concedes that Jung is closer ideologically to Spinoza than *either* Nietzsche or Freud (2015)!

There are two issues with the conclusion that Jung was passively influenced by Spinozism. First, as mentioned previously regarding *subspecie aeternitatis* and the archetypal, the subtlety with which Jung deploys Spinoza's concepts, whether explicitly or otherwise, suggests that Jung actually had more than a vague understanding of Spinoza's philosophy, that Jung's curious handling of Spinoza cannot be chalked up to him simply not 'getting' Spinoza. Second, sparse and ambivalent Jung's reception of Spinoza may be—but in many respects it is *anything* but passive. Cambray notices a clear trend in Jung's treatment of Spinoza: wherever Jung and Spinoza seem to converge upon an idea, moments where Jung *surely* could notice the resemblance of his ideas to Spinoza's, Jung instead chooses to rather confusedly and bizarrely denounce the Dutch philosopher. Cambray is left to conclude that Jung has some sort of unconscious block that prevents him from acknowledging the debt he owes Spinoza, that Jung, in effect, has a 'Spinoza complex'. What is the source of this complex? Cambray finds it interesting that just as Pauli was eager to distance himself from Albert Einstein, Jung sought to separate himself from Freud—and that both Freud and (especially) Einstein were influenced by Spinoza (2014, p. 49). This suggests, at best, that intellectual posturing is at play. At worst, it insinuates that Spinoza's Jewish heritage played into Jung's judgment.

Could Jung's 'Spinoza complex' be attributed to disappointing prejudice? Could it instead be a matter of theory, that perhaps the respective metaphysics of both thinkers are not so closely aligned after all (Langan, 2020)? Or is there a deeper cause that surpasses both these explanations?

Seeking Passage

Cambray posed the idea of Jung having a Spinoza complex around the same time I dropped out of school. It was not lost on me that Cambray's piece on Jung and Spinoza literally ends with him suggesting that *someone* ought to take on the task of exploring Jung's treatment of Spinoza in greater detail—and here I was, walking away from the opportunity to do just that! Yet during my unofficial sabbatical, I never really stopped reading Jung and Spinoza, as well as other thinkers who are intellectually adjacent to both men. I remained engaged enough with the literature that I was able to offer a possible explanation for Jung's curious reading of Spinoza, in a paper I presented at the *Holism: Possibilities and Problems* conference at the University of Essex in 2017, which was later published in a volume of the same name. Besides helping me realize I, in fact, missed university, that presentation also helped me consolidate the thoughts that had been simmering inside me for a while. I suggested that Jung's attitude toward Spinoza was not due to a personal issue but could instead be read purely as a matter of theory that it was worth scrutinizing whether or not Jung and Spinoza really believe in the same type of monism. To explain succinctly, I argued that the Jung–Pauli model risks tilting the scales in favor of the aspect of mind, at the expense of the aspect of matter, whereas Spinoza grants thought and extension parity. The result is that Jung's metaphysics, at least on the surface, has an introverted bias, where the inner world is given a metaphysical richness, while the outer world is diminished in comparison. This is a move that Spinoza, with his emphasis on transpersonal networks and *outbound connections*, simply rejects. Therefore, if Jung dismisses Spinoza, it might simply be because he and Spinoza are saying different things (2020).

In many ways that paper was a very belated explanation for why I abandoned this project. I felt there was a conceptual gulf between Jung and Spinoza that was not easily reconciled, that the introverted bias I perceived in Jungian thought was a roadblock to doing a Spinozist reading of Jung, and that it would be a mistake to simply highlight the ideas that Jung and Spinoza share without somehow addressing the differences as well. And clearly, I was not alone in thinking Jung's tendency to prioritize the inner was an issue. In contemporary Jungian literature there is a clear desire on the part of some scholars to 'even the score' between inner and outer. This is achieved by abolishing the metaphysical, and thus also the intrapsychic's exclusive access to it. For instance, Robin McCoy Brooks has proposed that the archetypal self's eternal qualities should be curtailed (2019). In a similar vein, Christian Roesler thinks that the archetypes should be best thought of as social constructs (2012, 2022). Certainly some Jungians of a cognitive science or phenomenological slant, like Jean Knox and Roger Brooke, have proposed jettisoning synchronicity as a relevant topic in Jungian studies (Knox, 2003; Brooke, 2015).

Hence another motive for going back to university and getting my doctorate: it seemed wrong to me to resolve difficulties in Jungian psychology by dispensing with the metaphysical underpinnings outright, and so I wanted to try and find a different way forward. Again, why is anyone drawn to Jung if not for the 'numinosity' of his thought, which in turn implicates the existence of his metaphysics? It seemed crucial to me to both address the potential issues in Jung's thought, while also preserving his implicit ontology. But this demand left me at the same impasse I had been at for some time: just as it felt dishonest to simply compare Jung and Spinoza's ideas in a vacuum, I was also not enthused about using Spinoza to simply point out where Jung goes wrong either. This was partly because such a critique, specifically the danger of the Jungian self potentially becoming a hermetically sealed whole, had already been performed with exacting and exhausting precision by my friend and colleague Christian McMillan, via Deleuze's philosophy (2015). I did not see what was to be gained by essentially restating the argument via a Spinozist lens.

But moreover I suppose I was a bit greedy—I wanted to excavate the concepts that Jung and Spinoza converge upon. These concepts are something of an obsession for me; my lasting interest in those ideas, whether inside or outside the university, is ultimately what led me back to this point. To put it in the most general terms for this introduction, the concepts shared by Spinoza and Jung are *God, affect,* and *destiny*, where God is the transcendental immanence that exceeds us yet constitutes us, and affect is the union of desire and knowledge; I will expand upon destiny later, but for now it suffices to say that it relates to the power of the individual. I believe these three ideas are, in a sense, at the core of Spinoza's philosophy; in my estimate, they also govern much of Jung's psychology as well; therefore, to tease these ideas out of Jung's thought is to give a Spinozist reading of Jung. This Spinozist reading is only possible, however, if the issue of intro-verted bias is dealt with—not by abolishing the metaphysical but rather by decoupling metaphysics from the inner world, so it can be experienced in the outer life as well. I came to realize that by thinking along with those concepts, or by thinking along with Jung and Spinoza, I would inevitably hit the points of disagreement between the two thinkers, and possibly eluci-date just why Jung treats Spinoza the way he does.

In his book on Bergson's philosophy, Deleuze writes that once one can correctly pose the problem, one has effectively solved it (1966/1988, pp. 29–30). That sentiment is all well and good, but it still remained for me to find the best way to *begin* a Spinozist reading of Jung. Until then, the issue seemed far from settled. But at this juncture, I was at least confident enough to email my former supervisor and gauge the prospects of picking up where I left off.

Charting the Passage

The main question of this text is whether or not Jung can be read as a Spinozist. If so, what implications does this have, not just for his meta-physics, but for his psychology as a whole? And why does Jung seemingly fail to recognize the connection that he and Spinoza share? My method-ology of 'thinking along' with Jung and Spinoza is lifted from the works of Deleuze, in particular his monographs of individual philosophers where he reconstructs their respective philosophies to tease out certain concepts, an approach later used by the philosopher Isabelle Stengers in her text *Thinking with Whitehead* (2011) and then adopted by Maxwell in his book *Integration and Difference* (2022).[3] Maxwell explains that this approach is not a history of philosophy, but instead "a kind of staging in a philosoph-ical theater, in which the theorists under consideration are playing out their problematic and variable relational drama, each enacting a distinct role in an often obscure and enigmatic narrative" (ibid., p. 2). In this case, the narrative concerns the Spinozist tendencies in Jung's thought—and Jung's strange reaction to those tendencies. By tracing the lines of thought where Jung and Spinoza meet, we will also inevitably encounter those moments where Jung dismisses Spinoza. For these encounters I also draw heavily upon *Hegel or Spinoza* by the French philosopher and Spinozist Pierre Macherey. Macherey retraces Hegel's reading of Spinoza to demonstrate that Hegel reads Spinoza deliberately and misleadingly so that he can defend his philosophy from elements of Spinozism that undermine it. In this retracing, Macherey discovers the 'points of tension' where the ideas of Spinoza and Hegel closely parallel, and consequently where Hegel is most likely to denounce Spinoza to protect his system. Thus, Macherey tells us something not just about the philosophies of Hegel and Spinoza but also about Hegel's motives as well (1979/2011). I use this same approach to analyze Jung's reading of Spinoza and conclude that Jung is similarly defending himself and his theories from what he sees as dangers within Spinoza's philosophy. Therefore the questions of "Can Jung be read as a Spinozist?" and "Why does Jung read Spinoza the way he does?" turn out to be interlinked; one cannot be answered sufficiently without addressing the other. Consequently, the six chapters of this book can be broken into two branches: Chapters 1, 5, and 6 articulate the metaphysics shared by Jung and Spinoza, and also explain how this ontology differs from contemporary versions of Jung's metaphysics in Jungian scholarship. Meanwhile, Chapters 2, 3, and 4 investigate Jung's reading of Spinoza, and are headlined as 'C.G. Jung, The Unlikely Spinozist'. Ultimately, I argue that Jung can indeed be read as a Spinozist, that in some respects he is even a quintessential Spinozist; yet at the same time, Jung greatly fears the Spinozist elements of his own thinking, because it undermines a cornerstone of his psychological theory, not to mention his own psyche: the sanctuary of the interior. To follow the Spinozist implications of Jung's thought is to also abolish the closed monad, to instead value the outer world as much as the inner. Yet I also find evidence that Jung on some level recognizes the necessity of this move, and in his work from the mid-1940s onward he makes concessions, however grudgingly and unwittingly, to a Spinozist viewpoint. Now as I alluded to earlier, this entire plan is moot if one does not know where to begin a Spinozist reading of Jung—or perhaps more precisely, where Jung *himself* articulates his own Spinozism. I believe I discovered such an instance in an exchange of letters between Jung and Pauli in 1953, and this correspondence acts as the set piece for Chapter 1. What Jung's discussion with Pauli demonstrates is that Jung, curiously, is not a dual-aspect monist after all: in addition to psyche and matter, Jung describes a *third* aspect of his monism. As he explains to Pauli, this lost aspect has been neglected over the centuries and confused with the psyche. Jung's distinction here effectively makes him a 'tripartite' monist, a maneuver that he gives ample justification for, both in the letters with Pauli and elsewhere in his writing. As it turns out, there is another figure in the history of thought who also explicates this tripartite setup, and who is similarly miscast as endorsing a traditional dual-aspect monism: *Spinoza*. Therefore, Jung's metaphysics is still something he inherited from Spinoza, but cast in a new light.

Yet as explained earlier, wherever Jung recognizes his proximity to Spinoza he seems to invariably criticize him, and it is no different with their parallel conceptions of God. Chapter 2 commences our analysis of Jung's duplicitous reading of Spinoza. This duplicity is most evident in 'The Phenomenology of the Spirit in Fairytales' (1948), where Jung denounces Spinoza's 'substance' as sterile and devoid of life—before arriving at a conception of the Divine that is quintessentially Spinozist. Despite Jung's attempts to distance himself from Spinoza, it becomes abundantly clear that they both see the world as inhering within God, that is, transcendental immanence. Is it possible that Jung thinks Spinoza's rendition of divinity is too abstract, that it is a kind of reified knowledge that fails to capture the vicissitudes of life in the way Jung's psychology calls for? Jung certainly sees philosophy at large as guilty of this charge. But it is *not* a crime he can accuse Spinoza of, because, like Jung, Spinoza sees our feelings as inseparable from our intellections. Some readers may wonder if Spinoza is indeed too 'rational' to be compatible with Jung. This is a notion I hope to dispel by conveying the dynamism in Spinoza's monism. Of course, the 'rationalist' canard is one that Jung ostensibly holds against Spinoza—but as I shall argue, this is really an excuse that Jung uses to gloss over the parts of Spinoza's philosophy that he identifies with yet also fears.

Chapter 3 explores how Spinoza's theory of knowledge and affectivity strongly aligns with Jung's theory of complexes and their archetypal cores. For both Jung and Spinoza, it is only when one confronts the affects that true knowledge of something is even possible—therefore, knowledge is always embodied. Their approaches to confronting affectivity show many similarities—yet here too we see Jung dismiss those agreements. It is true, however, that Jung prioritizes opposites and the symbolic in a way that Spinoza does not—for Jung, paradox is the language of his psychology and the only way one can discuss the unascertainable. Spinoza threatens to strip Jung of that language and force him to experience the metaphysical directly. This is a move that Jung finds dangerous, because it underscores Jung's fear about the psyche—*his* psyche—being subsumed by 'living spirit'. This is the chief reason, more than disappointing prejudice or a caricature of Spinoza's rationalism, why Jung treats Spinoza the way he does.

As explained by Jungian analyst and researcher Mark Saban (2019), Jung's usage of opposites is specifically meant to secure the sanctuary of the inner world. Of course, protecting the inner world comes at a cost, and is replete with drawbacks that even Jung seems to recognize. After demonstrating that Jung's predilection with paradox is, in fact, not so incompatible with Spinozist thought after all, Chapter 4 highlights Jung's introverted bias as the key difference between Spinoza and Jung. Yet if Jung maintains this primacy of the inward, his psychology in turn fails to address several key topics that he cannot ignore. Interpersonal relations, a necessary balance between ideal and material perspectives, and theorizing the archetypes as something that exist beyond the purely intrapsychic: Jung must choose between being able to explore these frontiers or to instead remain confined to interiority. The climax to this middle section of the book illustrates that Jung, despite all his reservations, surrenders *in part* to the Spinozist demands within his own psychological theory—hence the establishment of his tripartite monism and all the implications from it that follow. Hence Jung, the unlikely Spinozist.

Chapter 5 brings us back to this monism Jung and Spinoza jointly espouse; in particular, this chapter highlights how this monism differs from the Pauli–Jung conjecture as exposited by Harald Atmanspacher. While no doubt Atmanspacher's insights have been invaluable for setting the stage for a serious discussion of Jung's metaphysics, as well as giving Jung credence as a genuine contributor to the mind–body problem, the argument here is that his system risks conflating the psyche, that is, the individual subject, and all ideal things under the same category of 'the mind'—this conflation goes hand-in-hand with the inward bias mentioned earlier, and it is something that Jung and Spinoza both strongly caution against. Throughout this analysis, it is explored how best to think of key Jungian concepts—such as archetypes, synchronicity, and meaning—within this Spinozist framework. The intention here is to offer another way of looking at Jung's monism that complements the work done so far, while also enabling Jungians to avoid the pitfalls that arise when one confuses the ideal realm with the psyche proper.

Crucial to this tripartite monism is to conceive the psyche as a middle third between the ideal and material. Just what is the nature of this middle third? For Jung it is the self, which is realized through individuation; for Spinoza, it is what he calls essence, which is actualized through blessedness. Chapter 6 discusses what for the purposes of this introduction only I will call 'destiny'—at risk of offending both Jung and Spinoza, this term is something of a reification on my part, but it broadly describes what I argue individuation and blessedness get at: what does it mean to fulfill one's destiny? When I said at the start of this introduction that writing these words did not 'seem to be in my destiny', what exactly does that mean? Surely the answer, within a Spinozist framework, cannot be an idea one has of oneself, since so many of our ideas are inadequate; nor can it just be preprogrammed, biological wiring running its course. And similarly, for Jung, the self is something beyond both the ego and the body. The final chapter of this book explores what might be best thought of as 'the Blessed Self'; this is not a mere hybridization of analogous notions within Jungian psychology and Spinozist philosophy. Rather, this pursuit of the maximized realization of the individual is the ultimate rendezvous between Spinoza and Jung—and also the key goal within their respective systems of thought.

I must make a note about how Spinoza is deployed throughout this work. Spinoza's writing, the *Ethics* in particular, is famous (or perhaps notorious) for its labyrinth of propositions and demonstrations, what Henri Bergson described as being threatened by "an armored dreadnought" (1934). Yet within the margins Spinoza often offers easily digestible notes and digressions that illuminate his thinking; where he fails to do this, several centuries of Spinoza scholarship have tried to do the job. Throughout the text, I have done my best to explain key ideas in Spinoza's philosophy wherever we encounter them. I also have provided footnotes, wherever possible, highlighting debates and discussions within Spinozist scholarship.

Just as there are many different 'versions' of Jung, there are many different 'Spinozas'. For Spinozist scholar Steven Nadler, Spinoza is a secular champion who equates God with Nature in a very reductive sense—he is an atheist in all but name (2006, p. 119). For many of the German Romantics as well as artists and poets at large, Spinoza is an exemplar of esoteric spiritual belief—he is a "God-intoxicated man" (Förster and Melamed, 2012; Deleuze, 1970/1988, Ch. 6).[4] Clare Carlisle notes that the secularist label fails to do Spinoza's philosophy justice any better than if he were claimed, quite belatedly, by religious orthodoxy. Since the distinction between what is religious and what is secular rests on definitions that Spinoza himself deems obsolete, Carlisle decides to instead view Spinoza as practicing his own novel form of theology that radically differs from what came before and after (2021, pp. 2–3). That Spinozism represents something of a 'middle third' between physicalism and idealism, matter and spirit, and theology and science is a recurring theme throughout this text, and so I am certainly partial to this view. My version of Spinoza is influenced in significant part by literature originating from France and dating from the mid-twentieth century to modern day: thinkers such as Alexandre Matheron, Martial Gueroult, Deleuze, Macherey, Balibar, and Chantal Jaquet are prevalent throughout my citations. What originally drew me to these 'French Spinozists' is that the radical implications of Spinoza's thought are indeed recognized—but those implications are handled with the rigor and detail that Spinoza would undoubtedly demand. While all these scholars have their unique views and differing opinions, what one largely finds in this lineage of Spinoza studies is a premium on relations, a science of the affects, and a typology of finite individuals, or modes. In other words, how individuals move within the transcendental immanence of Spinoza's God is prioritized. Again, I have tried to offer contrasting points of view within the margins wherever possible.

Before I recede into the background and let this argument play out, I would like to risk one further personal note. One of the goals of this book was to get Jung 'out of his shell', so to speak, to abolish the hermetically sealed psyche. Spinoza was my pointman in this regard, and so I often imagined myself egging Spinoza on, to make him goad Jung further into opening up. Yet clearly this exercise could be turned around on myself. What good were all my ruminations about Jung's relationship to Spinoza if I never put them to paper? Does one even really understand one's own ideas unless one fully charts them, so that they may be viewed by the eyes of others? 'Destiny', for both Spinoza and Jung, is something never actualized unless it is truly lived—and life is an interaction with others. That is the only way the greatest kind of joy is achieved. And so perhaps my prime motive for completing this project was so that I held myself to that same standard, so that I too avoided the pitfalls of hermitude. Now that the argument has at last been put to page, I can only hope that I have done it justice.

Notes

1   L refers to 'Lemma', a term Spinoza used for a subset of points following the thirteenth proposition of Part II in the *Ethics*, where he explains a sort of physics regarding bodies and extension.
2   Gil Morejón illustrates how Spinoza was one of the early investigators of unconscious desires and affects (2022).
3   For examples of Deleuze's monographs, see *Nietzsche & Philosophy* (1962/ 1983), *Bergsonism* (1966/1991), and *Expressionism in Philosophy: Spinoza* (1968/1990), among others.
4   The description of Spinoza as a 'God-intoxicated man' is attributed to the German Romantic poet Novalis. Quoted in Melamed (2013, p. 69, footnote 37).

References

Atmanspacher, H. (2012). "Dual-Aspect Monism à la Pauli and Jung." *Journal of Consciousness Studies*, 19(9–10), 96–120.

Atmanspacher, H. (2018). "Synchronicity and the Experience of Psychophysical Correlations" (Ch. 14), in *Research in Analytical Psychology: Empirical Research*, edited by C. Roesler. London: Routledge.

Atmanspacher, H. & Fach, W. (2013). "A Structural–Phenomenological Typology of Mind–Matter Correlations." *Journal of Analytical Psychology*, 58, 219–244.

Atmanspacher, H. & Fach, W. (2014). "Introduction," in *The Pauli–Jung Conjecture and its Impact Today*, edited by H. Atmanspacher & W. Fach. Exeter: Imprint Academic.

Atmanspacher, H. & Fach, W. (2019). "Exceptional Experiences of Stable and Unstable Mental States, Understood from a Dual-Aspect Point of View." *Philosophies*, 4(1), 7.

Atmanspacher, H. & Kronz, F. (1999). "Relative Onticity," in *On Quanta, Mind and Matter: Hans Primas in Context*, edited by H. Atmanspacher, A. Amann & U. Muller-Herold. Dordrecht: Springer.

Atmanspacher, H. & Rickles, D. (2022). *Dual-Aspect Monism and the Deep Structure of Meaning*. London & New York: Routledge.

Balibar, E. (2018/2020). *Spinoza, the Transidividual*. Translated by M. Kelly. Edinburgh: Edinburgh University Press.

Bergson, H. (1934). *La Pensée et le mouvant: essais et conférences*, 5th ed. Paris: Alcan.

Bishop, P. (2007). *Analytical Psychology and German Classical Aesthetics: Goethe, Schiller, and Jung, Vol. 1: The Development of the Personality*. London & New York: Routledge.

Bishop, P. (2008). *Analytical Psychology and German Classical Aesthetics: Goethe, Schiller, and Jung, Vol. 1: Constellation of the Self*. London & New York: Routledge.

Brooke, R. (2015). *Jung and Phenomenology*. London & New York: Routledge.

Cambray, J. (2014). "The Influence of German Romantic Science on Jung and Pauli." in *The Pauli–Jung Conjecture and its Impact Today*, edited by H. Atmanspacher & C. Fuchs. Exeter: Imprint Academic.

Carlisle, C. (2021). *Spinoza's Religion: A New Reading of The Ethics*. Princeton: Princeton University Press.

Clark, G. (2006). "A Spinozan Lens onto the Confusions of Borderline Relations." *Journal of Analytical Psychology*, 51, 67–86.

Colacicchi, G. (2021). *Psychology as Ethics: Reading Jung with Kant, Nietzsche, and Aristotle.* London & New York: Routledge.

Deleuze, G. (1962/1983). *Nietzsche & Philosophy*. Translated by H. Tomlinson. New York: Columbia University Press.

Deleuze, G. (1966/1988). *Bergsonism*. Translated by H. Tomlinson & B. Habberjam. New York: Zone Books.

Deleuze, G. (1968/1990). *Expressionism in Philosophy: Spinoza*. Translated by M. Joughin. New York: Zone Books.

Deleuze, G. (1970/1988). *Spinoza: Practical Philosophy*. Translated by R. Hurley. San Francisco: City Light Books.

Förster, M. (2012). Herder and Spinoza" (Ch. 4), in *Spinoza and German Idealism*, edited by E. Förster & Yitzhak Y. Melamed. Cambridge: Cambridge University Press.

Förster, E. & Melamed, Y. (eds). (2012). *Spinoza and German Idealism*. Cambridge: Cambridge University Press.

Gieser, S. (2005). *The Innermost Kernel: Depth Psychology and Quantum Physics. Wolfgang Pauli's dialogue with C.G. Jung*. Berlin: Springer.

Jung, C.G. (1919). "Instinct and the Unconscious," in *The Structure and Dynamics of the Psyche*, 2nd ed. Translated by R. Hull. Collected Works of C.G. Jung, Vol. 8. Princeton: Princeton University Press, 1969a.

Jung, C.G. (1921). *Psychological Types,* 2nd ed. Translated by R. Hull. Collected Works of C.G. Jung, Vol. 6. Princeton: Princeton University Press, 1971.

Jung, C.G. (1946). "On the Nature of the Psyche," in *The Structure and Dynamics of the Psyche*, 2nd ed. Translated by R. Hull. Collected Works of C.G. Jung, Vol. 8. Princeton: Princeton University Press, 1969a.

Jung, C.G. (1948). "The Phenomenology of the Spirit in Fairytales," in *The Archetypes and the Collective Unconscious*, 2nd ed. Translated by R. Hull. Collected Works of C.G. Jung, Vol. 9i, 1969b.

Jung, C.G. (1952). "Synchronicity: An Acausal Connecting Principle," in *The Structure and Dynamics of the Psyche*, 2nd ed. Translated by R. Hull. Collected Works of C.G. Jung, Vol. 8. Princeton: Princeton University Press, 1969a.

Jung, C.G. (1921). Psychological Types, 2nd ed. Translated by R. Hull. Collected Works of C.G. Jung, Vol. 6. Princeton: Princeton University Press, 1971.

Jung, C.G. (1963). *Mysterium Coniunctionis*, 2nd ed. Translated by R. Hull. Collected Works of C.G. Jung, Vol. 14. Princeton: Princeton University Press, 1970.

Jung, C.G. (1963/1989). *Memories. Dreams, Reflections*. Edited by A. Jaffe, translated by R. Winston and C. Winston. New York: Vintage Books.

Jung, C.G. (1977). *C.G. Jung Speaking: Encounters and Interviews*. Edited by W. McGuire and R.F.C. Hull. Princeton: Princeton University Press.

Jung, C.G. (1979). *General Index*. Translated by R. Hull. Collected Works of C.G. Jung, Vol. 20. Princeton: Princeton University Press.

Kerslake, C. (2007). *Deleuze and the Unconscious*. London & New York: Continuum.

Knox, J. (2003). *Archetype, Attachment, Analysis: Jungian Psychology and the Emergent Mind*. London & New York: Routledge.

Langan, R. (2020). "Jung, Spinoza, Deleuze: A Move Towards Realism" (Ch. 10), in *Holism: Possibilities and Problems*, edited by C. McMillan, R. Main & D. Henderson. London & New York: Routledge.

Lindorff, D. (2013). *Pauli and Jung: The Meeting of Two Great Minds*, eBook edition. New York: Quest Books.

Macherey, P. (1979/2011). *Hegel or Spinoza*. Translated by S. Ruddick. Minnesota: University of Minnesota Press.

Main, R. (2007). *Revelations of Chance: Synchronicity as Spiritual Experience*. New York: State University of New York.

Main, R. (2022). *Breaking the Spell of Disenchantment: Mystery, Meaning, and Metaphysics in the Work of C.G. Jung*. The Zurich lecture Series: Vol. 8. Asheville, NC: Chiron Publications.

Maxwell, G. (2022). *Integration and Difference: Constructing a Mythical Dialectic*. London & New York: Routledge.

McCoy Brooks, R. (2019). "A Critique of C.G. Jung's Theoretical Basis for Selfhood: Theory Vexed by an Incorporeal Ontology" (Ch. 5), in *Jung and Philosophy*, edited by J. Mills. London & New York: Routledge.

McMillan, C. (2015). *The 'Image of Thought' in Jung's Whole-Self: A Critical Study*. Unpublished Ph.D. thesis. University of Essex, UK.

Meier, C.A. (ed.) (2001). *Atom and Archetype: The Pauli/Jung Letters 1932–1958*. London: Routledge.

Melamed, Y. (2013). *Spinoza's Metaphysics: Substance and Thought*. Oxford: Oxford University Press.

Mills, J. (2019). "Introduction: Philosophizing Jung," in *Jung and Philosophy*, edited by J. Mills. London: Routledge.

Mills, J. & Goodwyn, E. (2023). *Archetypal Ontology: New Directions in Analytical Psychology*. London & New York: Routledge.

Morejón, G. (2022). *The Unconscious of Thought in Leibniz, Spinoza, and Hume*. Edinburgh: Edinburgh University Press.

Myers, C. (2015). "C.G. Jung and the Inheritance of Immanence: Traces of Spinozistic, Nietzschean, and Freudian Influence in Analytical Psychology," in *Scientia et Humanitas: A Journal of Student Research*. Tennessee: Middle Tennessee State University.

Nadler, S. (1999/2018). *Spinoza: A Life*, 2nd ed. Cambridge: Cambridge University Press.

Nadler, S. (2006). *Spinoza's 'Ethics': An Introduction*. Cambridge: Cambridge University Press.

Nagy, M. (1991). *Philosophical Issues in the Psychology of C.G. Jung*. Albany, NY: State University of New York Press.

Peden, K. (2014). *Spinoza Contra Phenomenology*. Stanford: Stanford University Press.

Roesler, C. (2012). "Are Archetypes Transmitted More by Culture than Biology? Questions Arising from Conceptualizations of the Archetype." *The Journal of Analytical Psychology*, 57, 223–246.

Roesler, C. (2022). *C.G. Jung's Archetype Concept: Theory, Research, and Applications*. Translated by A. Ulyet & C. Roesler. London & New York: Routledge.

Saban, M. (2019). *'Two Souls Alas': Jung's Two Personalities and the Making of Analytical Psychology*. The Zurich Lecture Series: Vol. 2. Asheville, NC: Chiron Publications.

Stewart, M. (2006). *The Courtier and the Heretic: Leibniz, Spinoza, and the Fate of God in the Modern World*. New York & London: Norton & Company.

Spinoza, B. (1985). *The Collected Works of Spinoza*, Vol. I, Edited and translated by Edwin Curley. Princeton: Princeton University Press.

Stengers, I. (2011). *Thinking with Whitehead: A Free and Wild Creation of Concepts*. Translated by M. Chase. London & Cambridge, MA: Cambridge University Press.

Chapter 1

Matter, Psyche, *Spirit*
The Lost Aspect of C.G. Jung's Monism

If C.G. Jung is a dual-aspect monist, then for him the two aspects of the monist whole are not matter and psyche, but rather matter and what he calls *spirit*, with psyche acting as a mediating third between them. In the spring of 1953 Jung writes to his collaborator on the theory of synchronicity, the quantum physicist Wolfgang Pauli, that the opposing aspects of existence are not physis versus psyche, but instead physis versus pneuma, or spirit, "with psyche as the medium between the two."[1] Jung laments to Pauli that modern thought has collapsed spirit into psyche, rendering it a mere "function of the intellect" or even synonymous with it, thus robbing spirit of the same "autonomy and reality that we ascribe to matter without a moment's hesitation" (Meier, 2001, pp. 116–117). For Jung, psyche and spirit must be conceived as distinct concepts, even though both concern things of a 'psychic' or mental nature. If the psyche is the experience of an individual, the substance of "all the phenomena" in that individual's inner world, then spirit refers to a specific category of that substance: the objects of that individual's experience that "cannot be proved to exist" in the material world, such as thoughts, dreams, and unconscious complexes, as well as metaphysical and theological considerations. Spirit covers as wide a range of things as matter: just as our conception of physical reality ranges from the vastness of the entire universe to the intricacy of our own bodies, and ultimately to the smallest and least perceptible subatomic particles, spirit pertains to deliberate intellections such as metaphysical and theological beliefs, to irruptions of feeling and meaning within us such as with numinous experiences and the symbolism of the unconscious, and to the unknown regions of what might be considered paranormal phenomena (ibid., p. 125; CW. 8, 1926/1969a, par. 626). As with matter, spirit is a broad category of things that the psyche perceives—but these things are not equivalent to the psyche itself.

DOI: 10.4324/9781003516996-2

By what right does Jung make this distinction between psyche and spirit? How can he say that the very content that his psychology concerns itself with, these "manifestations of the unconscious," are strictly speaking *not the same as the psyche itself* (CW. 13, 1942/1967, par. 229)? This is more or less the question that Pauli asks Jung in their correspondence from 1953. Pauli initiates the exchange due to his dissatisfaction with 'Answer to Job', Jung's psychological polemic toward the biblical God. In 'Answer to Job' Jung argues for an enhanced psychological concept of God, or god-image, that can transcend opposites such as light and dark or masculine and feminine (CW. 11, 1952/1969c). Pauli's objection is that he believes Jung is mistaken to view this key theological problem purely through a psychological lens. He thinks Jung shortchanges matter's importance in the issue; psyche and matter are not treated as equal opposites, and much to Pauli's dismay the psychophysical union that is so central to their speculations concerning synchronicity is entirely ignored. Is Jung not, Pauli asks, interpreting this key issue exclusively through psychology and at the expense of the opposing view of materialism, even though the very balance of such opposites is something that Jung so frequently calls for? Indeed, what pair of opposites is more central to the question of the divine than psyche and matter? Are not the very fringes of matter, in the volatile subatomic world where, in Pauli's estimation, the perspective of the observer directly influences what is known, just as valid an entryway into whatever ontological realm lies beyond mind and matter as the unconscious is? Moreover, a theological topic like the god-image is contrary to materialism to begin with. By studying such an issue with a psychology that is also, by its very definition, opposite to physicalism, isn't Jung just overextending the psyche and contents of a 'psychic' nature (i.e., spirit) so that other viewpoints have no quarter? It is as if 'Answer to Job' left Pauli uncertain if he and Jung had really been arguing for the same thing. He writes that Jung has become psychology's version of King Midas, for whatever topic Jung studies inevitably becomes an object of the psyche. Surely the goal, writes Pauli, should be to instead synthesize these two fundamental opposites, to transcend materialism and psychism in order to better apprehend the underlying monist whole (Meier, 2001, pp. 84–97).[2] Instead, it would appear that Jung is making the psyche exempt from typical mind–matter oppositions. If left unjustified, such a maneuver seems to simply grant 'psychism'—whether that psychism is the psyche, idea, spirit, so forth—primacy over existence, to the diminishment of matter and other points of view.

Psyche as Middle Third

Jung's response is intricate and based on the fundamental points of his psychology. First, he argues that the psyche must be entrenched as a neutral medium, rather than part of the category that is contrary to matter—whether that opposing category be called Idea, or mistakenly called the psyche or mind, or, as Jung himself ultimately classifies it, spirit—because in Jung's estimation this is the only way to prevent precisely what Pauli is accusing him of: the inflation of the psyche into metaphysical realms it has no right to claim. Spirit is that category of ideas whose objects are not of the material world, or, as Jung says to Pauli near the end of the 1953 conversation, when Pauli has at last teased out of his collaborator the exact definitions of psyche and spirit, spirit is the content of the psyche that "cannot be derived either from the body or the external world." But spirit is not, however closely related to the psyche it may be, equivalent to the psyche itself (Meier, 2001, p. 125). The psyche is the basin of *all* experience, whether that experience is of spiritual things or material things—but it cannot be cast into either category of existence. To do so is to project the psyche into the outer world, into either spirit or matter, and such a projection inevitably introduces favoritism or one-sidedness into one's conception of existence. "All projections are unconscious identifications with the object," warns Jung, and such projections inevitably veil the true reality of things (CW. 14, 1963/1970, par. 696). It does not matter to Jung whether this unconscious identification is done by reducing the psyche to physiological processes, or if the psyche is depicted as the emissary of an eminent creator beyond our range of experience. Either route seeks to explain the psyche and its autonomous complexes rationalistically, "as the consequence of known causes, i.e., something secondary and unreal" (CW. 13, 1957/1967, par. 75). To install the psyche either in "Heaven or in earthly things" is to introduce a type of metaphysical judgment about its existence that Jung cannot condone (Meier, 2001, p. 100). The one-sidedness of such explanations tends to betray their inadequacy as well: for instance, someone who professes that all of reality can be explained by instinctual drives will be oblivious to the spirituality inherent in such a position, the implicit and outstanding metaphysical claim that reality somehow whispers to us from within blood and bone; similarly, an individual who suppresses the instincts out of fear or disdain or who attempts to subordinate bodily desires to the intellect will undoubtedly encounter a spiritual crisis of some sort, a crisis that tends to arise out of unmet demands of the biological drives that, although veiled in the unconscious, remained as influential as ever over the person who naively thought they conquered such things (CW. 8, 1946/1969a, par. 407). This is why Jung laments how alchemy was ultimately discredited as a discipline—the alchemists failed to understand that their methods were metaphors for psychic processes, instead choosing to "befuddle themselves with an ever more nebulous mysticism," or in other cases choosing to focus purely on matter, which ultimately led to the discovery of chemistry. The fact that focus on just one category of existence, one aspect of the monist whole, led to the establishment of a field full of admirable novelty, whether that field be chemistry or later microphysics, does not change the problem for Jung, no more than how preoccupation with spirit precipitated the world's great religions or ambitious metaphysical models. We feel sorry for one-sidedness that leads to delusion, notes Jung, just as we admire where success is yielded instead, "but no one asks about the fate of the psyche, which thereafter vanished from sight for several hundred years" (CW. 13, 1954/1967, par. 482).

If Jung denounces metaphysics, it is to denounce a specific type of metaphysics, one that confidently attributes the causes of things to some power that is inherently unverifiable and prior to experience. Philosophy scholar Bernado Kastrup notes that Jung specifically condemns any metaphysics that engages in "ungrounded, idiosyncratic explanation, detached from the world of actual experience and empirical evidence" (2021, p. 74).[3] Strict dichotomies, such as the Platonic notion of being or non-being, go beyond what is merely known through experience by introducing an ontological judgment, a claim to be able to say definitively what is or is not possible. Jung rejects this maneuver as a type of "primitive participation mystique," a projection of the psyche into objects outside of itself. Spirit and matter must not be depicted as reified entities, but rather categories that the psyche attributes to certain kinds of experience—in other words, they are simply labels for experiences of a spiritual origin or experiences of a material origin. These categories, while undoubtedly referring to something that exists independent of the psyche, are in truth "necessary elements" in the psyche's process of conceiving the world. After all, it is only through the psyche that experiences can be attributed to either the physical or the ideal—and therefore, Jung argues, it is only in the psyche that such distinctions are made. A dichotomy superior to 'being or non-being' is to instead speak of what is 'ascertainable or unascertainable', for the latter distinction concerns what can truly be known, and such knowledge is anchored in the psyche. To ignore that the psyche is the medium where these categories are distinguished, to speak as if any knowledge is mediated to us without passing through the psyche first, is to inevitably introduce a tendency toward either spiritualization or materialization in one's view of existence. Such an error eliminates the possibility of a middle perspective and sabotages any chance of understanding the true nature of things (Meier, 2001, pp. 99–101).

Thus, the psyche is not arbitrarily installed between spirit and matter; its middle placement is to ensure that our very knowledge of the ideal and physical doesn't fall back on unfounded philosophical mythologems, such as a *prima causa* or unified first cause that we must presume came before our present experience and from which the causal lines of mental and physical events then emanate (CW. 8, 1952/1969a, par. 828). Instead the psyche must be seen as something tantamount to Plato's concept of *Triton Eidos*, a medium that participates in *both* spirit and matter, which differentiates both aspects as sources of epistemology, without being collapsed into either (Meier, 2001, pp. 99–101). This insight is why Jung admires the alchemists, regardless of whether or not they truly understood the true nature of the 'gold' they sought. In his 'Commentary on "The Secret of the Golden Flower,"' Jung notes that the Western intellect had split apart spirit and matter for "epistemological purposes," yet nevertheless both aspects must "exist together in the psyche and psychology must recognize this fact. 'Psychic' means physical and spiritual." Jung credits alchemists such as the Chinese Taoists who authored *The Secret of the Golden Flower* for grasping the importance of the psyche as an intermediate world that "expresses life as it actually is," and without it, "spirit is as dead as matter, because both are artificial abstractions" (CW. 13, 1957/1967, par. 76 footnote). In other words, Jung is also clear that whatever the nature of spirit and matter truly is, they are divided as such "in the interests of human cognition," that is to say, by the psyche (Letters, Vol. 2, 1975, p. 620). Therefore, they must not be treated as lines emanating from a first cause, but one must start from the psyche and work outwards. Thus the "immediate reality" of the psyche (Letters, Vol. 1, 1973, p. 200).

Archetype via Instinct and Spirit (or Meaning)

Placing the psyche as the middle third does not just act as a safeguard against bad metaphysical positions; it also allows Jung to refine other concepts in his psychology, most notably the dominant patterns of the unconscious, the archetypes. It was Jung's research into the alchemical process of the conjunction that led him to speculate about the underlying monism beneath matter, psyche, and spirit, what the alchemists called the *unus mundus* (CW. 14, 1963/1970, pars. 766, 776–789). Jung does not speak of this monist whole with the same kind of metaphysical certainty that he chastises, but rather suggests our conceptions of this realm are inferred from what he calls the 'psychoid' aspect of the archetypes, or the substrate of the unconscious that "*cannot with certainty be designated as psychic*" (CW. 8, 1946/1969a, par. 439). While ultimately irrepresentable, we experience this psychoid level through the archetypal self, which offers "windows" into eternity. Such awareness comes from integration of the conscious and unconscious, and therefore it must always be seen as psychic first and foremost, since it is knowledge that passes through the psyche (CW. 14, 1963/1970, pars. 763, 776–789). It is certainly at the very boundaries of knowledge, and indeed self-knowledge, that one sees spirit in matter, and matter in spirit, and thus may postulate that they are expressions of the same thing (Meier, 2001, p. 101).

In 'On the Nature of the Psyche' Jung explains how the psychoid aspect of the archetypes explains archetypal manifestations in both matter and spirit. It is true that when Jung describes this psychoid factor, he is anchoring one end of the archetypes in biological patterns of behavior (Addison, 2009, 2019). However, Jung also states plainly that the psychoid refers to the archetype's *spiritual* manifestation as well. The spiritual character of archetypes can be found in the so-called archetypal images, the symbolic material the archetypes produce as irruptions into the psyche, such as in dream symbolism and the therapy practice of active imagination (CW. 8, 1946/1969a, par. 405). To use the definition of spirit that Jung gave Pauli, the archetypal images are ideas that have no direct object in the material world. Now undoubtedly an archetypal image may be complemented by a physical affectation too; for instance, spiritual experiences may be accompanied by a change in sexual libido, which would be indicative of a link to the instinctive (i.e., material) sphere. In cases of synchronicity, the material occurrence may even include the physical world beyond the body proper (CW. 8, 1952/1969a, par. 912). But any physical manifestation, as well as the archetypal image, ultimately are actualizations of something beyond spirit and matter, the psychoid aspect of the archetype, or the 'archetype as such'.[4] The 'archetype as such' has no content, and it is only proper to speak of it as being a pattern or form in a very limited sense. It is "empty and purely formal." Jung draws a comparison to the axial system of a crystal, which is the precursor to an actual crystal forming, despite having no material existence of its own (CW. 9i, 1954/1969b, par. 155). When Jung speaks of the psychoid archetype, he is referring not only to what under-writes the archetype's activation of instincts but also to whatever produces the symbolic and spiritual content of archetypal images—both are expressions of the archetype as such:

> The archetypal representations (images and ideas) mediated to us by the unconscious should not be confused with the archetype as such. They are very varied structures that all point back to one essentially 'irrepresentable' form. The latter is characterized by certain formal elements and by certain fundamental meanings, although these can be grasped only approximately. The archetype as such is a psychoid factor [...] It does not appear to be capable of reaching consciousness.
>
> (CW. 8, 1946/1969a, par. 417)

Jung's designation of archetypal images as spiritual content has ramifications for qualities associated with those images, most specifically the idea of *meaning*. In his earlier writings Jung sometimes writes of the archetype's relationship to instinct as if the archetype is the instinct's 'image of itself' (CW. 8, 1919a/1969a, pars. 270, 277). The introduction of the psychoid allows Jung to further articulate this relationship: it is not simply that the archetype emerges from instinctive processes, but rather that the archetype's manifestation in spirit is essentially the 'image' that the instincts (and, by implication, that the body and matter) are activated and subsumed by. By image Jung does not mean a literal, static picture, but rather that the image is the *meaning* of the instinct. The symbols that archetypes manifest as are not signs, not mere designations that connect known things and their referents as in semiotics, but rather expressions "for something that cannot be characterized in any other or better way," irruptions from the unconscious that bestow a profound effect upon the conscious psyche (CW. 6, 1921/1971, pars. 814–829). If instincts are biological drives, then the 'images' of the instincts are sort of assemblages, patterns that the instincts become involved in. For instance, in the animal kingdom, "the instinct of the leaf-cutting ant fulfills the image of ant, tree, leaf, cutting, transport, and the little ant-garden of fungi." This image is the meaning of the ant's instinctive behavior to interact with its environment in the way it does. "Image and meaning are identical; and as the first takes shape, so the latter becomes clear. Actually, the pattern needs no interpretation; it portrays its own meaning." The instinct cannot function properly without its total pattern or meaning (CW. 8, 1946/1969a, pars. 398, 402).

Jungian analyst and researcher Ann Addison postulates that Jung sharply differentiates between instinctual images, such as the example of the leaf-cutting ant, and the archetypal images that concern typical Jungian discourse; therefore, the so-called instinctual images would remain in the realm of instinct, whereas archetypal images and their symbolic content are of a higher order, that is, spirit (2019, pp. 32–33). Undoubtedly Jung would differentiate by some degree between, for example, the instinctive patterns of a crying infant and a responsive mother on the one hand, and the mother archetype and all its permutations through myth and culture on the other; he in fact does observe how some images are derived from the body, while others from a spiritual source that is "no less real" than matter (CW. 8, 1931/1969a, par. 681). However, in 'On the Nature of the Psyche' Jung uses the term *meaning* in relation to images irrespective of whether or not those images are associated with the 'lower' substrate of instincts or 'higher' realm of archetypal imagery.[5] This is a significant move, because in Jung's writings on synchronicity he will demarcate between events explained by causality and conventional laws of nature—that is, ideas related to the category of matter—versus acausal events explained by meaning (CW. 8, 1952/1969a, par. 915). Now, archetypal images and meaning are interconnected—as symbols, they are precisely what expresses something that cannot be articulated in any better way (CW. 6, 1921/1971, par. 816). In other words, they portray their own meaning. Archetypal images themselves are manifestations of spirit, and the hallmark of spirit is the spontaneous production of these images (CW. 9i, 1948/1969b, par. 393). Therefore meaning and spirit must also be deeply entwined. Jung's theory of synchronicity essentially sets up a ledger of existence that has matter and causality on one side, and spirit and meaning on the other. At times Jung even seems to refer to spirit and meaning as if they were synonymous with one another. Jung plainly makes an equivalence between spirit and meaning in his dialogue with Pauli, when Jung notes that examination of a dream chiefly for its metaphysical considerations, rather than through psychology proper, would lead to an analysis of a dream's objective meaning, or "what one might call spirit or the mind". At first, this passage is puzzling—after all that has been established regarding the difference between psyche and spirit, is Jung suddenly equating spirit with the 'mind'? However, in the original German text, the exact phrasing Jung uses is "Geistes bzw. Sinnes," which could also be translated to "spirit or sense," or "spirit or meaning" (Meier, 1992, p. 115; 2001, p. 114).[6] This latter phrase accords with the wording used in the opening passages of 'Answer to Job', where Jung explains that it is an error to believe psychic facts or experiences such as religious statements must have proof via physical truths, that even outstanding events like miracles appeal only to the person who does not understand that psychic facts are valid in terms of their "spirit or *meaning*," as "meaning is something that always demonstrates itself and is experienced on its own merits" (CW. 11, 1952/1969c, par. 554). In a letter from 1960 to Serrano, Jung states that much of what we do and make with our lives depends upon the "spirit, i.e., the meaning or significance" of how we live (Letters, Vol. 2, 1975, p. 596). And again in the exchange with Pauli, when Jung explains that, due to his professional work as a psychologist, his dreams often feature "the mythological aspect of nature, i.e., with what one might call the *spirit* (or the mind)," here the original German uses the phrasing "Geiste (oder Sinne)," which once more could be translated as "spirit (or meaning)" (Meier, 1992, p. 115; 2001, p. 115).[7]

In any event, by placing meaning in the sphere of spirit, Jung envisions a scale where, on one end, biological and physical, causal mechanisms occur, and on the other, where spirit *or meaning* is expressed. It is between these two extremes where the psyche lies. Jung describes his conception of psyche, spirit, and matter as a scale on which consciousness slides, toward one end (matter) or the other (spirit) (CW. 8, 1946/1969a, par. 408). One comparison he raises is the light spectrum, where the instincts could be considered the infra-red end, and the spiritual the ultra-violet side. Jung writes:

Just as the "psychic-infra-red," the biological instinctual psyche, gradually passes over into the physiology of the organism and thus merges with its chemical and physical conditions, so the "psychic ultra-violet," the archetype, describes a field which exhibits none of the peculiarities of the physiological and yet, in the last analysis, can no longer be regarded as psychic, although it manifests itself psychically. But physiological processes behave in the same way, without on that account being declared psychic. Although there is no form of existence that is not mediated to us psychically and only psychically, it would hardly do to say that everything is merely psychic. We must apply this argument logically to the archetypes as well. Since their essential being is unconscious to us, and still they are experienced as spontaneous agencies, there is probably no alternative now to describe their nature, in accordance with their chiefest effect, as "spirit" [...]. If so, the position of the archetype would be located beyond the psychic sphere, analogous to the position of the physiological instinct, which is immediately rooted in the stuff of the organism and, with its psychoid nature, forms the bridge to matter in general. In archetypal conceptions and instinctual perceptions, spirit and matter confront one another on the psychic plane. Matter and spirit both appear in the psychic realm as distinctive qualities of conscious contents. The ultimate nature of both is transcendental, that is, irrepresentable, since the psyche and its contents are the only reality which is given to us without a medium.

(ibid., par. 420)

The archetype is expressed both in spirit and matter: it is both "spirit and anti-spirit," instinct and its meaning. The way an archetype is expressed depends chiefly on the psychic state of the individual in question. One register, either matter or spirit, instinct or meaning, may be more prevalent in some cases than others, but it is only a cultivated psyche that can truly ascertain this relationship (ibid., par. 406). The introduction of the psychoid factor does not change the fact that the archetypes are to a degree psychic, as the investigation of the images and symbols that they manifest is inherently a psychological process. The psychoid merely allows Jung a degree of "conceptual differentiation," to acknowledge that the psyche is not equivalent to these spiritual or physical manifestations but rather is the witness of them (ibid., par. 419).

Psyche as Immediate Experience

If one accepts the necessity of a middle third, an objection could nonetheless be raised as to why it *must* be the psyche and not simply some neutral substance instead. This is precisely what Pauli says in reply to Jung's explanation of the psyche as *triton eidios*. Shouldn't the middle third be treated just like the psychoid level of the archetypes; that is to say, as something that is no longer strictly psychic or physical? A year before, off the heels of their joint publication on synchronicity, Pauli had written to Jung expressing his desire to discover a new psychophysically neutral language that would allow them to discuss that invisible, potential reality that they could otherwise only infer from its effects on psyche and matter. In Pauli's mind, this was the only way to develop a methodology to grapple with the psychophysical unity of the monist whole (Meier, 2001, p. 82). This desire to create a neutral framework has been taken up by the theoretical physicist and Jungian scholar Harald Atmanspacher, who argues that correlations between an individual's mental state and physical state may reveal which archetype has been activated and is expressing itself from the psychophysically neutral reality (Atmanspacher & Rickles, 2022, p. 51). Comparing the need for this new framework to how Maxwell's discovery of electromagnetism revolutionized how we think about electricity and magnetism, Atmanspacher writes:

> At present, we do not have a theoretical framework for psychophysical phenomena, just as the early 19th century did not have electrodynamics. The analogy [of the discovery of electromagnetism in relation to the psychophysical problem] tells us also that it is misleading to try and study psychophysical phenomena as if they were either mental or physical, exactly as electromagnetic phenomena are neither solely electric nor magnetic. It is likely that psychophysical phenomena need to be recast in a way even more radical than Maxwell's breakthrough has been.
>
> (Atmanspacher, 2018, p. 234)

Pauli was very much interested in this same project, and this is why he considers Jung's position of the psyche in this middle role as a step in the wrong direction. After all, when Jung introduced the psychoid level of the archetype he had essentially conceded that the archetypes were themselves not psychic. Why not then use neutral, general concepts to discuss this plane beneath mind and matter? For as Pauli says to Jung, one can label the origin of ideas in the psyche all they please; it does not change that the underlying monism is something unascertainable and that the language of psychology seems, to Pauli, ill-suited to chart such an unknown frontier. Pauli warns Jung that he is making too much of the psychic factor; instead of saying that the psyche is partly of a material nature, Pauli would prefer if Jung simply said that both psyche and matter are governed by these common, neutral ordering principles, and that these neutral factors should be what they are trying to infer. Notably at this point in the conversation, Pauli makes no mention of spirit as being separate from psyche—Pauli does not understand Jung's distinction of psyche from spirit, nor how Jung swapped psyche with spirit to be the aspect opposite to matter. To Pauli, it simply seems as if Jung has indeed indulged an "expansionist tendency" with the psyche (Meier, 2001, pp. 100–101, 105–106).

Jung concedes that any underlying monism would certainly *not* be equivalent to the psyche itself. Rather, the psyche is our only immediate data; that is to say, it is the only raw experience we have that is not filtered through something else. In Jung's mind it is impossible to avoid this fact, and to speak of general concepts in place of the psyche would again be a misstep into the metaphysical judgments that he abhors. No doubt some sort of neutral essence underlies the psyche, just as Jung stresses that both spirit and matter have a reality independent of our experience. However, the psyche is where our concepts of matter and spirit are conceived, and so it is only through the lens of the psyche that the two different categories of existence can be understood without raising metaphysical judgment. Spirit, the category of ideas that concern the non-material, is logically contrasted with any ideas or images that concern the material world—but, crucially, according to Jung, ideas that concern matter are nonetheless still a specific category of thoughts and images conceived by the psyche. Matter and spirit "are two different concepts that indicate opposites and—as ideas of different origins—are psychic." The psyche is "our only instrument of cognition" and thus cannot be dispensed with regarding any statement or perception concerning reality. At the very least, the psyche must be seen as a 'metaphorical' third; it may not be the whole truth, its sense of the truth may be as incomplete as the ego is compared to the archetypal self, but it is nonetheless "*the* conception of the truth that we have" (ibid., pp. 112–115). Therefore, Jung's neutral placement of the psyche is not just out of ontological necessity but also an epistemological priority. *The experience of the individual, the psyche, is that through which our ideas of both spirit and matter must pass.*

Jung allows that the psyche may be akin to the monads from Leibniz's philosophy, microcosms through which the world may be apprehended via an inner 'bodily' perception (CW. 8, 1952/1969a, par. 937). The difference for Jung however is that he sees no reason why the monads should be conceived of as 'windowless' wholes, as Leibniz does. Rather Jung contends "that the psyche does have windows and that from these windows we can perceive ever broader realistic backdrops." The psyche is the very boundary between what is ascertainable and unascertainable, and in a sense we are indeed sealed within it, but "it is within our power to extend our prison to the big, wide world outside" and thus abstract further elements from the unascertainable (Meier, 2001, pp. 111–115). But it is crucial, in Jung's view, to not mix or confuse the routes of inquiry. In the therapy room, for instance, he insists that one must never hold to a spiritual interpretation of a client's issues when it is their instincts that require cultivation; nor does it do good to claim the spiritual as an illusion when spirit demands recognition. For the therapist, the question of whether an explanation ought to be based in "physis" or spirit is sometimes, per Jung, a matter of life or death. The modern psychologist finds themself between these two opposites at all times, opposites that are the cause of turmoil in their clients—but this tension itself is caused by the failure to understand the psyche. All immediate experience is psychic, and "immediate reality can only be psychic." Therefore it is only through the psyche that these questions can be answered. This is not meant to diminish the reality of matter or spirit; on the contrary, *all* psychic facts are in some sense true: the fear of a ghost whose image is from a spiritual source is just as real as a fear of fire from the physical world, and just as it would never occur to someone in modern times to explain the nature of fire without chemistry or physics, neither would it do much good to explain a fear of ghosts outside of spiritual processes. It is the psyche and its experience of these fears that ought to be refined and cultivated, because only then will our understanding of these opposites improve, and the window of what is ascertainable may be widened (CW. 8, 1931/1969a, pars. 678–681). This is precisely why bad metaphysical judgment comes from psychic projection: psychological development or the Jungian project of individuation is inseparable from adequate knowledge of what the psyche actually is and what it conceives—psychology as a method cannot be distinguished from the psychic process itself (CW. 8, 1952/1969a, par. 429). This reflexive knowledge extends to what affects the psyche. Some years after their exchange on spirit, Jung writes to Pauli that it is the individuated person who can properly "perceive both the external sensory aspect of the world and also its hidden depths of meaning," that is, spirit and matter. An individual who has united the opposites of spirit and matter within oneself, who has withdrawn their projections, then has the opportunity to understand that spirit and matter are but split aspects of the world, and that these split aspects, while objectively real, are expressions of the monist whole, or *unus mundus* (Meier, 2001, pp. 156–157). The person who understands their psyche understands spirit, matter, and beyond.

A consequence of this epistemological priority for the psyche is that Jung does not seem as keen on constructing a neutral language as Pauli is—not because Jung doubts the existence of a monism beyond the psyche, but because it is evident to him that it would be pointless to speculate of such things without starting through the psyche first. Jung concurs with Pauli's desire for a neutral language—but only insofar as he considers the language of his psychology to already be a faithful reflection of the dual aspects, material and spiritual, which are the designations for "potentialities that transcend consciousness" (Letters, Vol. 2, 1975, p. 70). Quite simply, psychology *is* Jung's neutral language. The psyche is the arbiter between spirit and matter. This is why for Jung it was no issue at all to focus on the theological issues at stake in 'Answer to Job' purely through the lens of psychological truth, rather than trying to graft a materialist perspective onto a topic where it did not have anything to offer. To Jung's mind, this would be as large a folly as attempting to discuss the nature of matter without the lens of the physical sciences (Meier, 2001, p. 98). This is also why Jung is not particularly moved by Pauli's demonstration that he can interpret his own dreams through physical, psychological, and spiritual perspectives. Pauli aimed to prove that a physics-minded interpretation of his dream could be as enriching as any other from a psychological or spiritual perspective, and that therefore some neutral language underwrites the three approaches. For Jung however, this is not the point. It would be no better than if he approached his own dreams, which were as frequently laden with the images of mythology as Pauli's were with the symbols of physics, through a purely mythological attitude and tried to glean an impersonal meaning from them. Only the psychological approach yields a personal confrontation with the unconscious and a chance for psychic growth, and only through the microcosm can the greater horizons be seen (ibid., pp. 106–109, 113–114).[8]

If one wishes to verify that spirit and matter are different aspects of the same principle, Jung is very clear about what he believes is the best method to accomplish this. He imagines "setting up identical or parallel physical and psychological propositions on one hand, and on the other the psychological interpretability of religious revelations." It is not a matter of tracing correspondences between spirit and matter, but spirit to psyche and matter to psyche (ibid., p. 101).[9] The fact that theologians would dismiss this exercise on the basis that spirit might lose its luster before psyche's central role, just as physicists might believe matter is diminished under tandem of psyche and spirit (just as Pauli suspects), only proves Jung's point: traditional mind–matter distinctions, which set up mind and matter as separate but parallel lines to be traced back to a first cause, and with the promise that each aspect will be handled equally and in good faith, inevitably collapse due to bias toward one side or the other. Only the psyche can obviate this outcome. This is precisely why Jung responds to Pauli's objections, in a rare moment of possible irritation toward his colleague, that he fails to see Pauli's point about how psychology is "overburdened." Quite simply, Jung is ensuring that psychology performs the very job it is meant for (ibid., p. 113).

It should be clear that Jung is not advocating for any type of psychologism, nor even a 'psychism' or idealism, and that he believes both spirit and matter enjoy an existence independent of the psyche. Failure to acknowledge this and to instead render everything psychic thwarts the very purpose of psychology as an epistemology. This is why when Bernado Kastrup argues that 'Answer to Job' is really Jung's religious confession, that Jung uses the pretense of psychological analysis to make palatable a sort of theological manifesto, he is missing the point (Kastrup, 2021, pp. 104–108). Jung does not so often profess he is only a psychologist to simply mask his intentions, nor to diminish the importance of the topics he looks at through a psychological lens. Nor does he dismiss metaphysical speculation in his dialogue with Pauli out of fear of appearing unreasonable, as Kastrup suggests—it is Pauli, after all, who wants to seek out ordering structures, and Jung who seems skeptical of the whole enterprise (ibid., pp. 79–80; Meier, 2001, pp. 127–128). For Jung, such conjecture is irrelevant unless it starts from the psyche first. When Jung says he sticks to 'psychic facts', it is not so he can skirt around the issue of whether he really believes in the existence of God, or ghosts, or flying saucers, or the material world itself. Psychic facts are what affect the psyche directly, and it is only through understanding their impact upon the psyche that one can trace their lineaments into what was hitherto unascertainable, and to see what is really there.[10] This is not a deception on Jung's part—it is the very purpose of his psychology. On this point, we should take him at his word.

The Unio Mentalis

An outstanding issue remains: what of those instances where Jung speaks indeed *only* of psyche and matter, with no mention of spirit? If Jung insists that psyche and spirit must not be conflated nor confused, then why are there passages where Jung seems to do exactly that? In *Mysterium Coniunctionis* Jung talks of how psyche and matter are identical expressions of the *unus mundus* (CW. 14, 1963/1970, par. 766). He tends to speak of synchronicity as a correspondence between *psyche* and matter (CW. 8, 1952/1969a). And in the final letter Jung writes to Pauli in 1957, he speaks of the opposites *psyche* and *matter*, with no mention of the concept of spirit that he so assiduously defended the autonomy of just four years prior (Meier, 2001, pp. 166–169)! What of Jung's declaration that the true opposition is not matter versus psyche, but spirit and matter, and that spirit should not be folded into psyche?

The answer lies in the relationship between psyche and spirit, and how Jung highlights the importance of their relationship in the process of coming to consciousness while denying either metaphysical supremacy. While outlining how the use of the word spirit has changed throughout history, Jung takes to task thinkers who have either inflated spirit to a supernatural force contrary to nature, just as he is critical of anyone who reduces spirit to matter or intellect. In comparison, he is more favorable to so-called primitive beliefs that, while perhaps not fully articulating the nature of spirit, understood its connection to life, to that which vivifies and inspires—in other words, spirit as a dynamic principle (CW. 9i, 1948/1969b, par. 389). For instance, Jung observes that many primitive cultures consider the souls of the dead to be spirits, and therefore a belief in souls is a necessary premise for a belief in spirits (CW. 8, 1919b/1969a, pars. 577–578).[11] The implication here is that if one were to permit the existence of ghosts, and that if someone died and became a ghost, that ghost would be of their soul—however, relative to other people who were still alive, their ghost would be a spirit. Now this belief reflects something in psychic processes: for instance, the superstitious notion of being possessed by a spirit correlates with the modern theory of unconscious complexes. When something psychic happens to the primitive psyche, and this psychic event is perceived as belonging to the individual in question, they consider it as having come from their spirit or soul; but if it seems strange or foreign, then they will believe the experience came from someone else's spirit, or an entirely inhuman spirit. Thus at least from this perspective, *the psyche is spirit* (CW. 9i, 1948/1969b, par. 388).[12]

The passage from spirit to psyche and psyche to spirit is better understood in terms of how spirit affects psychic processes. In 'The Phenomenology of the Spirit in Fairytales', Jung illustrates how spirit often spontaneously appears to an individual when they are at some sort of psychological impasse. Using fairytales as a vignette, Jung demonstrates how, for instance, the archetypal old man often appears to give guidance to the hero, that is, the ego-consciousness, at a timely moment:

> Often the old man in fairytales asks questions like who? why? whence? And wither? For purposes of inducing self-reflection and mobilizing the moral forces, and more often still he gives the necessary magical talisman, the unexpected and improbable power to succeed, which is one of the peculiarities of the unified personality in good or bad alike. But the intervention of the old man—the spontaneous objectivation of the archetype—would seem to be equally indispensable, since the conscious will by itself is hardly ever capable of uniting the personality to the point where it acquires this extraordinary power to succeed. For that, not only in fairytales but in life generally, the objective intervention of the archetype is needed, which checks the purely affective reactions with a chain of inner confrontations and realizations. These cause the who? where? how? why? To emerge clearly and in this wise bring knowledge of the immediate situation as well as of the goal. The resultant enlightenment and untying of the fatal tangle often has something positive magical about it—an experience not unknown to the psychotherapist.
>
> (CW. 9i, 1948/1969b, par. 404)

Here Jung is describing the effect of spirit as the appearance of archetypal imagery during the process of psychological growth. Spirit is essentially the catalyst for the psyche's development. Now no doubt that the psyche's confrontation with the archetypes and the collective unconscious was already ably described by Jung before he decided that archetypal affects were best labeled as phenomena of spirit.[13] But once again Jung's spectrum of matter–psyche–spirit allows for further conceptual differentiation. It is through the interplay of psyche and spirit that psychological growth is enabled. As Jung scholar and synchronicity researcher Roderick Main notes, spirit is both an animating principle and an entity in its own right (2007, p. 24). Similarly with synchronicity Jung typically speaks of an inner psychic experience, such as a dream or premonition, that accords with an external event, such as something from said dream or premonition coming to pass in real life. *Meaning* is what ties these non-causal corresponding events together, that we "are so accustomed to regard meaning as a psychic process or content that it never enters our heads to suppose that it could also exist outside the psyche" (CW. 8, 1952/1969a, par. 915). When describing the role of spirit and matter in synchronicity, Jung tells Pauli that, considered under spirit, the archetypes are the "arrangers of physical circumstances" that imbue matter with meaning (Meier, 2001, p. 101). This is reminiscent of what elsewhere Jung calls the "natural spirit" that sways consciousness every bit as much as the "instinctual and reflex processes of the cortical centres." Both spiritual and instinctive powers emerge from the unconscious, but the difference is that spirit, with its ability to "anticipate future conscious processes," may just as easily be thought of as a "supraconsciousness" (CW. 13, 1942/1967, par. 229). Therefore even when synchronicity is described as psyche and matter reflecting one another, the third element of spirit still plays its part.[14]

This dynamism of psyche and spirit is perhaps best captured in the closing chapter of *Mysterium Coniunctionis*. Here Jung analyzes the alchemical conjunction as explained by the sixteenth-century alchemist Gerhard Dorn, and how this arcane process symbolized the crux of his psychology. As Jung explains to Pauli, Dorn at least partly understood that what alchemy really was groping at was a path to self-knowledge, which at the same time was knowledge of God (Meier, 2001, pp. 128–129; CW. 14, 1963/1970, par. 697).[15] This knowledge is brought about by the conjunction, a process that takes place in several stages. The first stage of the conjunction is called the *unio mentalis*, which is a uniting of spirit and soul. This frees the soul from the body, a body that is typically riddled with passions and affects. The original state of what we commonly call the mind was hardly conscious, animal-like and impulsive, an "inextricable weaving of the soul with the body, which together formed a dark unity" called the *unio naturalis*. Jung explains spirit's intervention is a way to "free the soul by means of the *separatio*, and establish a spiritual—psychic counterposition—conscious and rational insight—which would prove immune to the influences of the body." Jung compares this first stage of the conjunction to the psychotherapeutic goal of dissolving a client's projections to eliminate anything that impedes their path to self-knowledge. The aim of psychotherapy is in fact to help a client achieve this "rational, spiritual–psychic position" over the physical affects of the body (CW. 14, 1963/1970, par. 696). Thus the *unio mentalis* is the intervention of spirit, that is, the archetype, that helps cultivate a conscious mind or soul that is not simply slave to the reactive forces of instinct. The psychic–spiritual counterposition is central to the close relationship between psyche and spirit.

However, a further point must be made, which brings not just matter but the body itself back into the fold and reveals their relation to psyche and spirit. This unification of psyche and spirit would remain in a vacuum, abstract and removed from the world, if it did not in turn unite with the individual's actual life and experiences, of which the body is a sort of vanguard. So the second stage of the conjunction involves combining the *unio mentalis* with the body. In Dorn's understanding, this process produced a heavenly substance called the *caelum*; Jung seems to equate the *caelum* with the archetypal Self (ibid., par. 681).[16] Jung saw this part of the process as the psyche–spirit overcoming and transforming a body that had been previously caught in "worldly entanglements," as well as a realization that spirit was indeed trapped in "inert matter, or the God-image imprinted on the world." Ultimately when the ego-consciousness surrenders to the self, humankind is also reconnected with the world (ibid., par. 704). This is also where the importance of matter and the body is revealed; for if all of existence was just spirit, it is easy to imagine one being carried away by its wind-like nature.[17] Thus, it is only from the body that one's self can be realized. This leads to the third stage of the conjunction, which is a realization that the self is at one with the world, the *unus mundus*, and this affords one vistas where they can glimpse this one world (ibid., pars. 776–789).

Just as spirit is reflected in matter; the psyche is reflected in the body. Psyche and the body are microcosms within spirit and matter. God, says Jung, appears to us as two aspects, spirit and matter, but this is only because we "project a conception of him that corresponds to our own constitution: a body perceived by the senses and a spirit (=psyche) directly conscious of itself" (Letters, Vol. 2, 1975, p. 342). When Pauli struggles to understand to what extent psyche and spirit can be separated in the 1953 dialogue, the physicist attempts to compare the situation to archetypal images from his dreams that suggest a reciprocal relationship, or something similar to Athena springing forth from the head of Zeus (Meier, 2001, pp. 117–118). Jung responds with a technical explanation, that spirit is a specific category of psyche (ibid., p. 125). Yet he could just as easily have stated that psyche is a specific category of spirit. Indeed, not only does the relationship of psyche to spirit echo the relationship of body to matter, but Jung thinks that the psyche's connection with the body is much more apparent than the union of spirit and matter. Not only are the psyche and the body often thought of as being dependent on one another, but psychic processes themselves possess "a kind of materiality," Jung writes, "as in the idea of the subtle body and the Chinese *kuei*-soul clearly show. In view of the intimate connection that exists between certain psychic processes and their physical parallels we cannot," he flatly states, "very well accept the total immateriality of the psyche." Spirit too, however, despite seeming immaterial, seems to similarly be dependent on matter and vice versa. Jung cites the Tantrists, who described matter as being nothing but "the concreteness of God's thoughts." In any event, once again, the only "immediate reality" is the psyche, which labels its experiences as a "spiritual or material" origin (CW. 9i, 1948/1969b, par. 392). The additional differentiation that the psyche might make, as Jung says to Pauli, is that it might further differentiate those material experiences between the world and its own physical affectivity in that world, that is, the body (Meier, 2001, pp. 125–126).

Thus the psyche is spiritual, just as the body is material. When Jung speaks of psyche and matter in the same way that he speaks of spirit and matter, there is no contradiction or confusion within his thought. The psyche as we know it (i.e., our experiences) as well as the body may be two aspects of one union, just as with spirit and matter. Whatever the underlying substance, the *unus mundus*, might be, is the as yet unascertainable question at the heart of Jung's metaphysics.

3+1=4

Jung endorses a tripartite monism with two aspects, spirit and matter, with the psyche acting as a mediating third. According to Jung, the middle position of the psyche is the only way to avoid projection onto either spirit or matter. This understanding enables us to better grasp key concepts in Jung's thought such as the archetypes. Furthermore, the psyche must be seen as the middle third, not just any neutral language, because psyche is that through which our knowledge of spirit and matter passes through. Psyche and spirit enjoy a privileged relationship in the form of the *unio mentalis*, but this in turn involves the body and matter as well.

From all appearances, the 1953 exchange between Jung and Pauli wraps up amicably. Pauli concurs with why Jung argues for the psyche's middle position—so long as a possibility of a neutral language via the psychoid remains possible (Meier, 2001, p. 117). We know that Pauli was at times frustrated with the exchange. While it was ongoing he wrote to Jungian therapist Marie-Louise von Franz about how he felt Jung was dismissive of his concerns, both concerning his desire to give matter equal treatment to psyche, as well as his concern that Jung was expanding psychology beyond its proper boundaries (Lindorff, 2013, pp. 151–152). Ultimately Pauli told Jung that, much like the ideal and material, he hoped a medium would emerge between both of their viewpoints (Meier, 2001, p. 124). It is not evident that this ever occurred. The ideas that Jung fervently argues for in these letters—the opposition of spirit and matter instead of psyche and matter, and psyche's role as a mediating third that is a microcosm of some unknown, unitary substance—have not been addressed in the contemporary literature on Jung's dual-aspect monism, nor on the ideas developed between Jung and Pauli. David Lindorff's book on Jung and Pauli mentions that Jung saw the opposition of matter and spirit as more pertinent than one of matter and psyche, but he does not draw any implications from this concerning the differentiation of psyche and spirit beyond another factor to be reduced to a neutral language (2013, pp. 145–149). Susanne Geiser's text on Pauli and his collaboration with Jung makes note of Jung's declaration of the archetypes as spirit in 'On the Nature of the Psyche', and how such declarations certainly had a way of irritating Pauli. But she makes no mention in her analysis of the 1953 exchange of how Jung's defense of the psyche and spirit so radically differed from what Pauli had in mind until that point (2005, pp. 215–226). A 2014 book concerning the Pauli–Jung conjecture, edited by Harald Atanspacher, features a host of leading figures in Jungian psychology discussing a variety of topics concerning the work Jung and Pauli did together, including a chapter by William Seager about Pauli's version of dual-aspect monism. It is absent any discussion about spirit being a fundamental aspect of such a monism (2014, pp. 125–150). Nor is this trend exclusive to scholars who attend to the collaboration between Jung and Pauli. A chapter from *Jung & Philosophy* by Erik D. Goodwyn that focuses on how Jung contributes to the mind–body problem never mentions the role of spirit in this dynamic, nor the pertinent conclusions that Jung draws from it (2018, Ch. 3).

Most notably, Atmanspacher's reconstruction of the 'Pauli–Jung conjecture' conceives mind and matter as being 'local, epistemic aspects' of a 'non-local, ontological whole'. In this dual-aspect framework, the mental aspect encompasses both the individual subject, as well as the archetypal images and the collective unconscious. Thus, psyche and spirit are compressed into one category (Atmanspacher & Rickles, 2022, Ch. 3). What consequences there might be if compared to Jung's own views is a proposition that has yet to be reckoned with.

In any event, a major question remains for the monism sketched thus far. At one point in the letters with Pauli, Jung sketches a quaternity. Spirit and matter form the lateral arms, as the two aspects of the underlying substance. The vertical axis consists of the psyche, as well as whatever unknown transcendental world it is a microcosm of (Meier, 2001, p. 115). Later on, Jung notes the dilemma this quaternity suggests by posing a question, a question that echoes throughout the history of hermetic thought: "Oddly enough, the problem is still the same 2,000-year old one: How does one get from Three to Four?" (ibid., p. 129). In other words, *why* is the psyche a microcosm of the monist whole? On what ground can this be justified without resorting to a metaphysics that presumes to begin beyond the psyche? Jung's raising of Leibniz's monads may provide a clue. Jung not only suggests the monads might not be closed wholes, but he also does not see why they need to be beholden to an eminent creator that ensures all the monads cohere with one another, as Leibniz posited. Jungian and Deleuzian scholar Christian McMillan notes that this maneuver by Jung allows for 'transversal' relations, or rather outbound connections between separate but open wholes, rather than restricting connections to one fused whole (2018). This is the difference between psyche as a closed totality and psyche as an 'open monad' as Jung posits to Pauli (Meier, 2001, p. 115). This also would reflect an ontology that is a multiplicity, without the need of a transcendent first cause (CW. 8, 1952/1969a, par. 828). Still, it is difficult to see how such an ontology could be described without violating the epistemological standards that Jung's psychology is predicated on. A similar complaint could be raised against spirit. Even if we permit that spirit is a category conjured by the psyche, opposite and complementary to matter, there is still a question of *how* to discuss spirit in a way that does not risk falling back on ontological scaffolding. Jung says to Pauli that we find it difficult to grant spirit the same autonomy from the psyche that matter is afforded without hesitation

(Meier, 2001, pp. 116–117). Part of the reason for this however is surely the fact that, by and large, matter can be investigated by experimental methods that establish regular patterns, that is, natural laws. Spirit by its very nature thwarts this approach—it is ephemeral, seemingly based on chance (CW. 8, 1952/1969a, pars. 820–823). The problem is complicated when Jung nonetheless seems willing to make bold proclamations about the nature of spirit. In a letter to Father White, Jung says that "spirit is eternal and everywhere" (Letters, Vol. 1, 1973, p. 568). Presumably, Jung is impelled to make this claim in part due to the non-local, atemporal effects of meaning displayed in synchronicity. Still, it is very easy to see how such proclamations could be folded into the kind of metaphysics Jung condemns. Without a means to approach the 'fourth' in a way that satisfies Jung's epistemological standards, and despite all delineated in this chapter, it is difficult to see how the psyche's position as neutral third could be maintained without risking some poor metaphysical judgment.

As it turns out, and as the following chapters will demonstrate, this tripartite monism that Jung endorses has appeared before in the history of thought, albeit under a different name: *Spinozism*. For Spinoza agrees with Jung that the attributes of God, what he calls thought and extension, are wholly expressed through the individual, and it is only through the individual that knowledge of the Divine may be obtained. Furthermore, Spinoza can go a step further than Jung—it is through such bodily knowledge that Spinoza reaches his theory of God, in which the essences of all individual things are contained. Therefore the search for the *fourth* in Jung's metaphysics might be found by studying Jung through a Spinozist lens; but if this is indeed so, it is only because the Spinozist viewpoint—a middle between thought and matter, a knowledge of oneself that is inseparable from knowledge of the Divine, and a microcosm within the infinite—is what Jung inherently stood for to begin with.

Notes

1 For a breakdown of how the concept of spirit evolves in Jung's thought, see Main (2007, Ch. 2) and Gitz-Johansen (2020).
2 For more on Pauli's reaction to 'Answer to Job', see Lindorff (2013, Ch. 7–9). For more on Pauli's exchange with Jung regarding the nature of psyche, matter, and spirit, see also Geiser (2005, Ch. 4).
3 As Jon Mills notes, Jung's psychology *is* an ontology in the sense that it informs and is informed of our reality, and that this is something Jung himself would

not disagree with (Mills, 2019, pp. 4–6). Michael Howarth illustrates how Jung's sensitivity toward the limits on metaphysical speculation established that the critical philosophy of Immanuel Kant (1724–1804) places on cognition is in fact not an attempt by Jung to shut down metaphysical speculation but an awareness that he needed to find a sophisticated way *around* Kant's limits on cognition by working *through* them; that is, by finding a way to knowledge through the finite self (2012).

4 Sometimes Jung does simply conflate the term archetype with spirit, and instinct with matter, such as when he tells Pauli the archetypes as Ideas in the Platonic sense fall on the side of spirit. However, as Jung is unequivocal about spirit being a category of ideas, it is logical to conclude that when Jung speaks of the archetype as spirit, he is referring to how the archetype typically presents itself to the psyche, that is, as images and symbols, and that therefore he's simply short-handing the archetypal image's connection to spirit. This seems evident when Jung states that the "archetypes, or dominants of the collective unconscious" can be broken down phenomenologically, that is, by what we experience, into two categories: instinctual or archetypal. The instincts pertain to natural impulses, while the archetypal is the archetypal images and universal ideas that occur in the conscious psyche (CW. 8, 1946/1969a, par. 423). Elsewhere Jung plainly states that the instinct's formal aspect is indeed the archetype (1952/1969a, par. 846). One can conclude that in any instance where Jung speaks of the formal aspect of the archetype, whether in regards to spirit or matter, he is referring to the archetype as such, that is, the psychoid aspect. In this book, the term 'archetypal image' refers to archetypal content that falls under the category of spirit.

5 This is how Jung depicts meaning in a 1960 letter to Cornell, where Jung says that instincts appear in archetypal images and that the meaning they bestow is essentially the same as how instincts warn animals of impending catastrophe (Letters, Vol. 2, 1975, p. 542).

6 "Ich konnte aber auch, als Metaphysiker, die Traumaussage auf ihren objektiven Sinn, also von der Psychologie weg, untersuchen und kame dabei in das Gebiet des sog. Geistes bzw. Sinnes, von wo aus ich die archetypische Physik vielleicht erahnen mochte" (Meier, 1992, p. 114). In the English translation, this sentence was translated to: "But as a metaphysician I could also examine the dream statement for its objective meaning—in other words, not psychologically—which would take me into the sphere of what one might call spirit or the mind, and from there it might be possible for me to have an archetypal physics" (Meier, 2001, p. 114). It should be noted that even translating 'sinne' as sense, rather than meaning, would be a relevant change; Atmanspacher notes that the German word 'sinn' has also been used to denote a special type of 'sense' beyond ordinary perceptions (Atmanspacher & Rickles, 2022, pp. 51–52).

7 "Ich bin infolge meiner professionellen Beschiiftigung mit Psychologie mehr mit dem mythologischen Aspekt der Natur konfrontiert, d.h. also mit dem

sog. Geiste (oder Sinne)" (Meier, 1992, p. 115). In the English text, this reads as: "As a consequence as my professional work with psychology, I am more frequently confronted with the mythological aspect of nature, i.e., with what one might call the *spirit* (or the mind)" (Meier, 1992, p. 115).

8 Pauli also wanted to justify an impersonal interpretation of his dreams because he had an aversion to a personal interpretation. This is a point that Jung insisted was not tenable—as the psychic perspective was irrevocably personal. Eventually, Pauli concedes on this issue, at least to a degree (see Lindorff, 2013, Ch. 13).

9 Now Jung does concede near the close of the 1953 exchange with Pauli that finding some "common ground" between psychology and physics might be another way to investigate their common origin, and Jung believes that the study of numbers and their origins might be the way to do this. However, this is very different from trying to interpret one field with the other, to try and interpret psychology through physics or vice versa, or to find direct correlates between one branch and the other. Jung seems to think this is impossible because spirit and matter as aspects of the monist whole are incommensurable. In any event, finding common ground between the methodologies of physics and psychology is not strictly the same thing as finding correlations between the aspects of spirit and matter (Meier, 2001, pp. 127–128). This is exemplified in Jung's declaration that mathematics, the language of physics, is incompatible with psychology since there is no standard by which to quantify psychic qualities; that is, there is no reducible language between the two fields (CW. 8, 1946/1969a, par. 417).

10 The trouble with people, Jung writes in a letter to Sinclair in 1952, is that "they are still stuck with the silly question as to whether a metaphysical assertion is true or not, or whether a mythologem refers to a historical fact or not. They don't see, and they don't want to see, what the psyche can do. But there—alas—is the key" (Letters, Vol. 2, 1975, p. 97).

11 Such ancient cultures would also say some spirits do not come from human-kind at all, but are otherworldly (ibid., pars. 578–579).

12 This argument grants that there is some sort of correlation between the terms psyche and soul. This is by no means self-evident. It should be stressed that in some instances Jung uses the term soul in a technical sense to refer to parts of the psyche, such as the anima archetype (CW. 6, 1921/1971, pars. 797–811). In other places still, such as in his religious treatises, he uses it in a Christian or Neoplatonic sense. However, in the original German, Jung at times uses the German word *seele* in place of psyche. This word has no exact equivalent in English, as it expresses a combination of 'psyche' and 'soul' (CW. 12, 1953, par. 9, footnote). While this difference was mostly papered over with the term psyche in the English editions, occasionally this usage of a synonym for psyche that implies a connection to soul survived the translations. For instance, when Jung writes about how psychology emerged as a science in his own right, he says that the "hypothesis of the unconscious puts a large question-mark after the idea of the psyche. The *soul* [...] threatened to emerge from its chrysalis

as something with unexpected and uninvestigated properties" (CW. 8, 1946/1969a, par. 356; *emphasis mine*). Here an equivalency between psyche and soul, at least on some level, is implicit.

13 For example, in the 'Structure of the Unconscious' from 1916 (CW. 7, 1916/1966).

14 It may prove inadequate to restrict synchronistic experiences to an 'inner' psychic event complemented by an 'outer' physical event. For more, see Chapter 5 of this text.

15 Jung acknowledges that the alchemists never fully understood the true nature of their fantasies of transmuting gold, or in Dorn's case the extraction of the heavenly substance from the body, the caelum. They were never able to withdraw their projections and continued in a participation mystique. However, Jung stresses such an error continues through contemporary thought. Though we fancy that such erroneous fantasies could only occur in the Middle Ages, in Jung's estimate modern thinking has not yet gotten out of the woods regarding this danger (CW. 14, 1963/1970, par. 695). This warning seems to apply well to any metaphysical model that projects the psyche into the basins of either spirit or matter.

16 Also see Edinger's commentary, where he explains that when Jung speaks of the *imago Dei*, of which the *caelum* is equivalent, he is speaking of the self (1995, pp. 287–288).

17 In a letter to Thornton from 1958, Jung states: "The spirit is no merit in itself and it has a peculiarly irrealizing effect if not counter-balanced by its material opposite. Thus think again and if you feel enough solid ground under your feet, follow the call of spirit." In this same letter, Jung again says that spirit is always anchored within matter, and matter is dead and empty without spirit (Letters, Vol. 2, 1975, p. 460).

References

Addison, A. (2009). "Jung, Vitalism, and 'the Psychoid': A Historical Reconstruction." *Journal of Analytical Psychology*, 54, 123–142.

Addison, A. (2019). *Jung's Psychoid Concept Contexualised*. London: Routledge.

Adler, G. & Jaffe, A. (1973). *C.G. Jung Letters 1: 1906–1950*. Translated by R. Hull. Princeton: Princeton University Press.

Adler, G. & Jaffe, A. (1975). *C.G. Jung Letters 2: 1951–1961*. Translated by R. Hull. Princeton: Princeton University Press.

Atmanspacher, H. (2018). "Synchronicity and the Experience of Psychophysical Correlations" (Ch. 14), in *Research in Analytical Psychology: Empirical Research*, edited by C. Roesler. London: Routledge.

Atmanspacher, H. & Rickles, D. (2022). *Dual-Aspect Monism and the Deep Structure of Meaning*. London & New York: Routledge.

Edinger, E. (1995). *The Mysterium Lectures: A Journey through C.G. Jung's Mysterium Coniunctionis*. Transcribed and edited by J.D. Blackmer. Toronto: Inner City Books.

Gieser, S. (2005). *The Innermost Kernel: Depth Psychology and Quantum Physics. Wolfgang Pauli's dialogue with C.G. Jung.* Berlin: Springer.

Gitz-Johansen, T. (2020). "Jung and the Spirit: A Review of Jung's Discussions of the Phenomenon of Spirit." *Journal of Analytical Psychology*, 65(4), 653–671.

Goodwyn, E. (2018). "Jung and the Mind–Body Problem" (Ch. 3), in *Jung and Philosophy*, edited by J. Mills. London: Routledge.

Haworth, M. (2012). "Synchronicity and correlationism: Carl Jung as Speculative Realist." *Speculations: A Journal of Speculative Realism*, 3, 189–209.

Jung, C.G. (1919a). "Instinct and the Unconscious," in *The Structure and Dynamics of the Psyche*, 2nd ed. Translated by R. Hull. Collected Works of C.G. Jung, Vol. 8. Princeton: Princeton University Press, 1969a.

Jung, C.G. (1919b). "The Psychological Foundation of Belief in Spirits," in *The Structure and Dynamics of the Psyche*, 2nd ed. Translated by R. Hull. Collected Works of C.G. Jung, Vol. 8. Princeton: Princeton University Press, 1969a.

Jung, C.G. (1921). *Psychological Types*, 2nd ed. Translated by R. Hull. Collected Works of C.G. Jung, Vol. 6. Princeton: Princeton University Press, 1971.

Jung, C.G. (1926). "Spirit and Life," in *The Structure and Dynamics of the Psyche*, 2nd ed. Translated by R. Hull. Collected Works of C.G. Jung, Vol. 8. Princeton: Princeton University Press, 1969a.

Jung, C.G. (1931). "Basic Postulates of Analytical Psychology," in *The Structure and Dynamics of the Psyche*, 2nd ed. Translated by R. Hull. Collected Works of C.G. Jung, Vol. 8. Princeton: Princeton University Press, 1969a.

Jung, C.G. (1942). "Paracelsus as a Spiritual Phenomenon," in *Alchemical Studies*. Translated by R. Hull. Collected Works of C.G. Jung, Vol. 13. Princeton: Princeton University Press, 1967.

Jung, C.G. (1946). "On the Nature of the Psyche," in *The Structure and Dynamics of the Psyche*, 2nd ed. Translated by R. Hull. Collected Works of C.G. Jung, Vol. 8. Princeton: Princeton University Press, 1969a.

Jung, C.G. (1948). "The Phenomenology of the Spirit in Fairytales," in *The Archetypes and the Collective Unconscious*, 2nd ed. Translated by R. Hull. Collected Works of C.G. Jung, Vol. 9i, 1969b.

Jung, C.G. (1952). "Synchronicity: An Acausal Connecting Principle," in *The Structure and Dynamics of the Psyche*, 2nd ed. Translated by R. Hull. Collected Works of C.G. Jung, Vol. 8. Princeton: Princeton University Press, 1969a.

Jung, C.G. (1952). "Answer to Job," in *Psychology and Religion: east and West*, 2nd ed. Translated by R. Hull. Collected Works of C.G. Jung, Vol. 11. Princeton: Princeton University Press, 1969c.

Jung, C.G. (1954). "The Philosophical Tree," in *Alchemical Studies*. Translated by R. Hull. Collected Works of C.G. Jung, Vol. 13. Princeton: Princeton University Press, 1967.

Jung, C.G. (1954). "Psychological Aspects of the Mother Archetype," in *The Archetypes and the Collective Unconscious*, 2nd ed. Translated by R. Hull. Collected Works of C.G. Jung, Vol. 9i, 1969b.

Jung, C.G. (1957). "Commentary on 'The Secret of the Golden Flower,'" in *Alchemical Studies*. Translated by R. Hull. Collected Works of C.G. Jung, Vol. 13. Princeton: Princeton University Press, 1967.

Jung, C.G. (1963). *Mysterium Coniunctionis*, 2nd ed. Translated by R. Hull. Collected Works of C.G. Jung, Vol. 14. Princeton: Princeton University Press, 1970.

Kastrup, B. (2021). *Decoding Jung's Metaphysics*. Winchester: Iff Books.

Lindorff, D. (2013). *Pauli and Jung: The Meeting of Two Great Minds*, eBook edition. New York: Quest Books.

Main, R. (2007). *Revelations of Chance: Synchronicity as Spiritual Experience*. New York: State University of New York.

McMillan, C. (2018). "Jung and Deleuze: Enchanted Openings to the Other: A Philosophical Contribution." *International Journal of Jungian Studies*, 10(3), 184–198.

Meier, C.A. (ed.) (1992). *Wolfgang Pauli und C. G. Jung Ein Briefwechsel 1932–195 8*. Berlin: Springer-Verlag.

Meier, C.A. (ed.) (2001). *Atom and Archetype: The Pauli/Jung Letters 1932–1958*. London: Routledge.

Mills, J. (2019). "Introduction: Philosophizing Jung," in *Jung and Philosophy*, edited by J. Mills. London: Routledge.

Seager, W. (2014). "Dual Support for Pauli's Dual Aspects," in *The Pauli–Jung Conjecture and its Impact Today*, edited by H. Atmanspacher & C. Fuchs. Exeter: Imprint Academic.

Chapter 2

C.G. Jung, the Unlikely Spinozist I

The Meeting at the Middle Third

Of all the topics to commence an argument that Jung was in fact, however unwittingly, a consummate Spinozist, Jung's fervent argument for the existence of spirit would seem like a strange place to start. Jung does, after all, make Spinoza a chief antagonist in his essay 'The Phenomenology of the Spirit in Fairytales', where he claims that Spinoza robs spirit of all its power and autonomy that Jung so ardently defends (CW. 9i, 1948/1969b, pars. 385, 390–391). Nor can one easily picture Spinoza entertaining the more radical concepts associated with spirit that Jung readily embraces, such as spirit as a catalyzing force upon the psyche, or as the basis of paranormal phenomena. Spinoza critiques such views of spirit in the first chapter of his *Theological–Political Treatise*, specifically concerning the notion that the Biblical prophets had special access to the "Spirit, or mind, of God" (TTP I 25–48, CWS II pp. 85–93).[12] Consequently, one might protest that a discussion of spirit would work to only widen the gulf between Jung and Spinoza, to ultimately attribute to them both the worst canards one could cast at the other: Jung the obscure mystic, Spinoza the overt rationalist. Would it not then be more prudent to simply begin with a comparison of their respective metaphysics? Spinoza is, after all, credited as the originator of the dual-aspect monism sketched out by Pauli and Jung (Atmanspacher & Rickles, 2022, pp. 5, 8). Yet Jung's own monism differs from how the Pauli–Jung conjecture has been articulated in the contemporary discourse, because Jung does not view the two aspects of the monist whole to be psyche and matter. Rather, Jung deems the twin aspects to be spirit and matter, with the psyche playing the role of a mediating third. Therefore no study of a dual-aspect monism shared by Jung and Spinoza can avoid the topic of spirit.

DOI: 10.4324/9781003516996-3

In the first chapter, we saw that Jung distinguishes psyche from spirit for several reasons: first, in his estimation, it is the only way to avoid the projection of the psyche into either spirit or matter, which results in either cosmic idealism or reductive materialism, both of which are metaphysics built on unverifiable premises which Jung rejects. Furthermore, the placement of psyche as the middle third between spirit and matter honors the fact that the psyche is our only immediate experience, through which our knowledge of matter and spirit must pass. Finally, psyche and spirit are closely related, and the psyche in some sense *is* spirit, just as the body is matter—nevertheless, the psyche must be differentiated from the other ideal things it perceives. An outstanding issue with Jung's view, and the tripartite monism that follows from it, is that it remains unexplained *why* the psyche plays this middle role, and how the psyche's unique position can be established without falling back onto the type of ontological scaffolding that Jung abhors.

In the wake of German Idealism, the philosopher and historian of philosophy Friedrich Adolf Trendelenburg (1802–1872) analyzed the varied and sometimes contradictory ways in which Spinoza had been appropriated during the era. On one hand, Spinoza was depicted by Jacobi during the pantheist controversy as an atheist who wished to plunge the world into a sheer mechanistic nature; alternatively, for Schelling and Hegel, Spinoza was the launchpoint for cosmic idealism. Trendelenburg concludes that either route is an error and that Spinoza must not be seen as either an idealist or a materialist. Rather, his philosophy occupies a unique and fundamental place in the history of philosophy. Between idealism and materialism, says Trendelenburg, there is a *middle, third* option: Spinozism (1847, pp. 241–262, quoted in Beiser, 2012, p. 240). This is due to the absolute parity and equal valence with which Spinoza treats God's attributes. Thought and extension are both equal expressions of God's infinite and eternal power; neither attribute can affect the other, and certainly neither causes the other. Rather both equally express the exact same order and connection of what God produces, that is, finite or singular things (E IIP7, CWS I pp. 451–452). All singular things are contained *equally* in God's attributes. In Spinoza's philosophy, the problem of why the individual is contained within the attributes is already accounted for, because each individual is an expression of God's absolute power to create anything he conceives; each individual moves within the Divine whole in a kind of transcendental immanence (E IP16, CWS I pp. 424–425).

This third way between idealism and materialism is precisely what Jung seeks, not just in terms of a balanced worldview, but as the very starting point for any sort of ontology that he would willingly subscribe to. And while Jung certainly never acknowledges Spinoza as a precursor to his monism, nor is there any reason to believe Jung was entirely aware of the intellectual debt he owed the Dutch philosopher, it is nonetheless interesting that in the scant attention Jung affords Spinoza throughout his *Collected Works*, the only time Spinoza appears as more than just a passing figure is in the defense of spirit that Jung launches in the 'The Phenomenology of the Spirit in Fairytales'. It is this essay that Jung will refer back to when he openly declares his tripartite monism of matter, psyche, and spirit.[3] And while it is true that Jung casts Spinoza as an opponent in this piece, it is also paradoxically in this essay, and his distinction between spirit and psyche, that Jung reveals the Spinozist tendencies laden in his own thought.

Jung's Critique of Spinoza via Spirit

Jung begins 'The Phenomenology of the Spirit in Fairytales' with a historical survey of how the word spirit has been used throughout the ages. Here Jung defines spirit as "an immaterial substance or form of existence" that in the most universal or highest sense is sometimes considered to be God. Understood as a "principle that stands in opposition to matter," spirit is conceivably "the vehicle for psychic phenomena or even of life itself." In this way spirit, while contrary to matter, is every bit as much a part of nature. In contradistinction to this stance, however, is the notion that spirit is actually removed from nature, deemed to be opposed to it, and thus it becomes severed from its "connection with psyche and life." From this viewpoint spirit is seen as exclusively supernatural, something transcendent to the world. Jung argues this is precisely what Spinoza does by making spirit an attribute of God, or "the One Substance."

This move, in Jung's estimation, is not at all different from simply denying spirit's existence by making it reducible to matter (CW. 9i, 1948/1969b, par. 385). A sort of inevitable passage is implied here: the error of making spirit transcendent and otherworldly all too easily swings entirely the other way, where it instead becomes packaged as a mere epiphenomenon of brain and blood, or simply the psyche itself. It is, in fact, the "invisible presence" of spirit in the psyche, as something it experiences directly yet cannot pinpoint the source of, that causes the psyche to assume it and spirit have a shared identity, to confuse both psyche and spirit as "one's own spirit," and this causes the psyche to attribute properties to itself that belong to spirit alone. This conflation feeds the illusion of being part of a transcendent spirit vastly superior not only to matter but to nature itself, and so that in comparison nature is no better than death. Spirit becomes the highest, heavenly good—which naturally the psyche chooses to identify with—and therefore the physical realm must be the source of all evil, and it is to be shunned (ibid., par. 394; Meier, 2001, p. 126). Jung identifies this imbalanced line of thought within Christianity. The subsequent historical turn toward materialism against religion led to the opposite distortion: the reduction of spirit to matter. This mistake too is caused by the identification of spirit with psychic functions. The only difference in this instance is that the psyche is not seen as a heavenly vessel, but rather a product of physiology. Spirit becomes trapped in the body (ibid., pars. 389–391).

The conflation of spirit with the psyche and the problems this subsequently causes is precisely what Jung warns Pauli of in their 1953 exchange when he tells Pauli that modern thought has made the mistake of robbing spirit of the same autonomy granted to matter without hesitation (Meier, 2001, pp. 116–117). A primary reason for Jung's placement of the psyche between spirit and matter is to avoid carelessly projecting the psyche into either domain, which leads to seeing the source of existence solely in the heavens or in the earth (see Ch. 1, pp. 24–26). The misplacement of spirit is tantamount to the same error, for by misplacing spirit one is really misplacing the psyche by imagining that one can make spirit its subordinate. In the end, one is left with either the grandiose projections of cosmic idealism or instead the uncompromising austerity of eliminative materialism. The toggling from one extreme to the other is characteristic of unconscious projections left unchecked, a psyche in the throes of some underlying imbalance—reminiscent of what Jung calls enantiodromia (CW. 6, 1921/1971, pars. 708–709). Jung's insistence that psyche and spirit must remain unmixed is the correction of such an imbalance, so that projection and displacement may be avoided.

The second time Jung raises Spinoza's name in the essay, it is to reinforce the accusation that Spinoza renders spirit antinatural by warping it into some "supranatural and transmundane cosmic principle of order." This would tally Spinoza among the idealists who misappropriated spirit by rendering it transcendent to the world. Jung goes as far as to list Spinoza and

Christianity side by side for this offense, for both made spirit a "cosmic principle of order" tantamount to God or at least "an attribute of the One Substance (as in Spinoza) or one Person of the Godhead (as in Christianity)." This pairing of Spinoza and Christianity is curious, given Spinoza's views on the God of religion (CW. 9i, 1948/1969b, par. 390; E I Appendix, CWS I pp. 439–446; TTP, CWS II). But it becomes clearer why Jung makes this association when Spinoza is referenced implicitly a *third* time, in the very next paragraph where Jung describes the reversal toward the opposite error, the reduction of spirit to matter:

> One only had to give the One Substance another name and call it "matter" to produce the idea of a spirit which was entirely dependent on nutrition and environment, and whose highest form was the intellect or reason. This meant that the original pneumatic presence had taken up its abode in man's physiology [...] For it was into this latter concept that the original spontaneity of the spirit withdrew after it had been degraded to a servile attribute of matter.
>
> (ibid., par. 391)

In his analysis of these passages, the Jungian analyst and scholar Joseph Cambray correctly points out that Jung's accusations are not a fair portrayal of Spinoza's thought, that the absolute parity that Spinoza demands of God's attributes, and his refusal to reduce one to the other, goes unnoticed by Jung. He concludes that Jung's mistake was that he saw Spinoza as a kind of reductive materialist (2014, pp. 45–48). This is indeed ultimately where Jung claims Spinozism terminates—but only *after* Spinoza had committed the first fallacy, the direction toward grand idealism. Therefore, Jung is not simply accusing Spinoza of idealism *or* materialism. Rather, Spinoza's villainy, and why this thinker who Jung hardly pays attention to elsewhere figures so prominently here, in Jung's defense of a term that, as we shall see, Jung forcibly reads into Spinoza's philosophy, is because Jung sees Spinoza as the very passage from one blunder to the next, from a cosmic idealism to a barren materialism. In the history of thought, Jung singles out Spinoza as the fulcrum between both paths of displacement.

Why does Jung conclude that Spinoza ultimately fails to hold space between these two contrary positions, that his philosophy instead gets bandied about the erroneous extremes? Implicit in this question, and Jung's dismissal of Spinoza overall, is the fact that Jung here is acknowledging that Spinoza is relevant to the issue of this middle third, this neutral medium between thought and extension—or spirit and matter. There is no doubt that Jung's usage of Spinoza in 'The Phenomenology of the Spirit in Fairytales' is deliberate, that he is not just dispensing with any historical thinker to decorate the backdrop of his work. After God, Spinoza is the first figure Jung introduces in the section; he is the only person Jung references more than once, and he suggests that Spinoza has committed a very special offense, one that eclipses both Christianity and materialism for their respective biases. The question of why Jung singles out Spinoza for this critique is compounded by the fact that Jung is interjecting a word into Spinoza's philosophy that simply does not at all have the meaning there that Jung grants it: the term 'spirit' plays no significant role in Spinoza's metaphysics. Beyond the deconstruction of spirit in the *Theological–Political Treatise*, Spinoza deploys the word in some minor usages here and there in his writing, such as when he attacks Descartes' notion of the soul as master of the spirits of the body, in the preface of the *Ethics* Part V (CWS I pp. 594–597; CWS I p. 698). It is also used in a notable passage in one of Spinoza's early texts, the *Treatise of the Emendation of the Intellect*, when Spinoza compares the functions of the mind to a 'spiritual automaton' where thoughts reflect in the mind but the mind does not choose what thoughts to reflect on, a notion that Jung might readily approve of (TIE, 85; CWS I p. 37).[4] What Spinoza absolutely never does, however, is use the word spirit to refer to one of God's attributes. Thought and extension are the only attributes Spinoza names, and he is clear that they are the only attributes humankind can even be aware of since they involve our nature (E ID6, CWS I p. 409; IIP1–2, pp. 448–449). How did Jung conclude that spirit, too, was an expression of God's essence in Spinoza?[5] Does he have some reason to believe that spirit belongs besides thought and extension as a *third* attribute of Spinoza's God? Or rather, did he infer spirit was roughly equivalent to Spinoza's attribute of thought, given their shared ideal character?[6] This latter explanation is almost certainly the case. For Jung, spirit encompasses objects of psychic experience that cannot be proved to exist in the material world (Meier, 2001, p. 125). Similarly, according to Spinoza, the attribute of thought pertains to all minds and ideas, ranging from every conceivable idea in God's Infinite Intellect, all the way down to the finite human mind (E IP21–22, CWS I pp. 429–430; Ep. 64, CWS II pp. 438–439).[7] More specifically, an idea is the objective essence of something that has a formal essence, for example, the mind is the idea of the body, or the body's objective essence (E IIP13S, CWS I pp. 457–458).[8] One may point out that if ideas for Spinoza are simply the objective essence of something that exists formally in extension, like the mind is to the body, then thought always has a material reference, and therefore it is not analogous to the incorporeality that Jung grants spirit. However, Spinoza plainly states that ideas have their own formal essence as well, and this means that they in turn have an objective essence; in other words, there is an idea of the idea (E IIP20–21S, CWS I pp. 467–468).[9] The most extreme example of this is that the objective ideas of everything that God produces exist formally in God's Infinite Intellect, which is essentially God's power considered solely under the attribute of thought (E IIP7C, CWS I p. 451). Furthermore, Spinoza fully permits that there must be true ideas of things that do not currently exist, and therefore they would have no corporeal existence (E IIP8, pp. 452–453). Therefore, ideas have their own formality devoid of reference to matter or other possible attributes. There is accord here with Jung's definition of spirit as having no corporeal reference.

Jung's inference here is significant, since Spinoza's handling of spirit, despite the word never being used by Spinoza in the way that Jung deploys it, is Jung's justification for including Spinoza in the essay to begin with. The specific framing of Jung's critique as *spirit contra substance* is reminiscent of complaints raised against Spinoza more than a century prior by the German Idealist Georg W. F. Hegel. Hegel also read his own conception of spirit into Spinoza's philosophy; by making thought a mere attribute of God, Hegel declared that Spinoza had failed to do justice to the totalizing power of thought—or what Hegel calls spirit, and instead Spinoza was left with an inert substance, whose powerless determinations ultimately fade back into the featureless one (2018, pp. 252–289). While Jung professes no admiration for Hegel, Hegel's interpretation of Spinoza was hugely influential, and Jung's arguments echo key pieces of Hegel's critique (1963/1989, p. 69; Peden, 2014, p. 82).[10] It is just as likely, however, that Jung saw his version of spirit tantamount to Spinoza's attribute of thought because he simply recognized how Spinoza grasps the same fundamental split that Jung discovered from the Taoists who wrote *The Secret of the Golden Flower*— that is to say, the recognition that spirit and matter are different expressions of one and the same being (CW. 13, 1957/1967, par. 76, footnote). This is the insight that also informs Jung's tripartite monism of matter, psyche, and spirit (CW. 8, 1946/1969a, pars. 408, 420). Such a monism with spirit and matter as the twin aspects, with psyche as the middle third, is what Jung argues for in his letters to Pauli (Meier, 2001, pp. 116–117). It is this middle point, both between idealism and materialism and also the psyche itself expressing a unity between matter and spirit, where Jung and Spinoza meet.

Substance and Modes

In his *Lectures on the History of Philosophy*, Hegel assesses past philosophical systems through the successive development and concretization of individual and collective thought throughout history, that is, Hegel's own concept of spirit. Hegel admires Spinoza for recognizing that the two aspects of existence, thought and extension, are of one and the same unity. However, in Hegel's interpretation of Spinoza, the attributes that merely decompose from the One Substance are always exterior to it; in turn, finite individuals further decompose from the attributes, are even further removed from the absolute, which they perceive solely via the attributes. But this knowledge of how things decompose from substance is, according to Hegel, nominal if not outright illusory: in the fourth definition of *Ethics* Part I, Spinoza defines an attribute as "what the intellect perceives" of constituting God's essence (CWS I p. 408). From this definition Hegel famously raises, and in fact establishes, the subjective interpretation of Spinoza's attributes—Hegel takes Spinoza's definition to mean that the attributes are wholly an understanding of the finite intellect, and thus removed from substance proper; beyond this, the One Substance is utterly incomprehensible. Furthermore, both attributes and the finite things that follow from them are merely derived from substance, and so they enjoy no existence beyond this—or, to evoke Hegel's concept that he claims to have found the resources for in Spinoza, the attributes and finite things are nothing but *negations* of substance. In this view, the finite can do nothing except ultimately fade away into the substance from whence it came. Hegel chastises Spinoza for failing to follow through on the implications of equating finite modes with negation, for not considering the idea that the negative might have the ability to negate itself, to turn back onto substance as something opposed to it, and to ultimately surpass it—in other words, Hegel sees no dynamism in Spinoza, no ability for movement or succession. By rendering thought as a mere attribute of God rather than the very thing that determines itself internally, as Hegel conceives spirit, all Spinozism ultimately can accomplish in Hegel's estimation is to proceed from a faceless absolute to its powerless emanations, which ultimately collapse back into the faceless absolute. Consequently, Hegel sees both the individual and the attributes as weak points in Spinozist thought, for he contends that both are nothing but mere shadows cast by substance, that everything external to the absolute has only a provisional existence before it, and thus accusations of atheism against Spinoza miss the mark; rather, says Hegel, with Spinoza there is *too much* God (2018, 252–289).[11]

This misguided departure that Hegel speaks of, from an inert substance that can do nothing but emanate its derivations, to finite beings that can do nothing but fall back into the substance from whence they came, is what Jung reconstructs in his own dismissal of Spinoza: both critiques proceed from pretensions of a cosmic design, to collapse ultimately into a lifeless whole; each single out the attributes as the problem, as a bridge that fails to adequately connect the absolute with the singular. For Hegel, it is making thought exterior to substance that makes the attributes insufficient; for Jung, it is because he takes 'attribute' to mean a transcendent cosmic principle that is opposed to nature. In either case, it is argued that Spinoza loses something of spirit, by rendering it as something that is not internal to substance or nature.

Hegel's claim that the attributes are external to substance rests upon the assumption that the attributes are only conceived by the finite intellect but do not truly exist beyond this. This subjective interpretation of the attributes has been comprehensively rejected in contemporary Spinoza studies.[12] Even if one takes definition four of *Ethics* Part I to mean that attributes are only what the intellect perceives of substance, the word 'perception' is significant—later, when Spinoza embarks on his theory of the mind, he will define an idea as a concept that the mind forms by its being a thinking thing. Spinoza explicitly notes that he uses the word concept here, rather than perception, because concept seems to imply an action or activity of the mind, whereas "perception seems to indicate that the Mind is acted on by the object" (E IID3, CWS I p. 447). Spinoza therefore is suggesting in the definition of an attribute that the intellect is perceiving something that really does constitute the essence of substance, which the singular intellect accepts as is.[13]

This conclusion certainly accords with the way Spinoza generally writes about the attributes: there are numerous passages in the *Ethics* where he states that the attributes pertain to God's essence. What is essence in Spinoza? It is that which a thing "can neither be nor be conceived" without

(E IID2, CWS I p. 447). God's essence is his power (E IP34, CWS I p. 439). The attributes then are the very expressions of God's eternal and infinite power, and so therefore the attributes are as eternal and immutable as God himself (E IP19, P20C2, CWS I pp. 428–429). Our knowledge of God cannot be illusory—how could Spinoza claim that the human mind can have adequate knowledge of God's essence if this were so (E IIP47, CWS I pp. 482–483)? If the attributes pertain to God's power, this means that they are expressions of God's absolutely infinite power of existing and comprehending on which the very equality between thought and extension is based (E IIP7, CWS I p. 452).[14] Therefore the attributes cannot simply be shapeless emanations of substance that a finite mind projects form onto, nor exterior to substance itself.

What then of finite things, or what Spinoza calls the modes that God produces? According to Spinoza only two things exist: substance and modes. Substance is that "which is in itself and conceived through itself," whereas a mode is "that which is in another through which it is also conceived" (E ID3, D5, CWS I pp. 408–409). There can only be that which is, and that which is in another; in other words, there is only substance and modes (E IA1, CWS I p. 410). Now, Spinoza argues that the only substance that can exist is God (E IP1–11, CWS I pp. 408–419). Therefore, whatever is, must be in God (E IP15, CWS I p. 420). It is true then that modes are dependent on substance for their existence. But this is not due to the modes being nothing but the terminal emanations of an absolute that they dissolve back to, nor would it all be right to say that there is a division between spirit and nature. The attributes are expressions of God's absolute power, and everything he produces is wholly contained in those expressions (E IP16, CWS I pp. 424–425).[15] One may distinguish between the absolutely infinite power of God as *cause*, and everything God produces as *effect*; or rather substance is conceived through itself, and all its modifications follow from God's nature. Spinoza calls the former 'naturing nature', and the latter 'natured nature'.[16] The essence of God differs from the essence of singular things, yet the modes remain immanent to God, or rather the effects inhere within their cause, because attributes that express God's power must also pertain to the essence of everything God produces (E IP29S, CWS I p. 434). If the modes can be considered as following from the attributes, it is in the sense that the modes are what is expressed by the attributes; or that they are contained in the attributes just as they are contained within God. Contrary to being opposed to nature, in Spinoza's system it is the attributes such as thought, or 'spirit', that authorize the immanence between 'naturing nature' and 'natured nature', or between God and modes.[17]

Spinoza's mixing of nature with the Divine raises the question of whether or not he should be called a pantheist. Spinozist scholar Jonathan Bennett states that Spinoza is indeed a pantheist because he identifies "God with the whole of reality" (1984, p. 32). Yet 'reality' here demands a qualifier: if by pantheism one effectively means that God and the world are the same or interchangeable, Spinoza would definitely not accept this. It is the distinction of substance and modes that necessitates this qualification, because for Spinoza the world, as a mode of substance, absolutely does not exhaust all that exists. Modes cannot exist without that which causes itself to exist, that is, substance. And the Divine substance has an absolutely infinite power that produces an infinity of things, which surely always exceeds the world as it is given. Philosopher R.S. Woolhouse stresses that the corporeal world is not equivalent to the attribute of extension but rather a mode contained within it—so therefore, the world is not simply God conceived as extended substance (i.e., the world isn't simply the attribute of extension), but rather the world, or even the entire universe itself, is but one of an infinity of potential modes expressed under extension (Woolhouse, 1993).[18] There is always a demarcation between the infinite kinds of things that exist and the absolute power that produces those infinities—God is the latter. It is for this reason that Spinoza writes to his colleague Henry Oldenburg about critics who suspect Spinoza of covert atheism that they are missing the point, that when Spinoza equates God with Nature, what he really means is that:

> God is, as they say, the immanent, but not the transitive, cause of all things. That all things are in God and move in God, I affirm, I say with [the Apostle] Paul, and perhaps also with all the ancient philosophers, though in another way—I would also be so bold as to say, with all the ancient Hebrews, as far as we can conjecture from certain traditions, corrupted as they have been in many ways. Nevertheless, some people think [my philosophy] rests on the assumption that God is one and the same as Nature (by which they understand a certain mass, *or* corporeal matter). This is a complete mistake.
>
> (Ep. 73, CWS II p. 467)

Because of this, the French Spinozist Martial Gueroult prefers the term *panentheism* to describe Spinoza's God—the world is *not* God, but the world is definitely *in* God (1968, pp. 220–239). If this is the case though, it is not because God is strictly transcendent or eminent to the world despite his connection to it; rather, the relationship of substance to modes, of 'naturing nature' to 'natured nature,' demands a God that is *transcendentally immanent* to the world—that is to say, immanent as the cause of all things, yet always exceeding the singular things that move within it. Or, as Spinoza writes in Proposition 15 of *Ethics* Part I: "Whatever is, is in God" (CWS I p. 420).

Transcendental Immanence

How can something be immanent yet also transcendent? Is this not a contradiction? Are we left to accept paradox? Or is there a way of knowing—of experiencing—what Spinoza states in EIP15, that whatever exists, exists in God? Philosopher Clare Carlisle argues that this proposition is both the governing principle and ultimate goal of Spinoza's entire philosophy, that Spinoza's aim is to make his readers comprehend their own 'Being-in-God'. While Carlisle agrees with Gueroult that Spinoza is a panentheist, she prefers the term 'Being-in-God' because it conveys the immanence of being immersed in the Divine while also allowing for the transcendence that the Divine being must have, how God must always exceed what he creates. Carlisle stresses that Spinoza never opposes transcendence with immanence, that to place too much emphasis on the immanence of God can easily lead one to assume that Spinoza equates God with Nature in the strictest sense (i.e., God is the world or the universe).[19] This does no justice to the absolutely infinite power that Spinoza defines as the essence of God— a power that always surpasses the individual, and yet the individual is a direct expression of. "Spinoza recognizes immanence and transcendence as inseparable features" of reality (2021, pp. 67–68). Substance can never be confused with its modes. The universe must not be used as a synonym for the name of God, even though the universe moves within the Divine—just as humans and all other modes move within the Divine. Everything that exists is immanent to God, who also transcends all that exists. To know of our 'Being-in-God' is to experience transcendental immanence.

The philosopher Grant Maxwell explores this idea of transcendental immanence, tracing it from Spinoza to a lineage of thinkers that includes Jung, who in his late work, Maxwell notes, begins to write of the archetypes as "transcendental potencies" outside the psyche proper (Maxwell, 2022,

p. 182). This idea is also evoked when Jung speaks of spirit and matter as "potentialities that transcend consciousness," or aspects of one and the same thing that are a "discrimination in the interests of human cognition" (Letters, Vol. 2, 1975, pp. 70, 640). Now at first, it may sound as though Jung is proposing a version of spirit and matter closer to the subjectivist interpretation of Spinoza's attributes. However, Jung clearly does recognize that spirit and matter exist independently of the psyche, that it would "hardly do" to call everything psychic (CW. 8, 1946/1969a, par. 420). But as he writes at the end of his historical review of spirit in 'The Phenomenology of the Spirit in Fairytales', the two aspects may yet be "forms of one and the same transcendental being" (Letters, Vol. 2, 1975, p. 70; CW. 9i, 1948/1969b, par. 392). Jung is referring to the same unitary being he speaks of in works such as *Mysterium Coniunctionis* (CW. 14, 1963/1970, pars. 776–789). This implicit unity that the psyche finds itself immersed in is one of the reasons why Jungian scholar Roderick Main suggests that Jung himself should be considered a panentheist (2017).[20] Whatever the nature of this transcendental being Jung speaks of, spirit and matter constitute our experience of it because they involve "our own constitution: a body perceived by the senses and a spirit (=psyche) directly conscious of itself" (Letters, Vol. 2, 1975, p. 342). Now this sort of passive awareness of aspects that pertain to our own essence, and also to the world at large, evokes Spinoza's definition of the attributes as what the intellect perceives as constituting substance. Furthermore, Spinoza explains God has not just two but infinite attributes; however, the two attributes we humans know of are thought and extension—*because they pertain to our own essence* (E ID6, CWS I p. 409; IIP1–2, pp. 448–449).

What does it mean to be a singular thing immersed *in* God? Such knowledge is gleaned *through* oneself, as one finds oneself 'moving' within the Divine, and so one also recognizes that the attributes that constitute oneself also constitute God. This understanding that our essence involves the attributes has a further implication. Jung's formula that the psyche is, in a sense, one's 'own spirit' relative to other spirits—or, as he says above, that spirit (=psyche)—repeats his ardent contention that psyche and spirit enjoy a nuanced relationship in the sense that the psyche *is* spirit; but one cannot be folded into the other. Psyche is enfolded in spirit, just as the body is a composition of matter. But one would not equate *all* of spirit with the psyche, just as one wouldn't call all of corporeal existence the body (see Ch. 1, pp. 37–41). Now, Spinoza explicitly claims that the mind itself is but an idea, namely the idea of the body that is its object (E IIP13, CWS I pp. 457–458). There are the ideas that occur to us, and also the idea of ourselves and who we are. All ideas, whether of a human or a blade of grass, are conceived in God's Infinite Intellect, which is essentially God's power as expressed under the attribute of thought (E IIP1, P3, CWS I pp. 448–449; IIP8–9, pp. 452–454). So the human mind is contained within the attribute of thought, along with all other ideas that God has. But while the human mind is comprehended (i.e., created) by the mind of God, and is indeed part of that divine intellect, it would not at all be correct to say that the human mind and God's mind are in any way tantamount or equivalent with the other. Again, all singular things that God produces are contained within God's attributes. A person's mind and their body are the same thing, conceived as an idea in one instance, and as a mode of extension in the next (E IIP7S, CWS I pp. 451–452; E IIP21, pp. 467–468). Therefore, by divorcing spirit from psyche, to ensure both receive their proper autonomy and that their relationship is properly understood, Jung establishes a relationship identical to the one that Spinoza authors between singular minds and the attribute of thought. Despite the distances Jung attempts to cast between himself and Spinoza by insinuating that the Spinozist God fails to uphold itself amid the two aspects, in spite of the specter of the Hegelian critique and the intricate misunderstandings that ensue from it, the distinction of psyche and spirit, or the mind and thought, is an isomorphism that Jung and Spinoza indisputably share.

Hollow Knowledge

We are still left with the question as to why Jung fails to recognize this accordance with Spinoza—not just in regards to monism, but specifically with the relations he establishes between the individual and the aspects of the Divine, between psyche and spirit. Did Jung simply misunderstand Spinoza? Were his views perhaps shaped by the commonly held canard that Spinoza's God is inert and lifeless, that it utterly consumes and destroys all individuals it creates—the kind of reading propagated by Hegel? Or was Jung simply ignorant of Spinoza's philosophy beyond a sparse reading? One may get this latter impression from Jung's use of Spinoza in the essay 'Instinct and the Unconscious', where Jung laments how the metaphysical aspect of the archetype has been progressively devalued throughout history. Jung begins with Plato's initial conception of the archetype as a true metaphysical entity, before its ontological status gradually became nominal in the ensuing millennia, each successive definition becoming more and more constrained to the mind, until the archetype became a mere "internal condition of cognition," as clearly formulated by Spinoza: "By 'idea' I understand a conception of the mind which the mind forms by reason of its being a thinking thing" (CW. 8, 1919/1969a, pars. 275–276).

At face value, this is simply a poor reading of what Spinoza means by 'idea'. As already stated, the mind itself is but an idea, and all ideas exist in God's Infinite Intellect (E IIP1, P3, CWS I pp. 448–449; IIP8–9, pp. 452–454). There is a clear distinction between ideas that occur to us, and also the idea of ourselves and who we are. Thought precedes the mind, not the other way around. One would then be forgiven for having the impression that Jung simply plucked Spinoza's definition of idea out of the *Ethics* without realizing Spinoza's sensitivity to the relations between thought, mind, and idea. If someone were unaware of what has been established thus far, they might also be excused for wondering if it is in fact *Jung* who is insensitive to these relations between ideal things, that by failing to see how Spinoza decouples thought from the human mind and instead attributes it to the Divine, that Jung fails to make the same move of divorcing the archetype from the psyche. This would suggest a viewpoint that privileges the human mind in a way that is completely incompatible with Spinoza's philosophy (Langan, 2020).

This would prove too hasty of a conclusion to make. It is in the same stroke where Jung acknowledges spirit is separate from psyche that he also states that archetypes are not strictly psychic (CW. 8, 1946/1969a, pars. 420, 439). Besides, the idea that Jung's reading of Spinoza was careless fails to explain the few but significant occasions where Jung deploys Spinozist concepts in an incisive, even favorable, way. When Jung defines the psychological function of intuition in *Psychological Types*, he writes that since intuition is an apprehension of the unconscious, it "possesses an intrinsic certainty and conviction, which enabled Spinoza (and Bergson) to uphold the *scientia intuitiva* as the highest form of knowledge" (CW. 6, 1921/1971, par. 770). The French philosopher Henri Bergson was a much more apparent and acknowledged influence on Jung's thought, particularly for informing some of the vitalist strands evident earlier in his work (CW. 8, 1919/1969a; Shamdasani, 2003, pp. 208–210). And no doubt Bergson's conception of intuition as a method that unmixes and abstracts something essential from the whole accords well with Spinoza's intuition as a knowledge of the essence of singular things (2010; E IIP40S2, CWS I p. 478). But Jung chooses to prioritize Spinoza's name here, and explicitly raises the Latin term Spinoza deploys: *scientia intuitiva*, or intuitive knowledge (CWS I p. 697). Per Spinoza, intuitive knowledge allows one to see things as they appear *sub specie aeternitatis*, or under the view of eternity (E IIP44C2, CWS I p. 481). This term also appears but a handful of times in Jung's writing, but it does so at points where Jung attempts to bolster the metaphysical status of the archetypes and the collective unconscious, as something atemporal and outside the common flux of things. Jung describes the psychological function of introverted sensation as what gives one the ability to remove an object from its present state of affairs and to view it *sub specie aeternitatis*, in the same way it would appear to "a million-year old consciousness" (CW. 6, 1921/1971, par. 649). He evokes the eye of eternity concerning the hypothesis of a "supra-individual psyche" where the archetypal potency behind all individual things is revealed (CW. 8, 1931/1969a, par. 316). And in the introduction to his memoir, he states the way one's life appears through the inner vision of myth and symbols is to view one's life *sub specie aeternitatis* (1963/1989, p. 3). In other words, Jung sees resonance with archetypal knowledge and knowledge of things as they are under the eye of eternity.

It is wholly plausible that Jung stumbled upon this term in the writing of a philosopher who followed Spinoza, and who adopted the phrase for their own ends, and therefore it is also possible that Jung found affinity for this phrase from a thinker other than Spinoza. For example, the concept appears in the work of Arthur Schopenhauer (1788–1860), who directly cites Spinoza's definition of an eternal perspective while describing the strength of mind to suppress the rational categories one typically imparts on the world and to instead understand that one is never truly separate from it. Similarly, Nietzsche evokes the view from eternity in the ability to "rest from ourselves," to be able to look down upon oneself and either laugh or weep.[21] Certainly, the notion of viewing things from a timeless perspective has existed since at least Plato (1991, p. 465). But it must merely be pointed out that Jung adopts Spinoza's exact phrase, that he deploys the term in the same meaning that Spinoza intended, and that elsewhere Jung explicitly references Spinoza in defining the intuitive knowledge that leads to such an eternal perspective. It seems unlikely that Jung was unaware at least of how Spinoza had established the same line of thought that he subsequently follows and references. In 'The Love Problem of a Student' Jung even cites the love of God that Spinoza states is the result of intuitive knowledge, the *amor intellectualis Dei* (CW. 10, 1922/1970, par. 199). It may yet prove that Jung views the 'intellectual' portion of this love as a kind of qualifier, and this reveals where his reservations about Spinoza actually stem from. Nevertheless, the progression that Jung follows Spinoza along with, from intuition, to eternity, to love of the Divine, is proof that he was attentive to at least some of the nuance within Spinoza's philosophy. In any event, this is already clear from Jung's inference that spirit refers to the same thing as the attribute of thought. Jung's insight, and the way he reacts to this understanding, demonstrates that Jung could not have been as ambivalent toward Spinoza as one might assume—that Jung, on some level, *did* recognize the convergence of ideas he shared with Spinoza. The issue at hand is why, despite these similarities on issues at the heart of Jung's psychology, Jung concludes that Spinoza cannot maintain this middle position, that Spinoza's monism collapses upon itself.

A possible explanation is found in Jung's previous claim that Spinoza renders archetypes as an act of cognition. In Jung's critique of Spinoza in 'The Phenomenology of the Spirit in Fairytales' the ultimate failure is not just that spirit becomes tethered to matter, but that the highest form it could subsequently muster is merely "intellect or reason" (CW. 9i, 1948/1969b, par. 391). Jung clearly sees the intellect as insufficient, that the emphasis on conceptualizing a thing rather than paying heed to the visceral reaction that the thing evokes is a mistake typical of philosophers. In the parlance of psychological types, the error here is to prioritize the thinking function, or a judgment of what a thing is—that is, its objective meaning—over the feeling function, or rather a judgment of the thing's value, a subjective acceptance or rejection of the said thing (CW. 6, 1921/1971, pars. 724, 834, 958). This is exemplified in Jung's explanation to Pauli about how one could analyze a dream from a purely metaphysical perspective and glean an *objective* meaning from the dream's contents; yet this type of analysis would say utterly nothing of the dreamer's psychology or how the dream affected them (Meier, 2001, p. 114). Similarly, the theory of complexes, those knots of unconscious thoughts and feelings on the periphery of the psyche, are not all sufficiently accounted for by mere classification or taxonomy; the feelings that specific complexes provoke are key to unwinding them and uncovering their archetypal core; furthermore, the severity of these feelings, and the affects that they can trigger throughout the body, are the very marker of how strong the complex's pull on the psyche is (CW. 8, 1934/1969a). The union of these feeling-toned complexes and knowledge of the archetypal is in many ways the bedrock of Jung's psychology—and it is psychology that Jung sees as the sole method of investigation into the unconscious (see Ch. 1, pp. 31–36). In comparison, the "philosophic intellect" performs an illusion in the sense that it pretends to have possession of the object that it has an idea of; but in truth, "one has acquired nothing more than its name." This may be useful in other sciences, but not in psychology, where feelings and affects cannot be discounted. In psychology "one possesses nothing unless one has experienced it in reality. Hence a purely intellectual insight is not enough, because one knows only the words and not the substance of the thing from the outside" (CW. 9ii, 1959/1969c, pars. 50–61). And in Jung's opinion, no discipline is guilty of performing more "unintentional psychology" than philosophy (CW. 8, 1946/1969a, par. 360).

It is not that Jung believes philosophical conjecture is without merit, but rather that all too often it is hollow—*rootless*. A philosopher who attempts to explain that which can only be experienced by the psyche will have the same results as someone attempting to discuss zoological theory with "a duck-billed platypus." Jung insists that it "is not the concept that matters; the concept is only the word, a counter, and it has meaning and use only because it stands for a certain sum of experience." In other words, metaphysical ideas all too easily become reified, abstracted from the dynamism that was originally their object. Without being reconnected to that dynamism—and the feelings and affects that it generates—metaphysical ideas become completely brittle, an impediment to psychic development, and ultimately meaningless. Jung goes as far as to say that this "is unfortunately the fate of metaphysical ideas" (CW. 9ii, 1959/1969c, par. 63). Philosophy deludes itself with its pretensions of being "able to pull itself up by its own bootstraps and know things that were right outside the range of human understanding" (CW. 8, 1946/1969a, par. 358).

Jung's bleak forecast for metaphysical ideas evokes his distrust of metaphysics that we previously covered: metaphysics too often errs by presuming to begin beyond the bounds of the psyche (see Ch. 1, pp. 31–36). This added layer expands the problem because we see Jung attribute the issue to overreliance on reason itself. The two complaints may be entwined: overreliance on reason leads to extrinsic explanations that remain 'outside' the psyche. This again evokes Hegel's critique, in that he saw Spinoza's geometric demonstrations as deployed in the *Ethics* as the result of an intellectualization that is always exterior and static compared with what it discusses—much like Spinoza's metaphysics itself (2018, pp. 283–285). Could this be the cause of Jung's double-handed treatment of Spinoza? Could Jung have profited from some of Spinoza's concepts that he did find alluring, such as the intuitive intellect or the view from eternity, or even possibly transcendental immanence itself, while dismissing Spinoza's philosophy as a whole for failing to capture the visceral nature of life? It would not be unprecedented—Jung does something similar in his judgment of Bergson, for while on the whole Jung writes much more favorably of Bergson than he does Spinoza, Jung does claim that while Bergson's method of intuition is an indication of something beyond intellection, on the whole "the Bergsonian method is intellectual and not intuitive" (CW. 6, 1921/1971, par. 540). Shamdasani has pointed out that this is not a fair treatment of Bergson's sensitivity to how concepts are articulated, and how they always can meld back into the fringe (2003, p. 230). Similarly, we once again will find that Spinoza actually meets Jung's demands—he in fact anticipates them, with his theories of knowledge and affects.

Notes

1 TTP is an abbreviation of the *Theological–Political Treatise*. I 25–48 is the chapter and paragraphs within the TTP being cited. CWS II refers to volume two of *The Collected Works of Spinoza*, with pages 85–93 being the respective page numbers.

2 All references to 'CWS I' belong to Spinoza (1985) and all references to 'CWS II' belong to Spinoza (2016). These are the two editions edited by Curley.

3 In 'On the Nature of the Psyche', where Jung explicitly states that the archetypes must be seen as manifestations of spirit beyond the psyche itself, he directs readers to 'Phenomenology' as the paper that best explains spirit's role in this regard (CW. 8, 1946/1969a, par. 420).

4 TIE is an abbreviation for *Treatise of the Emendation of the Intellect*. The paragraphs in the *Treatise* are numbered; so, for instance, this citation refers to paragraph 85 of the text.

5 Quality translations of Spinoza's work were lacking for many years. A critical edition of his complete works was not published until 1925. Given the varied and intermingling ways in which words like thought, spirit, and mind translate across languages, it is worth asking if Jung's overlaying of spirit over thought came from a translation oddity in whatever edition of Spinoza's texts that he had at his disposal. There is no bibliographic reference for what version of Spinoza's work Jung might have used, if any, for writing 'The Phenomenology

of the Spirit in Fairytales'. However, Jung does directly quote Spinoza in 'Instinct of the Unconscious', an essay in Volume Eight of the Collected Works. According to the bibliography in the German edition of Volume Eight, the version of the Ethics that Jung used was a German translation published in the late 1880s by a Rabbi and scholar named Jakob Stern. The Foundation of the Works of C.G. Jung has confirmed that this is the sole text of Spinoza that Jung had in his personal library (Personal Correspondence, 2022). Stern does translate Spinoza's usage of mind as the German word for spirit, Geist; however, the attribute of thought is translated as 'Attribut des Denkens' (1888). Furthermore, despite citing Stern's edition of the Ethics in the German version of 'Instinct and the Unconscious', or 'Instinkt and Unbewußtes', Jung writes the quotation he uses in that essay in the language Spinoza originally wrote the Ethics, Latin: "Per ideam intelligo mentis conceptum, quem mens format." Or rather: "By 'idea' I understand a conception of the mind which the mind forms by reason of its being a thinking thing" (CW. 8, 1919/1969a, pars. 275–278). Therefore, Jung's reading of spirit into Spinoza's philosophy does not appear to be an accident by translation. Instead, it is a deliberate inference made by Jung. See 'Bibliographie' in *Die Dynamik des Unbewußteni*, Vol. 8 of *Gesammelte Werke* (1995). For context on Jakob Stern and his contributions to Spinozist thought, particularly in context of German Marxism, see Steila (2021). For a textual history of Spinoza, see Steenbakkers (2009).

6 A work from 1921, by the emergentist thinker Samuel Alexander, actually attempts something similar by arguing the attribute of thought is equivalent to the Bergsonian version of time (see Alexander, 2015).

7 Ep. refers to one of Spinoza's letters. So Ep. 64 refers to Letter 64 in Spinoza's correspondences.

8 Spinoza, following Descartes, takes the term 'objective' from scholastic ter-minology. It by no means should be understood as the opposite of subjectivity. Rather, an 'objective thought' refers to a thing that is taken as an object of that thought, and thus the thought becomes a representation of it (see Jaquet, 2019, p. 11).

9 And in fact, the idea of the idea has its own objective essence, and therefore there is an idea of the idea of the idea, which in turn would have its own objective essence, etc. This duplication process, of formal and objective essence, goes on to infinity.

10 Hegel's objective spirit even features in 'Phenomenology' as another rendition of the term that Jung finds unsatisfactory, for—at least according to Jung—it is a mere summation of humankind's intellectual and cultural achievements rather than something Divine (CW. 9i, 1948/1969b, par. 386, footnote 392).

11 Also see Yovel (Ch. 2, 1989) and Macherey (1979/2010).

12 For another subjectivist interpretation, see Wolfson (1962). Though the sub-jective interpretation of the attributes has been rejected in modern Spinoza scholarship, an alternative is by no means agreed upon. Most Spinozist schol-ars fall into the 'objective' camp, which believes the attributes really exist, and

therefore the question becomes how to reconcile an infinity of attributes with only one substance—especially when Spinoza at times talks as if the attributes are identical to substance (Ep. 9, CWS I p. 195). For variations of how this issue is approached, see Bennett (1984, pp. 60–66), Curley (1969, p. 16), and Donagan (1966). There are also commentators who treat the attributes as relatively distinct, but logically the same; or, similarly, that the attributes are formally distinct but numerically the same, or expressions of the same power (see Jarrett, 1978; Deleuze, 1968/1990; Della Rocca, 2008).

13 This is hardly the only part of ID4 which has been disputed. Most notably, it has been debated how the original Latin word *tanquam* should be translated, whether it should be rendered 'as if' or 'as'. The former would cause the definition to read as "By attribute I understand what the intellect perceives of a substance, *as if* constituting its essence," which would favor a subjective interpretation. Another issue is whether Spinoza is referring to singular intellects here, or the Infinite Intellect (see CWS I pp. 408–409). Arguably whether Spinoza means a finite or infinite intellect here is irrelevant however, since all intellects are part of God's Infinite Intellect.

14 How does one distinguish between God, God's essence, and the attributes? Deveaux (2007) endorses a similar line of thought to Della Rocca, who believes that essence refers to the power a being has, and that the attributes are expressions of that power (Della Rocca, 2008). So in this respect, God is the being who has absolutely infinite and eternal power; God's essence is to *have* absolutely infinite and eternal power; and the attributes are *expressions* of that power. This emphasis on power being equivalent to essence in Spinoza's philosophy, as well as the importance of expressionism, is also highlighted by Deleuze (1968/1990).

15 The fact that Spinoza unquestionably sees the world of modes as real and not illusory is precisely what has been argued in defense of Spinoza in response to Hegel's accusations (see Parkinson, 1977; Yovel, Ch. 2, 1989; and Macherey, 1979/2010).

16 Or, to use the Latin Spinoza deploys in IP29S, *Natura naturans* and *Natura naturata.* Also see Bennett (1984, pp. 118–119).

17 The mutual immanence between substance and modes and the attributes that they share is why Deleuze applies the scholastic term 'univocity' to Spinoza's metaphysics, a term borrowed from Duns Scotus. The univocity of the attributes means that although God and singular things differ in essence, the words or forms that pertain to their essence are one and the same (Ch. 3, 1968/1990).

18 And while the corporeal world is contained within the attribute of extension, and the corporeal world can be divided into the finite things that compose it, extended substance itself is indivisible as the infinite power of existing that extended things are expressed by (E IP15S, CWS I pp. 421–424; see Genevieve Lloyd, 1996, pp. 38–41).

19 Secularist interpretations of Spinoza often latch onto a phrase Spinoza uses, *Deus sive Natura,* or 'God or Nature', as evidence that Spinoza asserts a strict

identity between God and nature. Yet Spinoza uses this term but a handful of times in the *Ethics*, and Carlisle argues that when Spinoza deploys this phrase, he is either referring to the 'naturing nature' of substance, which is very different from nature as we typically experience it; or the dependent nature of modes upon substance (see Carlisle, 2021, pp. 64–67).

20 Main gives a systematic account for why Jung should be considered a panentheist, based on a set of criteria established by Michael Brierley (2008). Brierley's criteria state that in panentheism, God is more than the cosmos, God is not separate from the cosmos, and God is affected by the cosmos. Main (2017) argues that Jung fulfills these stipulations. In the case of Spinoza, however, the first two qualifiers are met, but the last seems to be violated, as there is certainly a unilateral direction between substance and modes, in the sense of substance as the cause and modes as the effect. There is, however, much to be parsed out here in respect to 'naturing nature' versus 'natured nature', since singular things are the extrinsic cause of other singular things to exist, which therefore affect what God expresses, certainly not in eternity, but in duration (more on this in Ch. 6).

21 See Schopenhauer (2010, pp. 201–204) and Nietzsche (1974, prop. 107).

References

Adler, G. & Jaffe, A. (1975). *C.G. Jung Letters 2: 1951–1961*. Translated by R. Hull. Princeton: Princeton University Press.

Alexander, S. (2015). *Spinoza and Time*. London: Forgotten Books.

Atmanspacher, H. & Rickles, D. (2022). *Dual-Aspect Monism and the Deep Structure of Meaning*. London & New York: Routledge.

Beiser, F. (2012). "Trendelenburg and Spinoza" (Ch. 13), in *Spinoza and German Idealism*, edited by E. Förster & Yitzhak Y. Melamed. Cambridge: Cambridge University Press.

Bennett, J. (1984). *A Study of Spinoza's Ethics*. Indiana: Hackett Publishing.

Bergson, H. (2010). *The Creative Mind*. New York: Dover Publications.

Brierley, M. (2008). "The Potential of Panentheism for Dialogue between Science and Religion," in *The Oxford Handbook of Religion and Science*, edited by P. Clayton & Z. Simpson, pp. 635–651. Oxford: Oxford University Press.

Cambray, J. (2014). "The Influence of German Romantic Science on Jung and Pauli," in *The Pauli–Jung Conjecture and its Impact Today*, edited by H. Atmanspacher & C. Fuchs. Exeter: Imprint Academic.

Carlisle, C. (2021). *Spinoza's Religion: A New Reading of The Ethics*. Princeton: Princeton University Press.

Curley, E. (1969). *Spinnoza's Metaphysics: An Essay in Interpretation*. Harvard: Harvard University Press.

Deleuze, G. (1968/1990). *Expressionism in Philosophy: Spinoza*. Translated by M. Joughin. New York: Zone Books.

Della Rocca, M. (2008). *Spinoza*. London & New York: Routledge.

Deveaux, S. (2007). *The Role of God in Spinoza's Metaphysics*. London: Continuum.

Donagan, A. (1966). "A Note on Spinoza, Ethics I, 10." *Philosophical Review*, 75(3), 380–382.

Gueroult, M. (1968). *Spinoza vol. I: Dieu (Ethique I); vol. II: L'Ame (Ethique II)*. Paris: Aubier-Montaigne.

Hegel, G.W.F. (2018). *Hegel's Lectures on the History of Philosophy Volume Three*. Project Gutenberg. Produced by Fritz Ohrenschall and the Online Distributed Proofreading Team at www.pgdp.net (Accessed October 2022).

Jaquet, C. (2019). *Affects, Actions and Passions in Spinoza: The Unity of Body and Mind*. Translated by T. Reznichenko. Edinburgh: Edinburgh University Press.

Jarrett, C. (1978). "The Logical Structure of Spinoza's *Ethics*, Part I", *Synthese*, 37, 15–65.

Jung, C.G. (1919). "Instinct and the Unconscious," in *The Structure and Dynamics of the Psyche*, 2nd ed. Translated by R. Hull. Collected Works of C.G. Jung, Vol. 8. Princeton: Princeton University Press, 1969a.

Jung, C.G. (1921). *Psychological Types*, 2nd ed. Translated by R. Hull. Collected Works of C.G. Jung, Vol. 6. Princeton: Princeton University Press, 1971.

Jung, C.G. (1922). "The Love Problem of a Student," in *Civilization in Transition*, 2nd ed. Translated by R. Hull. Collected Works of C.G. Jung, Vol. 10. Princeton: Princeton University Press, 1970.

Jung, C.G. (1931). "Basic Postulates of Analytical Psychology," in *The Structure and Dynamics of the Psyche*, 2nd ed. Translated by R. Hull. Collected Works of C.G. Jung, Vol. 8. Princeton: Princeton University Press, 1969a.

Jung, C.G. (1934). "A Review of the Complex Theory," in *The Structure and Dynamics of the Psyche*, 2nd ed. Translated by R. Hull. Collected Works of C.G. Jung, Vol. 8. Princeton: Princeton University Press, 1969a.

Jung, C.G. (1946). "On the Nature of the Psyche," in *The Structure and Dynamics of the Psyche*, 2nd ed. Translated by R. Hull. Collected Works of C.G. Jung, Vol. 8. Princeton: Princeton University Press, 1969a.

Jung, C.G. (1948). "'The Phenomenology of the Spirit in Fairytales," in *The Archetypes and the Collective Unconscious*, 2nd ed. Translated by R. Hull. Collected Works of C.G. Jung, Vol. 9i. Princeton: Princeton University Press, 1969b.

Jung, C.G. (1957). "Commentary on 'The Secret of the Golden Flower,'" in *Alchemical Studies*. Translated by R. Hull. Collected Works of C.G. Jung, Vol. 13. Princeton: Princeton University Press, 1967.

Jung, C.G. (1959). *Aion: Researches into the Phenomenology of the Self*, 2nd ed. Translated by R. Hull. Collected Works of C.G. Jung, Vol. 9ii. Princeton: Princeton University Press,1969c.

Jung, C.G. (1963). *Mysterium Coniunctionis*, 2nd ed. Translated by R. Hull. Collected Works of C.G. Jung, Vol. 14. Princeton: Princeton University Press, 1970.

Jung, C.G. (1963/1989). *Memories. Dreams, Reflections*. Edited by A. Jaffe, Translated by R. Winston and C. Winston. New York: Vintage Books.

Jung, C.G. (1995). *Die Dynamik des Unbewußteni*. Gesammelte Werke, Vol. 8. Berlin: De Gruyter.

Langan, R. (2020). "Jung, Spinoza, Deleuze: A Move Towards Realism" (Ch. 10), in *Holism: Possibilities and Problems*, edited by C. McMillan, R. Main & D. Henderson. London: Routledge.

Lloyd, G. (1996). *Routledge Philosophy Guidebook to Spinoza and the Ethics*. London: Routledge.

Macherey, P. (1979/2010). *Hegel or Spinoza*. Translated by S. Ruddick. Minnesota: University of Minnesota Press.

Main, R. (2017). "Panentheism and the Undoing of Disenchantment," in *Zygon*, 52(4), 1098–1122.

Maxwell, G. (2022). *Integration and Difference: Constructing a Mythical Dialectic*. London & New York: Routledge.

Meier, C.A. (ed.) (2001). *Atom and Archetype: The Pauli/Jung Letters 1932–1958*. London: Routledge.

Nietzsche, F. (1974). *The Gay Science*. New York: Vintage Books.

Parkinson, G.H.R. (1977). "Hegel, Pantheism, and Spinoza," *Journal of the History of Ideas*, 38(3), 449–459.

Peden, K. (2014). *Spinoza Contra Phenomenology*. Stanford: Stanford University Press.

Plato. (1991). *The Republic*, 2nd ed. Translated by A. Bloom. New York: Basic Books.

Schopenhauer, A. (2010). *The World as Will and Representation*. Edited and Translated by J. Norman, C. Janaway & A. Welchman. Cambridge University Press Online. www-cambridge-org.uniessexlib.idm.oclc.org/core/books/schopenhauer-the-world-as-will-and-representation/contents/15885E5E3DA6A643E238CB1E7F6C9D1B (Accessed October 2022).

Shamdasani, S. (2003). *Jung and the Making of Modern Psychology: The Dream of a Science*. Cambridge: Cambridge University Press.

Spinoza, B. (1888). *Die Ethik*. Translated by J. Stern & P. Leipzig. Reclaim. Republished Online at: www.ethicadb.org/index.php?lg=en (Accessed September 2022).

Spinoza, B. (1985). *The Collected Works of Spinoza*, Vol. I, Edited and Translated by Edwin Curley. Princeton: Princeton University Press.

Spinoza, B. (2016). *The Collected Works of Spinoza*, Vol. II, Edited and Translated by Edwin Curley. Princeton: Princeton University Press.

Steenbakkers, P. (2009). "The Textual History of Spinoza's *Ethics*" (Ch. 1), in *The Cambridge Companion to Spinoza's Ethics*. Cambridge: Cambridge University Press.

Steila, D. (2021). "Interpretations of Spinoza in Early Russian Marxism," in *Studies in Eastern European Thought*, 2022(74), 279–296.

Trendelenburg, A. (1847). *Philologische und historiche Abhandlungen der königlichen Akadamie der Wissenschaften zu Berlin*. Berlin: Drummer, pp. 241–262.

Wolfson, H. (1962). *The Philosophy of Spinoza: Unfolding the Latent Processes of His Reasoning*. Harvard: Harvard University Press.

Woolhouse, R.S. (1993). *Descartes, Spinoza, Leibniz: The Concept of Substance in Seventeenth Century Metaphysics*. London: Routledge.

Yovel, Y. (1989). "Spinoza and Hegel: The Immanent God—Substance or Spirit?" (Ch. 2), in *Spinoza and Other Heretics: The Adventures of Immanence*. Princeton: Princeton University Press.

Chapter 3

C.G. Jung, the Unlikely Spinozist II

Affective Knowledge

The previous chapter demonstrated a pair of meeting points between Jung and Spinoza. First, just as Jung distinguishes psyche from spirit, Spinoza differentiates the idea of oneself (i.e., the mind) from the ideas of other things. Second, both thinkers place the individual between thought and extension—or, in Jung's parlance, the psyche is seated between spirit and matter. This leads us to a third point of convergence: both Jung and Spinoza see knowledge of the whole as necessarily routed through knowledge of oneself.

Affections and Projections

Spinoza distinguishes between definitions of things that are based on abstractions and classification, versus definitions that adequately reproduce the thing, or at least some aspect of the thing (Matheron, 2020, p. 72). For instance, if a circle "is defined as a figure in which the lines drawn from the center to the circumference are equal," Spinoza sees this as a poor definition because it describes only an abstract, arbitrary means of conceiving a circle (TIE 93–95, CWS I, p. 39).[1] This type of abstraction is indicative of how we normally conceive things: for instance, Spinoza considers universal notions we take for granted like man, horse, or dog to be these same types of abstractions, since they arise from the fact that we encounter so many beings of similar constitution—other people, to name an example—that the sheer number of encounters surpasses our ability to form singular impressions of each specific being. Instead we create a reification that is based on what those other beings had most in common, and ascribe a single word to encompass all of them—in this case, *human*.

For Spinoza, a reification always remains extrinsic to the thing being described, and is thus an example of what he considers the lowest form of

DOI: 10.4324/9781003516996-4

knowledge, an inadequate idea (E IP40, CWS I, pp. 475–478). Inadequate ideas are derived from our random encounters with other singular things and how they affect us—or rather, how they increase or diminish our power of existence.[2] Indeed, affections—or the encounters that change our power of existence—*are nothing else than these stochastic impacts upon us.* Therefore, as stated by the French Spinozist Alexandre Matheron, every affection, and consequently the idea we have of any affection, carries with it *the mark of the world* (2020, p. 69). But these ideas only comprehend a trace of what has affected us, or what Spinoza calls the image; therefore, in and of themselves, affections tell us nothing true about the foreign mode that we have encountered.[3] Furthermore, because we understand so little of our own body and mind to begin with, our affections also do not even necessarily tell us anything adequate about ourselves. The mind is the idea of the body, but while it exists it can only perceive that which affects the body or itself—in other words, an innate understanding of one's own mind or body is not a given for Spinoza (E IIP28–29, CWS I, pp. 470–471). Because of this dual inadequacy in our understanding, both of ourselves and other things, the ideas of our affections are always confused. The excess of affections that we regularly experience only compounds this confusion, and this is precisely why we form abstractions, because we are simply unable to imagine the sheer multitude of things we encounter. Yet this process itself is fraught with error—for example, if we are affected by two modes simultaneously, we readily confuse the affection of one mode with the other; and subsequently, if only one of those two modes affects us again, we may readily assume that both modes are present (E IIP17–18, CWS I, pp. 463–466). Inadequate ideas then are the result of our failure to adequately comprehend the affections that continually bombard us (E IIP40S2, pp. 477–478).

This concatenation of affections, as well as our complete inability to often understand *why* something affects us the way it does and the appeal to abstractions that ensues, shares an affinity with Jung's observation of how when psychic energy is transferred from one object to another, it often carries traces of the previous object of attachment, which leads to all sorts of false conclusions. Per Jung, this transference often causes us to overvalue the similarities between two objects, while their "equally essential differences" are overlooked (CW. 8, 1928/1969a, par. 38). Likewise, Spinoza notes that everyone constructs reifications based on their own particular biases and prejudices—for some, *man* may merely be "an animal of erect stature," but for others, a human is "an animal capable of laughter, or a featherless biped, or a rational animal." The universals that someone forms are in fact predicated on their own personal disposition (E IIP40S2, CWS I, p. 478). Hence Jung says that just "as we tend to assume the world is as we see it, we naively suppose that people are as we imagine them to be." We are always "naively projecting our own psychology into our fellow human beings. In this way everyone creates for himself a series of more or less imaginary relationships based essentially on projection" (CW. 8, 1916/1969a, par. 507). In other words, for Jung, the act of reification is closely related to the psychological phenomenon of projection, or the expulsion of personal content onto the world (CW. 6, 1921/1971, par. 783). Projections are a product not of the conscious but unconscious mind— just like Spinoza's affections, they are not made but instead *encountered*. Projections isolate the individual from the world, "since instead of a real relation there is now only an illusory one. They change the world into a replica of one's own unknown face," that is, their unconscious or shadow (CW. 9ii, 1959/1969c, par. 17).[4] We have already seen a special example of this in Chapter 1, concerning Jung's belief that overly idealist or physicalist viewpoints betray a psyche guilty of projective identification, or of throwing itself into either the realm or spirit or matter—in other words, personal biases have been plastered upon reality itself (pp. 24–26). Yet we are constantly at risk of incurring such imbalances, at any scale and any event in life. States Jung:

> A person whom I perceive mainly through my projections is an *imago* or, alternatively, a *carrier* of imagos or symbols. All contents of our unconscious are constantly being projected into our surroundings, and it is only by recognizing certain properties of the objects as projections or imagos that we are able to distinguish them from the real properties of the objects. But if we are not aware that a property of the object is a projection, we cannot do anything else but be naively convinced that it really does belong to the object. All human relationships swarm with these projections […] Unless we are possessed of an unusual degree of self-awareness we shall never see through our projections but must always succumb to them, because the mind in its natural state presupposes the existence of such projections. It is the natural and given thing for unconscious contents to be projected.
>
> (CW. 8, 1916/1969a, par. 507)

This dire state of affairs leads one to believe that one has control where one truly does not. To admit the truth, says Spinoza, would be to also admit that one's worldview is built on completely false pretenses. This is why we naturally prefer to think that we choose the ideas our mind reflects upon, yet in actuality it is the ideas that reflect upon the mind; hence why Spinoza compares the mind to a "spiritual automaton" (TIE 85; CWS I, p. 37). We fancy that we freely select the things that we love and shun things we hate; but we seldom understand the nature of *why* we love or hate, which in truth is predicated upon whether or not something increases or diminishes our affective powers; that is to say, whether or not something gives us joy or sorrow. In reality we have little choice in what we love or hate; instead we are reacting to the excess of affections that we have no control over. This reaction, and the change in our power to exist that it encapsulates, is what Spinoza calls the passions (E III, CWS I, pp. 491–543).[5] Ideas steeped in the passions are explanations we create *post hoc* to justify desires of ours that we do not truly understand, rather than seeking any knowledge that constitutes the actual lived experience. "For each one governs everything from his affect," says Spinzoa, and "those who are torn by contrary affects do not know what they want, and those who are not moved by any affect are very easily driven here and there." Hence, he states:

> The infant believes he freely wants milk; the angry child that he wants vengeance; and the timid, flight. So the drunk believes it is from a free decision of the Mind that he speaks the things he later, when sober, wishes he had not said. So the madman, the chatterbox, the child, and a great many people of this kind believe they speak from a free decision of the Mind, when really they cannot contain their impulse to speak [...] So experience itself, no less clearly than reason, teaches that men believe themselves free because they are conscious of their own actions, and ignorant of the causes by which they are determined, that the decisions of the Mind are nothing but the appetites themselves, which therefore vary as the disposition of the Body varies.
>
> (E IIIP2S, CWS I, pp. 496–497)

Jung and Spinoza jointly reject knowledge that remains extrinsic to the thing it attempts to define. Both thinkers deny this hollow understanding not just because it provides insufficient explanations of the world, but because it betrays insufficient knowledge of oneself. According to Jung, so long as someone does not withdraw projections that are in discordance with what is really there, the person will never know things as they actually are (CW. 6, 1921/1971, par. 783). And similarly for Spinoza, it is only freedom from the passions that allows someone to know their own powers as well as the powers of other things (E IVP26, CWS I, p. 559). This task is the very goal at the heart of the *Ethics*. Therefore, if Jung charges Spinoza with taking an overly intellectualist approach, it cannot be due to Spinoza championing an abstract understanding of things, since Spinoza also denounces this kind of knowledge. But in Jung's estimate, *rooted* knowledge must be grounded in the psyche, or rather routed directly through it. Adequate understanding of the world cannot come without an understanding of oneself as a being within that world. The psyche is our only immediate datum of experience, and so it must be the starting point for any metaphysics not dependent upon a transcendent scaffolding that Jung flatly rejects (see Ch. 1, pp. 24–26). And just as Spinoza and Jung meet at the middle third between thought and extension—or, to use Jung's parlance, spirit and matter—so too are they both insistent that knowledge of the whole comes via knowledge of oneself, and how one *finds* oneself in that whole; that is to say, ontology is inseparable from self-knowledge.

Common Notions

Adequate ideas are obtained through an understanding of the actual connections between oneself and other things. They are always predicated upon what Spinoza calls common notions. Rather than an understanding based on extrinsic, "fortuitous encounters with things," a common notion apprehends the *intrinsic* relationship between oneself and another thing, "to understand their disagreements, differences, and oppositions" (E IIP29S, CWS I, p. 471). Spinoza stresses that common notions are not the same as universals, which again would be in the realm of abstraction, that is, terms of summation like *dog*, *cat*, or *human* (E IIP40S1, CWS I, pp. 475–477). Rather, common notions represent things that are either common to all bodies, and therefore equally in the part and in the whole, or common to us and at least one other body, and equally in the part and in the whole of each (E IIP38–39, CWS I, pp. 474–475).

For example, if *A* is something that is equally common to us and another mode that affects us, then *A* is something within that affection that can actually be explained by our nature alone. Because this gives us an idea we can conceive independently of other affections, we can conceive it adequately. Furthermore, because A is something common to the other mode that affects us, it allows us to grasp something true of that other mode as well. If Spinoza thinks that to explain a circle as a collection of points equidistant from a centerpoint is a bad and arbitrary definition, then he also thinks that to describe a circle as any line where one end is fixed and the other movable is a good definition (TIE 96, CWS I, p. 40). Why is the latter explanation acceptable? Deleuze notes that Spinoza likes the second definition because it is *genetic*; it describes the genesis of a circle as a geometric figure. But at the same time it clearly is still a fiction; after all, no one sees circles birthed in nature from one-dimensional lines that rotate (1970/1988, pp. 47–48). Yet whether the definition applies to the genesis of all circles existing in nature has no bearing on whether or not it is an adequate idea. Rather, the definition of a circle as a rotating line is adequate because *the definition of rotation forms a common notion between ourselves and the idea of a circle*; as Matheron observes, the connection "is explained very simply by the fact that our body is capable of performing rotations" (2020, p. 71). Therefore in this instance *rotation* is a property common to ourselves and the geometric figure of a circle, or also any other mode that *affects* us with the idea of a circle, whether it be the sun or a tennis ball.

A consequence of this is that *in all inadequate ideas, there is a kernel of adequate understanding to be discovered*, for inadequate thought is simply the error of our minds and not the things that our mind perceives (E IIP35, CWS I, pp. 472–473). We may not understand the myriad ways in which the sun affects us, nor the intricacies of how a tennis ball spins through the air after it is hit; yet the notion of rotation forges a relation between us and these other modes that we can conceive adequately.

Another example is our understanding of water. One may argue that to state that water is the combination of two hydrogen atoms and one oxygen atom is manifestly a true idea; but, had Spinoza been around to witness the discovery of atoms and the periodic table of elements, he would likely argue that to simply recite this explanation is no better than a merchant who remembers how to do calculations because they remember "what they heard from their teacher without any" intrinsic understanding (E IIP40S2, CWS I, p. 478). Such an understanding based on memorization is essentially another example of a reified image, and therefore is necessarily an inadequate idea. This particular example underscores why Spinoza's epistemology is *not* simply an endorsement of rational or scientific knowledge as it is typically conceived.

On the other hand, a swimmer who innately understands the flow of water around their body, who knows how to manipulate that flow with the stroke of their limbs to create propulsion demonstrates an adequate understanding of the relation between their body and water. It is evident that an 'intellectual' knowledge of the physics or mathematical formulas relevant to this movement is unnecessary. Olympian swimmer Michael Phelps, for instance, was able to dominate his sport without using theoretical formulas concerning the movement of dense objects in water. It is in this sense that common notions are "more biological than mathematical" or rather they are "relations of agreement or composition" between two bodies. An intellection of this relation is secondary to the physical reality of the composition itself (Deleuze, 1970/1988, pp. 54–55).

This is not at all to say that scientific knowledge is invariably inadequate. It is just that our ability to form a common notion depends on the nature of the things that connect with one another. For example, a chemist who understands the molecular properties of water, who knows how to manipulate water's intensive properties such as boiling and freezing points, develops a connection between themselves and water via experimentation. For the chemist this is knowledge gleaned through a relation between themself and water, rather than theory abstracted into a reification. It is the difference between that merchant who vaguely remembers classroom formulas to do their accounting, versus a merchant who has worked with numbers enough to infer what answers might be, even if they've never seen the exact problem before (E IIP40S, CWS I, p. 478). Clearly science can help one understand the compositions as described in the disciplines of physics, chemistry, or biology. But the concepts those fields describe are tangential to a true, tactile understanding.[6] Professional golfer Bryson DeChambeau differs from our earlier example of swimmer Michael Phelps because DeChambeau actually does credit the application of physics to the golf swing as a key factor in his success. On the other hand, while Tiger Woods has voiced admiration for DeChambeau's approach, and has acknowledged that the scientific way in which DeChambeau approaches his craft gets at the same problems other golfers might discuss in more instinctive terms, Tiger has nevertheless not found it useful to adopt the same methods to his own game. Certainly no golf commentator would argue that choice has diminished Tiger Woods' career. So when we state that the formation of a common notion depends on the nature of the individual things entering into a relationship with one another, this must include the *nature of the individual person* too: in the case of an athlete who profits from applying a theoretical approach to their craft, like DeChambeau, there is evidently something in the theoretical approach—an element X—that is shared by the actual hitting of the golf ball as well. Yet this element X is idiosyncratic to DeChambeau and his own relation to the golf swing, possibly due to his background in physics. Physics was DeChambeau's major in college, it is a subject he greatly enjoys, so it is not a reach to suggest he has formed an intimate relationship with using numbers just like the example of our more astute merchant, or that Michael Phelps has with the water (Wacker, 2018; Jiwani, 2021). Furthermore, DeChambeau's specific relationship with physics would be absent in other golfers who lacked such a background. In this hypothesis, DeChambeau's *love for physics is itself a common notion*, which allowed him to *apprehend the golf swing intrinsically and therefore form another common notion;* indeed, Spinoza explicitly states that our ideas of common notions can compound to form new adequate ideas (E IP40, CWS I, p. 475).

Thus the nature of the entities involved within a given composition always determines the common notion that can be extracted; furthermore, the compounds that we have already established allow us to form and comprehend new compositions. This is precisely why Deleuze cites the scholium of proposition two in *Ethics* Part III as Spinoza's most important statement, the 'scream' at the heart of his philosophy: that no one has determined in its entirety what the body can do, much less than what the mind can do (CWS I, pp. 494–497; Deleuze, 1970/1988, pp. 17–18). How many common relations can be determined between one's own body and other things? How many affects are we capable of experiencing? Spinoza submits the possibilities are limitless, which is why reification is so dangerous: by abstracting and paraphrasing what is there, a cap is put on that very potential of direct experience. There is always a direct relation between a common notion and the bodies it represents, including our own; because a common notion is always an understanding of affections that can be explained by our singular nature alone (Matheron, 2020, p. 70).

Affective Knowledge

One can see how the common notion's emphasis on intrinsic relations between things, rather than on an intellection of what has occurred, antici- pates Jung's demand that true knowledge must be *embodied* (CW. 9ii, 1959/ 1969c, par. 61). Of course, just because Spinoza agrees with Jung on the shortcomings of intellectual abstractions does not mean that Spinoza, in Jung's estimate, goes on to achieve an intrinsic type of understanding. How does one know that knowledge they have is anchored sufficiently in the psyche? Does Spinoza's common notion truly meet this standard? Per Jung, one way of assuring that knowledge is truly embodied is to account for the *feeling* evoked by experience. Says Jung:

> The function of value—feeling—is an integral part of our conscious orientation and ought not to be missing in a psychological judgment of any scope, otherwise the model we are trying to build of the real process will be incomplete. Every psychic process has a value quality attached to it, namely its feeling-tone. This indicates the degree to which the sub- ject is *affected* by the process or how much it means to him (in so far as the process reaches consciousness at all). It is through the "affect" that the subject becomes involved and so comes to feel the whole weight of reality. The difference amounts roughly to that between a severe ill- ness that one reads about in a textbook and a real illness that one has. In psychology one possesses nothing unless one has experienced it in reality. Hence a purely intellectual insight is not enough, because one knows only the words and not the substance of the thing from inside.
>
> (CW. 9ii, 1959/1969c, par. 61)

Jung defines feeling as the *value* judgment a subject makes, or in other words whether the subject perceives something as good or bad (CW. 6, 1921/1971, pars. 724, 834, 958). Whenever the intellect tries to separate these value judgments from an idea, the result is a "great cheat," a facsimile of an actual experience that has "no weight or substance" (CW. 9ii, 1959/ 1969c, par. 60). What Jung defines as the psychological functions of think- ing *and* feeling are equally necessary to apprehend experience. Thinking may indeed tell us what something is, or rather its objective meaning, but only feeling tells us a thing's subjective value (ibid., par. 52). For Jung, feeling is inseparable from embodied knowledge. And for Spinoza this is no different: an adequate idea is nothing more than knowledge of how another thing affects us. One cannot speak of achieving any sort of adequate understanding without navigating the affects that continually bombard us—for in the end, all of our ideas are implicated by affects to begin with.

To help us fend off affections that we have no control over, the passions, Spinoza formulates a typology of different affects and the emotions they generate within us. Spinoza's aim here is absolutely not to make an exhaustive classification. He cautions that it would be impossible for him to show "all the conflicts of the mind there can be." Outside of the desire for something that increases our power, the joy of having our power increased, and the sadness of having our power diminished, the "various affects can be compounded in so many ways," and "so many variations can arise from this composition that they cannot be defined by any number" (E IIIP59S, CWS I, p. 530; III Def XLVIII, p. 542).[7] Spinoza's move here is reminiscent of the circumspect way in which Jung devises his theory of psychological types, which Jung describes as "the four points of the compass; they are just as arbitrary and just as indispensable. Jung's typology of psychological functions is necessary for a critical method of exploring personality but never ought to be reified as a strict taxonomy (CW. 6, 1921/1971, pars. 958, 959). Knowledge of the affects for Spinoza is similarly fluid: it is quite literally the lived passage from either a lesser or greater state of existence that the affection caused. When Spinoza speaks of this passage, he emphasizes that he does not mean that the mind compares the body's "present constitution with a past constitution, but rather" that the idea of an affect "affirms of the body something which really involves more or less of reality than before" (E III, Gen. Def, CWS I, p. 542). Therefore Spinoza rejects any intellectualist interpretation of his affects theory; not only does his philosophy problematize abstract ideas, but true understanding avoids them as well because it is nothing other than the immanent passage from one state of existence to the next.

What does it mean to have an increase in our affective power? What is 'joy' in Spinoza's philosophy? Effectively it means an increase in our power of acting and comprehending (i.e., the powers of the mind and body). Understanding of affections that agree with us gives us joy, which in turn allows us to form more common notions, to effectively find joy in other encounters—even in encounters that we may otherwise disagree with (E IIIP59, CWS I, pp. 579–590; V10S, pp. 601–602). The common notion is simply the knowledge of an agreement between us and at least one other mode, predicated on a factor that can be explained by our nature alone. Such an agreement increases our affective power—that is to say, it brings us joy. Therefore true understanding always brings us joy (E IVP30–31, CWS I, pp. 560–561). In other words, the very exploration of our affects is what gives us adequate ideas—for Spinoza, no true knowledge can be gleaned without passing first through that which affects us.

Complexes, etc.

It is not just a convergence upon this general concept of 'affective knowledge' where Jung and Spinoza agree—they share an affinity in the consequences of this approach as well. Again, for Spinoza there is always a kernel of adequacy to be uncovered in an inadequate idea; that is to say, error is really just a "privation" of knowledge—but that missing knowledge nevertheless does already exist, implicitly or virtually, within the mind of God (E IIP35, CWS I, pp. 472–473). And this same principle is evident in how Jung treats complexes. In the complexes, certain personal experiences cluster around a nuclear element, a singular point acts as a "vehicle for meaning" for the thoughts and memories caught within its orbit (Jacobi, 1959, p. 23). Because the nuclear core of the complex is submerged in the unconscious, an individual often has no idea when they are arrested by one's power. Someone who had a dominating mother who was impossible to please may project the same expectations, fears, and judgment onto every romantic partner in their life; conversely, they may become demanding and impossible to please themselves. In either case the person is in the throes of a singular complex that they are entirely unaware of (Samuels, 1985, p. 48). Of course, what is unconscious is invariably projected outward (CW. 9ii, 1959/1969c, par. 16). Thus the sort of extrinsic judgments that we saw Jung (and Spinoza) condemn are typical of being caught in the grip of a complex: projections and identifications, dissociations and delusions are the products of either a willful or brittle ego that always remains external to the thing encountered, indicative of an individual whose depth of understanding is far more shallow than they would ever dare admit.[8] Even someone who claims they "know" that they have a complex ("I know I've had a mother complex my whole life!") likely may not *understand* that complex's true nature; in other words, they have not encountered the complex on the emotional, intrinsic level that Jung demands. But conversely, within the complex is the possibility for true understanding, and moreover for "new possibilities" of growth for the psyche (Jung, 1933/2001, pp. 81–82). Confrontation with the complex in order to bring it to consciousness can not only ameliorate the deleterious affects that it radiates—it allows one to apprehend *the true cause behind those affects*. Implicit within the subject who projects his dominating mother's expectations onto his romantic partners is the insight that his behavior stems from a complex first constellated in the relationship with his mother; just as the person who is affected unusually by the color *white* comes to learn that she associates white with the sheet that covers the dead, and that she is still mourning the loss of a loved one (CW. 3, 1907/1960, par. 94).

Of course, such an understanding can only be achieved if the *affectivity* of the complex is properly accounted for, hence why attentiveness to feeling is necessary for such a confrontation. Here the convergence between the extraction of a common notion in Spinoza's philosophy and the process of glimpsing the nuclear core of the complex in Jung's therapeutic approach is evident. Through an unrelated intellectual lineage and tradition, Jung nevertheless deploys the concept of affects in exactly the same way Spinoza does: the *affect* is not the same as feeling itself, which can be restricted to a mental function. Rather, it encompasses both the emotion experienced as well as the unconscious and physical innervations that it triggers—therefore the affect signals reciprocal impacts upon both the mind and the body (CW. 6, 1921/1971, par. 681).[9] But while the affect envelops both the mental and the physical, it is nevertheless the psyche that perceives that affect, as the psyche is our raw datum of experience—therefore, it must be the feeling function, as part of the psyche, that helps us apprehend the nature of a complex affecting us. The entire mass of thoughts and memories that gravitate around the nuclear element of the complex are imbued with a certain "feeling-tone," or a sort of thematic affect that Jung compares to a recurring leitmotif within a song that is in effect 'heard' whenever a complex is triggered by something that happens in the present (CW. 3, 1907/1960, par. 80, footnote 4). Complexes act like "living units" or "splinter psyches" that arrest the ego with an overwhelming feeling, effectively possessing it—hence why Jung argues they are deeply related to the universal belief in spirits (CW. 8, 1934/1969a, pars. 204, 210). Emotion "is not an activity of the individual but something that happens to him." Attention itself is an affective state, and the attention of the ego is constantly disrupted "by ideas with a strong feeling-tone, that is, by affects." A strong complex can inhibit all other ideas, totally seizing our attention. "Thus we should not say that we direct our attention to something, but that the state of attention sets in" with the given affect (CW. 3, 1907/1960, par. 84). It is for the exact same reason that Spinoza claims it is folly to believe that we choose our affects and desires; similarly, it is why he states that our passions cannot be explained by our essence alone, but rather is defined "by the power of an external cause compared with our own." Spinoza describes the arresting power of the passions in the same way that Jung does the affectivity of complexes: so long as the passion's power surpasses the power of the individual, it can stubbornly cling to the person, and it cannot be restrained or taken away except by an affect "opposite to, and stronger than" itself. This is why for Spinoza knowledge of good and evil is "nothing but an affect of Joy or Sadness, insofar as we are conscious of it" (E IVP5–8, CWS I, pp. 549–551). It is only when we correctly perceive what affections agree with ourselves, that our mind becomes capable of rearranging the affections according to adequate ideas (E VP10, CWS I, p. 601).

It must be clarified that it is not just a simple choice of joy over sorrow that constitutes freedom from the passions for Spinoza. It is not simply that adequate ideas give us joy, and inadequate ideas do not. Many kinds of affections in fact do give us joy. Yet the majority of those affections come from outside us and cannot be explained by our essence alone; therefore, even though these joys increase our power, it is only on a provisional and contingent basis; we understand nothing of it, and are not truly in control of it. *These joys then are still ultimately passions* (E IVP59, CWS I, pp. 579–580). Binge-eating may bring someone temporary joy, but if they are eating wantonly out of comfort or to blot out unrelated anxiety, this demonstrates no true understanding of oneself or the food that they eat, and one can readily imagine this enjoyment quickly turning to regret and discomfort. Whether they are joys or sorrows, inadequate ideas are always bound with passions. Conversely, the common notion can be explained by an individual's own essence, and so it allows them to better understand their own essence as well as the essence of other things involved in that common notion. Furthermore, this allows an individual to enjoy affects explained internally by their essence alone. Because these affects invariably lead to an increase in one's power, they *must* be joys—but they are joys in an *active* sense, as nothing outside of our power is necessary to explain them. Therefore, the formation of common notions leads to an *active* kind of joy, and the true dichotomy of Spinoza's theory of affects is not between joys and sorrows, but really between *actions* and *passions* (E

IIIP58–59, CWS I, p. 529). A golfer who simply tries to recite instructions a coach gave them may not, in Spinoza's opinion, have any better understanding than the merchant who recalls calculations learned in the classroom; but the golfer who forms an intrinsic relationship with their swing, no matter the exact method used to achieve it, is expressing an active joy with their craft.

In Jung we find a similar discernment in finding a resolution to the complex. One can easily imagine the short-lived relief a person may have when they find a person suitable for receiving the needs of their unconscious complex—for instance, a romantic interest that is capable of receiving the projection of a mother image. Whatever relief found here may prove to be quite tenuous, and the true cause of psychic disturbance remains hidden. But a similar 'false solution' can be found even within the actual therapeutic process of treating the complex, and this is essentially how Jung distinguishes between his synthetic method and the analytic approach of his erstwhile mentor, Sigmund Freud. In the case of an individual with a mother complex, a Freudian approach may conclude that the source of the complex was the initial relationship the person had with his mother, and whatever dysfunction, disappointment, or trauma arose from those formative years. Yet for Jung this analytic method is not sufficient. It is only when one casts off the personal histories and memories surrounding the core of the complex that one can find the true cause—an archetype. Then, an individual is no longer confronted with the image of their own mother, but with the archetype of the maternal; they are no longer consumed with their own personal history, but all peoples and all histories that have engaged with all the possibilities and problems expressed by the mother archetype. The woman who associates the color of white with death due to the loss of a loved one suddenly no longer focuses on that past trauma, but rather an archetypal notion of death—and perhaps rebirth as well. Suddenly the complex is no longer an immense burden that the individual struggles to find the most suitable figures, past and present, to project it onto; but rather something atemporal and experienced by all. Yet at the same time it can be explained by oneself alone, by the very nature of their being human (Jacobi, 1959, pp. 26–27).

A final consequence can be drawn from this. The archetypal perspective on complexes allows one to view their cause *sub specie aeternitatis* (CW. 8, 1931/1969a, par. 316). We have already seen Jung use this phrase in the exact meaning Spinoza crafted (Ch. 2, pp. 63–68). For Spinoza it is the accumulation of adequate ideas, this increased understanding of how the essences of singular things intrinsically agree with one another even despite differences that appear in existence, that enables one to pass over into Spinoza's third kind of knowledge, the intuitive intellect where one can understand things as they exist eternally in the mind of God (E IIP40S2, CWS I, p. 478; EVP29, pp. 609–610). In both Jung and Spinoza we find that all knowledge is affective, and therefore predicated on knowledge of oneself—but that this does not place a handicap on what one can know. The 'monad with windows' can constantly push into unknown territories, into what was heretofore unconscious and "unascertainable" (Meier, 2001, pp. 111–115).

The Problem of Symbols

To summarize, Jung and Spinoza both endorse an embodied knowledge that treats understanding and affect as inseparable. Therefore Spinoza anticipates another of Jung's reasons for the tripartite monism established in Chapter 1: knowledge of existence is routed through knowledge of the self. For Jung, this is an acknowledgment that the psyche is our only immediate datum of experience, and consequently our understanding of spirit and matter must pass through the psyche. For Spinoza it is the same: all common notions, whether they are ideas of intrinsic relations between ourselves and just one other mode or *all* other modes, begin with an understanding of what affections can be explained by our singular essence alone. And the formulation of these initial common notions can lead to the formation of more general notions, until one perceives that all bodies and minds are conceived by the absolute power of God, whether that power is conceived under the attribute of extension or of thought (E IIP37–40S, CWS I, pp. 474–478). This union of knowledge and affective power is precisely what Nietzsche found so alluring in Spinoza, why he considered Spinoza a precursor to his own 'psychological' approach to philosophy (Schacht, 1999). Grant Maxwell draws a historical lineage between this exploration of affective potencies in Spinoza, with the *Naturalphilosophie* of Schelling and the theory of forces in Nietzsche, all the way to archetypal complexes of Jung (Maxwell, 2022). It is in a sense as if Jung has been dealing with *two different Spinozas*: the negative caricature as authored by Hegel, and the philosopher from whom he inherited a sort of transcendental immanence—if not Spinozism itself.

Once again we are left wondering why Jung does not recognize this affinity. Can Jung's rejection of Spinoza simply be explained by an aversion to philosophy, perhaps due to a suspicion that it will always lean too far into the intellect, even when it claims not to? Or perhaps, as Jungian scholar Jon Mills has posited, Jung was instead motivated by a desire to not have his psychology scrutinized by a philosophical lens (Mills, 2019, pp. 4–6). Is it a matter of petty intellectual posturing? One might even be inclined at this point to ask if antisemitism is at play; namely, if Jung's embarrassing opinions on the dangerousness of "rootless" secular Jews played any role in his view of Spinoza (Letters, Vol. 1, 1973, p. 164). Spinoza, among his many other accomplishments, was the original "Renegade Jew" (Goldstein, 2006). Yet it would not do justice to the nuance Jung displays on the issues discussed thus far to attribute his treatment of Spinoza to prejudice alone. Consider, for instance, how Jung shows much more outright contempt for Hegel, a German protestant, than he ever does toward Spinoza. Jung refers to Hegel's inflation of "philosophical reason with Spirit" as a megalomaniacal act; he describes Hegel's prose as reminiscent of the ramblings of a schizophrenic; and he claims that the intellectual "victory of Hegel over Kant dealt the gravest blow to reason" throughout Europe, leading to a chain reaction that Jung astonishingly traces through German Romanticism all the way to the catastrophes of the Second World War (CW. 8, 1946/1969a, pars. 358–360). The raising of Immanuel Kant brings up a further point: in contrast to his views on other philosophers, Jung's allegiance to the limits placed on human cognition in Kant's critical philosophy has puzzled some Jungian scholars, since it seems to at times hold Jung's thinking back unnecessarily.[10] Yet in Jung's mind, a passing allegiance to Kantian epistemology is perhaps a measure taken to protect the psyche's sovereignty—particularly from the non-psychic. The tool that Jung uses to secure that sovereignty is precisely what he finds absent in Spinoza's philosophy: the symbolic.

The symbol actually plays a similar role in Jung's psychology to that of the common notion in Spinoza's epistemology. As discussed, the common notion is what allows one to conceive what connects oneself to other modes. Similarly, the symbol is what connects the personal with the archetypal; in the case of complexes, the archetypal imagery that is extracted from one's personal experiences is precisely how one perceives the complex's archetypal core. The archetype is only ever glimpsed through the symbolic: the archetype *itself* is purely psychoid—that is to say, beyond spirit and matter, and therefore purely eternal, or virtual. But when actualized as a symbol or archetypal image, the archetype expresses a specific meaning within that time and history, whether we mean a collective history or simply one's own life (CW. 13, 1954/1967b, par. 350). Jung uses Anatole France's story of the pious priest Abbé Oegger, who had dreamt of Judas Iscariot before ultimately leaving the church, as an example of how mythological figures illustrate and hasten "certain tendencies in the personality" which would remain unconscious otherwise—in other words, grappling with the symbolic is the key to understanding the unconscious (CW. 5, 1956/1967a, pars. 41–45). The "symbol is a living thing, it is an expression for something that cannot be characterized in any other or better way." Once a meaning has been rigidly defined—in other words when a symbol is reified and abstracted—it is dead (CW. 6, 1921/1971, par. 816).

This again harkens to the difference between extrinsic and intrinsic knowledge that Jung and Spinoza jointly espouse. However, another element of the symbolic that is ostensibly absent in Spinoza's treatment of adequate ideas is the involvement of *opposites and paradoxes*. In an anecdote Jung uses to portray synchronicity, one of his patients possessed a highly intellectual attitude that made Jung's brand of analysis difficult. The symbolic manifestation of a scarab beetle (both in the patient's dreams and literally at Jung's window) caused a breakthrough in the patient and allowed productive work to begin (CW. 8, 1952/1969a, par. 982). In this example, the symbol caused a resolution between the patient's rationalist outward views and the opposing needs of the inner life. This is indeed the function of a symbol, to bridge the gap between the personal and universal layers of the complex, or between the individual and the archetypal (Jacobi, 1959, pp. 25–26). Therefore the symbol is crucial to the union of opposites such as *inner* and *outer*; it is the language of paradox that Jung sees as the *only* way to navigate the unconscious.[11]

Now while Jung and Spinoza both treat mere *signs* as a form of extrinsic knowledge, and thus inadequate, there is no discussion of symbols in Spinoza's philosophy. Any adequate idea *must* be expressed perfectly— therefore, any sort of equivocation or merely *implied* meaning has no place beyond the realm of error and passions. Nor does Spinoza have any use for discussion of unifying opposites: in his view opposites are just another form of abstraction, a way of framing a universal category against a pure negative, such as being versus non-being, or order versus disorder (E IV, Preface, CWS I, p. 544). For Spinoza there is only affirmation—what is seen as negative is only what is not yet known (Deleuze, 1970/1988, pp. 68–69).

The argument that Spinoza fails to see the value of uniting opposites somehow due to him being a Jew is a canard that Jung indeed may have held—it in fact preceded him, once again with Hegel. Hegel comments that Spinoza's 'oriental' or Jewish background allowed him to only see God as a dyad where the individual is inevitably consumed by the whole, whereas the Christian trinity meanwhile allows for a *middle* term between the infinite and finite, for the incarnation of God *in* man, and—most importantly to Hegel—the ability to view God in human terms, as in Hegel's version of spirit (2018, p. 252). Jung may have a similar thought in mind when he states that Spinoza's Love of God, an *intellectual* love, is a rung lower than the Christian version of love, which allows for more mystery (CW. 10, 1922/1970, par. 199). Moreover, in 'Role of the Unconscious' Jung tells the story of a young rabbi who was almost cast out of his synagogue as a heretic—Jung explicitly notes that this echoes Spinoza's own herem. Is it a coincidence that Jung notes how the symbolic nature of the ram's horn that the elders threatened to use to signal the young rabbi's condemnation, the *shofar*, meant nothing to the young rabbi, *since he saw the horn as not a symbol but only a mere object* (CW. 10, 1918/1970, pars. 27–29)? In other words, does Jung see in Spinoza a failure to appreciate the true symbolic power of the unconscious, the same failure he saw in his former mentor Freud? That there is an antisemitic lineament in Jung and Hegel's thoughts that is worthy of criticism is not the point, nor would it be accurate to say that this prejudice is the root cause of Jung's grievance toward Spinoza— even if it gave him an excuse, however objectionable, to fashion his complaints. Rather, *Jung condemns what he sees as the fatal absence of the symbolic in Spinoza's philosophy*. For Jung this criticism goes far beyond mere prejudice or intellectual posturing—symbols are the language of the unconscious; without them, Jung thinks any further statements of the unascertainable or metaphysical are purely farcical. With that in mind, it is easier to see why Jung would dismiss Spinoza despite agreeing with him on so many other points. One cannot readily imagine Jung flipping open his copy of the *Ethics*, reviewing the uncompromising precision of Spinoza's 'geometric method', and finding it to be satisfactory. Indeed, Jung mentions that the patient whose breakthrough came via the synchronistic occurrence of the scarab beetle initially had the intellect of a polished Cartesian who viewed the world in perfect "geometric order" (CW. 8, 1952/1969a, par.

982). Clearly Jung viewed such an intellect as imbalanced. It would be difficult to imagine him viewing Spinoza, who infamously wrote the *Ethics* in that very same sort of geometric method, any differently.

Therefore, despite all the isomorphisms between Jung and Spinoza that have been described thus far—their transcendental immanence, the union of knowledge and affect, and the distinction of mind and spirit that all their other affinities inevitably demand—Jung still ultimately finds Spinoza to fail to uphold the middle; not because Spinoza's philosophy is in itself reductionist or mechanistic, but because without the symbolic and the mysterious power it commands, Jung believes a one-sided intellectualization is inevitable anyways. For Jung this approach leads to a severance from the sacred, or 'numinous', culminating in a certain disenchantment with the world that much of Jung's project was dedicated to combating (Main, 2022, pp. 19–22, 26–30). Jung's accusation of Spinoza likely would be that he proceeds too hastily into the unknown, ill-equipped and lacking the necessary tools to survive. In turn, Spinoza might reply that Jung is too tepid, too content to hide behind analogy and equivocation rather than to proceed into what is *really* there. Yet for Jung, inattentiveness to the symbolic is not merely a failure to describe the unascertainable. Jung believes there is an actual danger to this type of 'imbalanced' approach.

At What Price?

In his book *Hegel or Spinoza*, the French philosopher Pierre Macherey identifies the key ways in which Hegel misreads Spinoza's philosophy. Macherey does not merely highlight what Hegel gets wrong about Spinoza; rather, he asks *why* Hegel interprets Spinoza the way that he does. He concludes that Hegel recognizes both the proximity his philosophy has to Spinoza's, as well as certain elements in Spinoza's thought that would effectively refute parts of Hegel's system. Therefore, Hegel formulates a reading of Spinoza that is meant to put distance between the two of them and to protect Hegel's idealism from a Spinozist attack. These defenses chiefly concern the notion of a subject that is given guaranteed protection with Hegel's version of spirit, as well as spirit's inherent ability to totalize the differences in all things in order to reach a final absolute (Macherey, 1979/2011). Hence Hegel's claim that the individual has no true home in Spinoza's philosophy. As we saw in Chapter 2, this accusation depends in large part on a subjective reading of Spinoza's God, and that this interpretation has been widely discredited (pp. 57–61).[12] Spinoza, like Hegel, conceives individual things as being within God; however, Spinoza's placement of thought as *anterior* to any notion of a subject dispenses with all use for an absolute teleology within his metaphysics. Thought is not an internal movement toward an all-encompassing final cause; rather, the attribute of thought expresses God's ability to absolutely and completely comprehend all the things that he produces. For Hegel, the progression of history is the movement of spirit itself; but for Spinoza, history is just one of the infinity of things that God creates, just another singular mode of substance—and anything that God can think of he *must* also produce. All modes, whether they be histories, persons, things, or otherwise, are expressions of God's absolutely infinite capacity to conceive and create (E IP15–17S, CWS I, pp. 420–428). According to Macherey, it is this unmooring of a totalizing subject that Hegel could not accept, and so, despite their mutual dedication to an immanent God and a rejection of dualism, Hegel tries to cast space between himself and Spinoza by producing a reading of the Dutch philosopher's metaphysics that ultimately cannot sustain itself beyond the guarantee of a featureless One Substance (1979/2011).

Hegel is pertinent to this discussion because, as we have seen, some of Jung's dismissals of Spinoza echo Hegel's own influential critique (see Ch. 2, pp. 57–61). Another reason however is that on some level Jung does seem to understand the proximity he shares with Spinoza, while at the same time he clearly disapproves of Spinoza's philosophy as a whole. Macherey writes that

> Hegel is never so close to Spinoza as the moments when he distances himself from him, because this refusal has the value of a symptom and indicates the obstinate presence of a common object, if not a common project, that links these two philosophers inseparably without conflating them.
>
> (1979/2011, p. 11)

Is this the same case for Jung? In other words, would a direct meeting with Spinoza force Jung to cede some crucial portion of his own psychology? This is not at all to say that Spinoza was in any way as important for Jung as he was for Hegel. Hegel quite deliberately makes Spinoza the starting point for his own philosophy, and, in his opinion, *all* philosophy commences with Spinoza—it is Hegel who even says that one is "either a

Spinozist or not a philosopher at all" (2018, pp. 258, 283). But as demonstrated in the previous chapter, Jung is at least aware of Spinoza's relevance to the problem of spirit and the psyche, to the distinction of spirit and matter, and his metaphysical position as a whole. It is at this juncture in fact where Jung finds he is closest to Spinoza—and indeed, where he pushes him away.

This is not the first instance where Jung has been alleged to behave in such a manner toward an intellectual predecessor. Jungian and Nietzschean scholar Lucy Huskinson has chronicled Jung's peculiar reception of Nietzsche, how Jung is hesitant to admit Nietzsche's philosophy as a forerunner to his psychology despite the similar ways in which they treat psychological opposites, as well as the affinity between Nietzsche's *Übermensch* and the Jungian self. Instead Jung claims that Nietzsche's philosophy fails to truly uphold itself because it valorizes the conscious over the unconscious psyche—because of this, Jung claims Nietzsche fails *to maintain a middle third* between these opposite views. In Huskinson's opinion, Jung selectively reads Nietzsche to reach this conclusion by omitting portions of Nietzsche's work where Nietzsche clearly recognizes the nuance that Jung claims he misses. Huskinson believes Jung does this not merely to protect his psychology from any criticism on Nietzsche's part. Rather, Jung perpetuates the canard that Nietzsche's philosophical mindset ultimately drove him mad. Jung himself had his own bout with possible psychosis after his fallout with Freud. Therefore, to admit that his psychological project bears resemblance to the philosophy of Nietzsche might also allow that Jung shares the same madness as Nietzsche (Huskinson, 2004).[13]

What is the specific part of Spinoza's philosophy that might cause such tension for Jung? What is it in the 'unascertainable' that Jung fears so much, that he insists cannot be reckoned with head-on and without the necessary defenses, those armaments of symbolism, paradox, and myth? Is there anything in Spinozism that possibly even reminds Jung of his own madness? In Part II of the *Ethics*, Spinoza explains the nature of individuals. Each individual is in fact a composition of other individuals, with each composite being defined by their specific ratio of relations, what Spinoza calls "motion and rest." Now each individual composite may lose and gain some of the individuals that compose its relations—but so long as its specific ratio of motion and rest is maintained, the individual is not destroyed. And Spinoza is clear that each and every individual is part of a composition greater than itself: blood is within man, man is within the state, the state is within the world, and the world is within the cosmos. This proceeds to infinity, until one can conceive all of nature as a single individual, "whose parts, i.e., all bodies, vary in infinite ways, without any change of the whole Individual" (E IIP13SL6–7; CWS I, pp. 461–462). For Spinoza this is essentially all of nature as conceived under the attribute of extension (E IP15S, CWS I, pp. 421–424). Because all modes can be conceived equally under different attributes, this composite theory would apply as well to the attribute of thought (E IIP7S, CWS I, pp. 451–452). And indeed, Spinoza notes that the human mind is a complex idea made of many smaller ideas, and ultimately all ideas are contained within God's Infinite Intellect (E IIP3, CWS I, p. 449; IIP15, p. 463).[14] It is these very relations, both within ourselves and between modes, that the common notions are predicated upon, why they are elements that are equally "in the parts and the whole"; in a sense, common notions are when two or more modes compound into a more powerful assemblage. This is true whether we speak of chyle and lymph forming blood, or of two people falling in love (Ep. 32, CWS II, pp. 18–22).[15]

For Hegel, the individual as composite is something he cannot tolerate with the Spinozist system (2018, pp. 272–273). That for Spinoza the extrinsic parts that make up an individual are not as important as the intrinsic ratio of relations that define them—or that this ratio is an expression of a singular essence that is eternal—is little consolation for Hegel, who in any event does not want the Divine separate from history (Yovel, 1989, Ch. 2). Macherey claims this is in fact what Hegel fears most in Spinoza: the dynamism that *does* exist in Spinoza's monism leaves no room for any totalizing teleology, nor a succession of movements determined by negation. Instead there is the perpetual composition and decomposition of extrinsic things, as well as the intrinsic essences that those extrinsic modes express intermittently (Macherey, 1979/2011, Ch. 4). A determination of God is not a lesser emanation but instead an expression of a singular degree or essence of his power.

Now this notion of extrinsic encounters forming the individual is not foreign to Jung's psychology. In many respects this is precisely what his complex theory suggests, with its implications regarding the dissociability and new connections between "splinter psyches" (CW. 8, 1934/1969a). *The ego itself is actually a complex*, the whole mass of ideas pertaining to one's own consciousness as well as the "ever-present feeling-tone of" one's own body

(CW. 3, 1907/1960, par. 82). Jung's psychology in a sense describes a lateral plane of different complexes colliding and interacting with one another— our own selves being just one of many complexes within this plane. Jung even paints a very similar analog to Spinoza's composite theory of bodies in 'Spirit and Life', where he speculates that ego-consciousness might merely be subordinate to a wider consciousness, "just as simpler complexes are subordinate to the ego-complex." Jung supposes that the optical system possessed consciousness or had an "eye-personality." These conscious eyes would only know the perception of the world through light. When the auditory system hears, for instance, a passing car, the whole body will respond to it; but this perception remains unknown to the optical system. If the eyes were conscious, Jung notes, they would surely find the world of light to be full of turbulent disturbances, never knowing the disturbances were in fact caused by the body of which they were part. Are there, Jung asks, similar disturbances that happen to us, which we have no will over, and would suggest that we too are involved in a composition greater than ourselves? Jung affirms this, noting the random mood swings associated with neurotics and how unconscious complexes affect the psyche in dramatic ways that defy ready explanation (CW. 8, 1926/1969a, pars. 637–639). Writes Jung:

> Our imaginary "eye-personality" might doubt that sudden disturbances of its light-world came from another consciousness. Similarly, we can be sceptical about a wider consciousness, though with no more ground for scepticism than the eye-personality would have. But as we cannot attain to such a state of wider consciousness or understand it, we would do well to call that dark region, from our point of view, the "unconscious," without jumping to the conclusion that it is necessarily unconscious itself.
>
> (ibid., par. 641)

What is the collective unconscious for Jung if not some type of "supraconsciousness" that anticipates and envelops the individual (CW. 13, 1942/1967b, par. 229)? Is this not where the transformative power that spirit bestows upon the psyche is derived (CW. 9i, 1948/1969, par. 392)? But if Spinoza encourages exploration of the composition of things and ideas, it is Jung who counsels restraint. The unconscious is not some "parlour game." Jung compares it to digging a well and running "the risk of stumbling on a volcano." The rewards are great to be sure but only if one is capable of cultivating a personal psyche that can transcend the depths; otherwise, the unconscious may break forth: "uncontrollable fantasies" and even "latent psychoses" may ensue. And Jung claims it is not just a matter of psyche and spirit too: manifestations in the physical world, like freak accidents or ill health, may result, a cruel synchronistic outcome from reckless investigation of the psyche (CW. 7, 1916/1966, pars. 192–195).

With this warning in mind, there is no longer any need to posit that Jung simply misread Spinoza, that he found Spinoza's philosophy hollow and devoid of affect, a mechanistic dreadnought lacking in life and *spirit* itself—in fact, in Spinoza Jung recognizes a "highly imaginative" person susceptible to the same visions that Jung, both professionally and personally, was so consumed with.[16] The Spinozist viewpoint aggressively plunges one into an infinite composition, to knowingly move within the Divine, and to Jung's mind this leaves the individual ill-equipped and unprepared to withstand the forces that could readily tear them apart. This was a danger that Jung himself was acutely aware of. "I wanted the proof of a living Spirit and I got it," Jung writes to Father White in 1948. "Don't ask me at what a price" (Letters, Vol. 1, 1973, p. 492). When Jung insists that no philosophy can be of any use to confront the unconscious, it is not a mere cynical ploy to promote the merits of psychology (Letters, Vol. 2, 1975, p. 620). Without psychology—moreover, *without the language of symbols and contradiction to act as the only viable 'chain mail' to defend oneself*—the confrontation with the unconscious can only end in disaster. The psyche's separation from spirit is not only an ontological and epistemological necessity for Jung—it is also an issue of one's own survival.

Whether Spinoza's philosophy truly fails in this regard is not as important as knowing that this reveals what Jung is most resistant to in Spinoza—to be overwhelmed by *spirit*. Spirit is the point of tension on which they perplexingly unite, yet also diverge; it is the vista where Jung writes most intensely on Spinoza, where he realizes they meet, yet he also insists that Spinoza ultimately slips from this summit, having reached for a cosmic scheme only to tumble down into the realm of dead materialism—or, worse yet, an all-consuming *spirit* embedded within that One Substance. To embrace Spinozism would potentially force Jung to cede territory he claims for the psyche alone. Consider that Jung will not compromise his psychology for the world's great religions, nor the science of his day; small wonder then he would not do so for a long-dead philosopher whose views he otherwise had much in common with. For it is Jung's most ardent belief that only psychology can perform this middle role. We have seen it as the basis for his metaphysics; it is also what he truly insisted was what the world in his time needed. It is not that Jung sees Spinoza as the zoologist attempting to give the duck-billed platypus a zoological critique; rather, Jung judges Spinoza's attempts to interact *directly* with the platypus, or with any other singular mode or affection, as ill-advised and dangerous.

Following this long foray into the common ground that Jung and Spinoza *do* share concerning their monism and the theory of affects, before ultimately stumbling upon their point of contention, one might ask if it is really necessary to go any further, if we really need to investigate these apparently irreconcilable issues in any more detail; or, if instead we can simply accept Jung and Spinoza have significant differences that can't be solved, but nonetheless some of Spinoza's ideas can be retrofitted nicely onto Jung's psychology to bolster his metaphysical position. Yet Jung's criticism here also belies a potential problem in his own psychology, a vulnerability that Spinoza's philosophy exposes, engages, and possibly even solves. It is this problem we must next analyze, because in turn it provides clarity regarding Jung's move toward Spinozism.

Notes

1 All references to 'CWS I' belong to Spinoza (1985) and all references to 'CWS II' belong to Spinoza (2016). These are the two editions edited by Curley.

2 The power of existence is also what Spinoza calls the 'striving' or 'persevering' of each thing to exist. The original Latin term, *conatus*, is commonly used in Spinoza scholarship (E IIP7, CWS I, p. 499; CWS I, p. 699).

3 It is worth noting that the sense in which Spinoza uses the term 'image' is not, technically speaking, an idea or in the domain of thought. Rather, an image is a corporeal trace of an affection. Now, the corresponding idea our mind has of that trace gives us the impression that the thing that affected us is still present. Hence the mind 'imagines' something that isn't really there (E IP17S2, CWS I, p. 465). This speaks to the nuanced roles which both corporeal and ideal things share in Spinoza's theory of affects (Jaquet, 2019).

4 A knowledgeable reader may point out a looming discrepancy between Jung and Spinoza's approaches here: ostensibly for Jung, the withdrawal of the projection leads to an inward search for an archetypal cause, at expense of the outer world; whereas for Spinoza, as we shall see, true knowledge lies in a better understanding of outward relations. This difference in the priority of inner or outer is discussed in Chapter 4.

5 In regards to the affects, Spinoza actually uses two different terms, *affectio* and *affectus*. *Affectio* refers to the affections of other modes we encounter, as discussed. *Affectus* refers to the affect itself, that is, the change in one's own power of existing that results from the affection. Some translators conflate both words and simply use 'affect', which loses the nuance Spinoza meant to convey. Other translators, including Samuel Shirley and George Eliot, translate *affectus* as emotion, which makes sense to a degree since Spinoza considers emotions to be nothing other than the change in one's power of existence. The term emotion however implies that affects are purely of the intellect, when in fact they have an impact upon the body *and* the mind (see Deleuze 1970/1988, pp. 48–51; also Jaquet, 2019, p. 78, footnote 12).

6 This is similar to why Matheron points out that it is important to not confuse just *what* we are forming common notions of. When we form a genetic idea of a circle in our head, for instance, the important factor that makes it a common notion is the idea of rotation—that is, the common factor that both we and the circle are capable of. One could object that we don't know how our brain forms the picture of a circle to begin with; however, if we were to understand those intricacies, the adequate idea we would subsequently form would no longer be of a circle, but rather the neurological processes in question. There is always an excess of things we have inadequate knowledge of, but common notions are those affections that can be explained by our specific nature (2020, pp. 70–71).

7 At the end of *Ethics* Part III Spinoza provides a list of definitions for the affects. He stresses again that it is just a mapping of common occurrences, not a total taxonomy (E III, CWS I, pp. 531–543).

8 Per Jacobi, four of the ways the ego can approach a complex include total ignorance, projection, identification, and, finally, confrontation (1959, p. 17).

9 Jung outright describes the *affect* as a combination of the feeling and sensing functions. He credits his teacher Eugene Bleuler for the notion of *affectivity*. Jung, in contrast to Bleuler, distinguishes *affect* from feeling (CW. 6, 1921/ 1971, par. 681).

10 For more on the ways Jung uses (and misuses) Kant's philosophy, see de Voogd (1977), Bishop (2000), and Giegerich (1987).

11 Many thanks to Roderick Main for insights on this (Personal Correspondence, 2022).

12 Other Spinozist scholars are more open to the idea that at least some of Hegel's criticisms of Spinoza have merit (see Yovel, 1989, Ch. 2).

13 Interestingly, Nietzsche himself treats Spinoza in a similar way, admiring his predecessor for his insights into the union of knowledge and affect while also criticizing Spinoza for pretending his philosophy was an adequate "mail and mask" to protect him from the onslaught of the passions. In doing this, Nietzsche describes Spinoza as a philosopher trying to compensate for his loneliness and declining health—an obvious projection of Nietzsche's own state at the time (Schact, 1999; Wollenburg, 2015, Ch. 2).

14 Though, technically, this infinite composition would be what Spinoza calls a 'mediate infinite mode' under thought, whereas the infinite intellect is an 'immediate' infinite mode that produces the mediate infinite mode. For an explanation of this enigmatic difference, see Ch. 5, p. 170, footnote 1.

15 "For if, for example, two individuals of entirely the same nature are joined to one another, they compose an individual twice as powerful as each one" (E IVP18S, CWS I p. 556).

16 Jung describes a waking vision Spinoza had of a dark Brazilian man in his room to suggest that "highly imaginative people" are susceptible to such visions. At the very least, such a reference suggests that Jung recognized within Spinoza more than a mere rationalist (CW. 1, 1957/1970, par. 100, footnote 49).

References

Adler, G. & Jaffe, A. (1973). *C.G. Jung Letters 1: 1906–1950*. Translated by R. Hull. Princeton: Princeton University Press.

Adler, G. & Jaffe, A. (1975). *C.G. Jung Letters 2: 1951–1961*. Translated by R. Hull. Princeton: Princeton University Press.

Bishop, P. (2000). *Synchronicity and Intellectual Intuition in Kant, Swedenborg, and Jung*. Lampeter, UK: Edwin Mellen Press.

de Voogd, S. (1977). "C.G. Jung: Psychologist of the Future, 'Philosopher' of the Past," in *Spring 1997*, 175–182.

Deleuze, G. (1970/1988). *Spinoza: Practical Philosophy*. Translated by R. Hurley. San Francisco: City Light Books.

Giegerich, W. (1987). "The Rescue of the World: Jung, Hegel, and the Subjective Universe," in *Spring 1987*, 107–114.

Goldstein, R. (2006). *Betraying Spinoza: The Renegade Jew Who Gave Us Modernity*. New York: Nextbooks/Schocken.

Hegel, G.W.F. (2018). *Hegel's Lectures on the History of Philosophy*, Vol. 3. Project Gutenberg. Produced by Fritz Ohrenschall and the Online Distributed Proofreading Team at www.pgdp.net (Accessed October 2022).

Huskinson, L. (2004). *Nietzsche and Jung: Whole Self in the Union of Opposites*. Hove and New York: Brunner Routledge.

Jacobi, J. (1959). *Complex, Archetype, Symbol in the Psychology of C.G. Jung*. Translated by Ralph Manheim. Princeton: Princeton University Press.

Jaquet, C. (2019). *Affects, Actions and Passions in Spinoza: The Unity of Body and Mind*. Translated by T. Reznichenko. Edinburgh: Edinburgh University Press.

Jiwani, R. (2021). "Bryson DeChambeau: What Makes 'The Scientist' tick?" in *Olympics.com*. https://olympics.com/en/news/golf-bryson-dechambeau-five-things-to-know-the-scientist (Accessed July 2024).

Jung, C.G. (1907). "The Psychology of Dementia Praecox," in *The Psychogenesis of Mental Disease*. Translated by R. Hull. Collected Works of C.G. Jung, Vol. 3. Princeton: Princeton University Press, 1960.

Jung, C.G. (1916). *Two Essays on Analytical Psychology*, 2nd ed. Translated by R. Hull. Collected Works of C.G. Jung, Vol. 7. Princeton: Princeton University Press, 1966.

Jung, C.G. (1916). 'General Aspects of Dream Psychology', in *The Structure and Dynamics of the Psyche*, 2nd ed. Translated by R. Hull. Collected Works of C.G. Jung, Vol. 8. Princeton: Princeton University Press, 1969a.

Jung, C.G. (1918). 'The Role of the Unconscious', in *Civilization in Transition*, 2nd ed. Translated by R. Hull. Collected Works of C.G. Jung, Vol. 10. Princeton: Princeton University Press, 1970.

Jung, C.G. (1921). *Psychological Types*, 2nd ed. Translated by R. Hull. Collected Works of C.G. Jung, Vol. 6. Princeton: Princeton University Press, 1971.

Jung, C.G. (1922). 'The Love Problem of a Student', in *Civilization in Transition*, 2nd ed. Translated by R. Hull. Collected Works of C.G. Jung, Vol. 10. Princeton: Princeton University Press, 1970.

Jung, C.G. (1926) 'Spirit and Life', in *The Structure and Dynamics of the Psyche*, 2nd ed. Translated by R. Hull. Collected Works of C.G. Jung, Vol. 8. Princeton: Princeton University Press, 1969a.

Jung, C.G. (1928) 'On Psychic Energy', in *The Structure and Dynamics of the Psyche*, 2nd ed. Translated by R. Hull. Collected Works of C.G. Jung, Vol. 8. Princeton: Princeton University Press, 1969a.

Jung, C.G. (1931). 'Basic Postulates of Analytical psychology', in *The Structure and Dynamics of the Psyche*, 2nd ed. Translated by R. Hull. Collected Works of C.G. Jung, Vol. 8. Princeton: Princeton University Press, 1969a.

Jung, C.G. (1933). *Modern Man in Search of a Soul*. New York & London: Routledge, 2001.

Jung, C.G. (1934). 'A Review of the Complex Theory', in *The Structure and Dynamics of the Psyche*, 2nd ed. Translated by R. Hull. Collected Works of C.G. Jung, Vol. 8. Princeton: Princeton University Press, 1969a.

Jung, C.G. (1942). 'Paracelsus as a Spiritual Phenomenon', in *Alchemical Studies*. Translated by R. Hull. Collected Works of C.G. Jung, Vol. 13. Princeton: Princeton University Press, 1967b.

Jung, C.G. (1946). 'On the Nature of the Psyche', in *The Structure and Dynamics of the Psyche*, 2nd ed. Translated by R. Hull. Collected Works of C.G. Jung, Vol. 8. Princeton: Princeton University Press, 1969a.

Jung, C.G. (1948). 'The Phenomenology of the Spirit in Fairytales', in *The Archetypes and the Collective Unconscious*, 2nd ed. Translated by R. Hull. Collected Works of C.G. Jung, Vol. 9i. Princeton: Princeton University Press, 1969b.

Jung, C.G. (1952). 'Synchronicity: An Acausal Connecting Principle', in *The Structure and Dynamics of the Psyche*, 2nd ed. Translated by R. Hull. Collected Works of C.G. Jung, Vol. 8. Princeton: Princeton University Press, 1969a.

Jung, C.G. (1954). 'The Philosophical Tree', in *Alchemical Studies*. Translated by R. Hull. Collected Works of C.G. Jung, Vol. 13. Princeton: Princeton University Press, 1967b.

Jung, C.G. (1956). *Symbols of Transformation*. 2nd ed. Translated by R. Hull. Collected Works of C.G. Jung, Vol. 5. Princeton: Princeton University Press, 1967a.

Jung, C.G. (1957). *Psychiatric Studies*. 2nd ed. Translated by R. Hull. Collected Works of C.G. Jung, Vol. 1. Princeton: Princeton University Press, 1970.

Jung, C.G. (1959). *Aion: Researches into the Phenomenology of the Self*. 2nd ed. Translated by R. Hull. Collected Works of C.G. Jung, Vol. 9ii. Princeton: Princeton University Press, 1969c.

Macherey, P. (1979/2011). *Hegel or Spinoza*. Translated by S. Ruddick. Minnesota: University of Minnesota Press.

Main, R. (2022). *Breaking the Spell of Disenchantment: Mystery, Meaning, and Metaphysics in the Work of C.G. Jung*. The Zurich Lecture Series: Volume 8. Asheville, NC: Chiron Publications.

Matheron, A. (2020). *Politics, Ontology, and Knowledge in Spinoza*. Translated by D. Maruzzella & G. Morejon. Edinburgh: Edinburgh University Press.

Maxwell, G. (2022). *Integration and Difference: Constructing a Mythical Dialectic*. London & New York: Routledge.

Meier, C.A. (ed.) (2001). *Atom and Archetype: The Pauli/Jung Letters 1932–1958*. London: Routledge.

Mills, J. (2019). "Introduction: Philosophizing Jung," in *Jung and Philosophy*. Edited by J. Mills. London: Routledge.

Samuels, A. (1985). *Jung and the Post-Jungians*. London & New York: Routledge.

Schact, R. (1999). "The Spinoza–Nietzsche Problem," in *Desire and Affect: Spinoza as Psychologist*, edited by Y. Yovel. New York: Little Room Press.

Spinoza, B. (1985). *The Collected Works of Spinoza*, Vol. I, Edited and translated by Edwin Curley. Princeton: Princeton University Press.

Spinoza, B. (2016). *The Collected Works of Spinoza*, Vol. II, Edited and Translated by Edwin Curley. Princeton: Princeton University Press.

Wacker, B. (2018). "The Woods–Dechambeau Bromance Continues with Tiger Singing Bryson's Praises," *Golf Digest*. www.golfdigest.com/story/the-tiger-woods-bryson-dechambeau-bromance-continues-with-tiger-singing-brysons-praises (Accessed March 2023).

Wollenburg, D. (2015). "Power, Affect, Knowledge: Nietzsche on Spinoza" (Ch. 2), in *Nietzsche and the Problem of Subjectivity*. Berlin: De Gruyter.

Yovel, Y. (1989). "Spinoza and Hegel: The Immanent God—Substance or Spirit?" (Ch. 2), in *Spinoza and Other Heretics: The Adventures of Immanence*. Princeton: Princeton University Press.

Chapter 4

C.G. Jung, the Unlikely Spinozist III

Outbound Connections

What is the origin of this 'antimonial' thinking, this play of opposites at the heart of Jung's psychology? Jung's interest in this subject, at least initially, can be attributed to his *own* psyche. Jungian scholar Mark Saban explains that Jung's prioritization of opposites originated from Jung's belief from a very early age that he had two distinct personalities (2019). Jung labeled these aspects of himself as his 'Number 1' and 'Number 2' personalities. He associated the Number 1 personality with the familiar and everyday, the obligations of being a responsible human in society, as well as his inclinations toward the natural sciences. In contrast, the Number 2 personality was timeless, mysterious, and dwelling within "God's world" (Jung, 1963/1989, pp. 19, 35, 67). Jung came to view the familiar, science-based Number 1 personality with the outer world, whereas the spiritual, atemporal Number 2 character was of his inner realm. It is on the tension between these inner and outer selves and the need to balance them that all other opposites Jung discusses—whether it be the personal and the universal, Logos and Eros, rational and irrational—are based; Saban argues that Jung's grappling with his two personalities is the very foundation of his psychology (Saban, 2019; also see Papadopoulos, 1991).

Now on the surface, it seems Spinoza would lump this discussion of opposites and paradoxes in with abstract thinking, and thus deem this crucial Jungian concern a mere product of inadequate thought (see Ch. 3, pp. 89–93). Yet there is a major omission in this apparent break between Jung and Spinoza: we have already seen that the reconciliation of the inner and outer *does* play a significant role in Spinoza's theory of knowledge— it is, after all, how the common notions from which we enjoy adequate knowledge of things are formed. From the tension of our own existence against another mode that affects us, a common third can be formed that

DOI: 10.4324/9781003516996-5

resolves that tension through active joy (ibid., pp. 79–85). Inner and outer for Spinoza are really the division of passions that come from without and actions that come from within—the division that defines Spinoza's theory of affects (E IIIP58–59, CWS I, p. 529). As it turns out, the transformation of passions into actions requires the very same elements that Jung demands of his psychology, those tools that he may have otherwise thought lacking in Spinoza's philosophy: the rejection of rote causation in favor of a blend of intrinsic reason and a discriminating imagination; the transcending of opposites via a middle third that has a *transformative* effect; and, finally, the priority of meaning within that transformation.

To argue that Spinoza in fact has the capacity for mystery and meaning, for the mythopoeic and the numinous, is not to proclaim, once more, that Jung has misread Spinoza. The extrapolation of these points requires a deep interrogation of Spinoza's writing, and it would be entirely unreasonable to assume that Jung, the self-confessed 'not a philosopher', had performed such a reading. Rather, it is important to highlight the way Jung's concepts emerge in Spinoza's philosophy because they do so in a way that, for all their similarity, Jung *still* cannot accept. This final moment of tension, this last knot of affinity and rejection between Jung and Spinoza, goes beyond Jung's reverence toward spirit or his belief that only psychology—*his* psychology—can confront the unconscious (Ch. 3, pp. 93–99). It will also betray a problem in Jung's thinking, a dilemma related to his very use of opposites, and ironically he must ultimately surrender to a Spinozist viewpoint in order to solve it.

Disenchantment and the Storm Lantern Dream

Roderick Main depicts Jung as a thinker concerned with the problem of disenchantment.[1] He derives this view from the work of German social scientist Max Weber (1864–1920). In this framework, the modern world is characterized by "disenchantment," where existence is stripped of "genuine mystery" in favor of "empiricism and reason," where the pursuit of "the true reality of being, art, nature, God, or happiness" has been superseded by the relentless march of incremental progress and technological achievement. This results in a world devoid of meaning or value, much less any knowledge of the spiritual or divine (Main, 2022, pp. 15–19). Jung's entire project can arguably be viewed as a response to disenchantment: his ardent defense of spiritualism against reductive materialism, his occupation with "meaning, mystery, and the sacred" and all other things that scientific empiricism cannot sufficiently address, as well as the goal of individuation and the resolution of opposites at the heart of his psychology, all make him a thinker of reenchantment; that is to say, Jung aims to "break the spell" of disenchantment (ibid., pp. 20–45).

Main frames Jung's championing of reenchantment in two different ways: via Jung's model of individuation, as well as the alchemical symbolism that Jung uses to illustrate that process. In the case of individuation, the path to reenchantment begins with "an initial undifferentiated and unconscious state, a preconscious fusion of subjectivity with the world." This state of *participation mystique* is what Main compares to enchantment in its most naive and uncritical form, where everything in the world seems "to behave according to the influence of magical forces" (ibid., p. 33). It is no different than what Jung warns Pauli about regarding metaphysical judgments that do not account for the psyche first (Meier, 2001, pp. 99–101). As it turns out, disenchantment is a *necessary process* that allows one to break free from this naive enchantment, to "come to terms with life's realities" and to withdraw "animistic delusions" and projections from the world. This correlates with the development of the ego as separate from the unconscious; therefore, disenchantment is actually necessary to achieve a more sophisticated level of enchantment via reenchantment (Main, 2022, pp. 33–34).

This entire process of disenchantment is reflected not just in Jung's theories of ego development but also in the *development of his own psyche* and his experiences as a young boy, namely when the struggle between his Number 1 and Number 2 personalities was especially pronounced. As a child, Jung's mythical and timeless personality, the Number 2, seemed to consume him entirely, occupying all his attention with myriad dreams and fantasies, until at last he was compelled to live more within the world via the responsible, everyday Number 1 personality. Thus Jung began to live by what he calls 'the spirit of the time' (Saban, 2019, Ch. 1, also pp. 140–142). This progression is encapsulated by a dream that Jung had around this time that he dubbed his 'Storm Lantern Dream'. In the vision, Jung found himself caught in particularly inclement weather and cupping a sole light in his hands for guidance. A giant dark figure stalked him, which terrified Jung until he realized that the light he carried was drawing the phantom out, even guiding it. Jung realized that his Number 1 personality was the "bearer of light" on which the Number 2, personified by the dark figure, depended, and that it was therefore incumbent upon Jung to heed the demands of the Number 1, and that therefore he had to venture into the real world of "study, moneymaking, responsibilities, entanglements, confusions, errors, submissions, defeats" (Jung, 1963/1989, pp. 87–88). Hence Jung's resolve to cultivate an ego-personality that no longer identified wholly with the archetypal domain of his Number 2 personality. This cultivation of an ego strong enough to carry its own identity is reminiscent of how Main describes disenchantment in the alchemical metaphor: he compares this first stage to the *unio mentalis*, when the soul breaks free of the body and unites with spirit, to establish a "rational, spiritual-psychic" position over the turbulence of both the bodily affects and the "original, half-animal state of unconsciousness" (CW. 14, 1963/1970, par. 696, quoted in Main, 2022, pp. 33–38). We have already seen how the *unio mentalis* demonstrates the nuanced relationship between psyche and spirit (see Ch. 1, pp. 37–41). In theory, at this stage of disenchantment all progress is "purely intrapsychic," and the body as well as the material world are not reunited with psyche and spirit until the later stages of the conjunction (CW. 14, 1963/1970, par. 664). Jung also seems to associate arrested development at this stage, that is, being mired in disenchantment, with the careless mixing of psyche and spirit that he laments in his letters with Pauli (Meier, 2001, pp. 116–117).

Jung and some of his adherents have at times summarized the Storm Lantern Dream and Jung's subsequent foray into the natural sciences, and ultimately traditional psychoanalysis, as Jung going 'all-in' with the Number 1 personality, at expense of the mythical Number 2. Saban argues that this is a gross simplification of Jung's fledgling attempt to achieve a sort of 'binocular vision' via both aspects of himself (2019, pp. 17–28). Further implications of this misleading narrative, which Jung himself ultimately adopts, will be the focus toward the end of this chapter. For now, it is sufficient to say that Jung's cultivation of the Number 1 personality, and the breaking of his naive enchantment with "God's world" of the Number 2, can be correlated with the *necessary* process of disenchantment (Main, 2022, p. 29).

Spinoza: A Thinker of Reenchantment?

Can Spinoza be considered a fellow traveler in the battle against disenchantment? There are immediate objections to this question, not the least of which is that Spinoza precedes Weber's formulation of the problem, as well as any responses to disenchantment such as Jung's, by several hundred years. How could Spinoza, a philosopher from the dawn of the Enlightenment, and who in many respects was a key ghostwriter for the unmooring of religion and the triumph of the scientific revolution that ensued the period, be seen as a thinker *counter* to those trends (Israel, 2002; Stewart, 2006)? It is after all the Enlightenment that helped "rapidly accelerate" the current era of disenchantment to begin with (Main, 2022, p. 37). Yet while Spinoza is a forerunner to the modern and secular intellectual, he is also the last of the premodern philosophers: the final figure in a chain of thinkers dating back a millennium who were dedicated to the hermetic mystery of what it is to know and experience the true nature of God (Carlisle, 2021, pp. 71–78). Just as Spinoza occupies the middle space between materialism and idealism, so too is he a fulcrum between modern science and esoteric philosophy. This unique space that Spinoza occupies in the history of thought is why he could chastise a friend who was convinced of the existence of ghosts, while at the same time be open-minded toward the alchemical experiments going on in his day (Ep. 40, CWS II, p. 37; Ep. 52, pp. 408–409).[2] He is of course not exceptional on this latter point; other intellectuals of the era such as Leibniz and Isaac Newton (1643–1727) also held an interest in alchemy alongside their scientific, philosophical, and mathematical achievements (Newman, 2018). The difference with Spinoza is that he offers not just a countervailing philosophy against theism and the era of religion's dominance that preceded him—but he also rejects the divorce of the Divine from existence in the age that followed him as well. Main observes that Weber sees theism just as much culpable for disenchantment as he does the age of rationalism that succeeded it; monotheism may have made God supreme, yet it also helped inform the modern assumption that God is separate from the world—a demand made by deism, atheism, and reductive materialism alike (Main, 2022, pp. 142–144). This separation was implicitly endorsed by the philosophy of Spinoza's contemporary, Leibniz, and Matthew Stewart argues that Leibniz's desire to protect a transcendent God against the implications of Spinoza's philosophy led to the very conditions of modernity where God is cut off from existence (2016). Spinoza strongly dissents from this separation of God and world—his transcendental or divine immanence is the culmination of a thousand-year problem of how to place oneself *within* God. This is precisely why Carlisle suggests that Spinoza offers a new conception of religion that is neither the orthodoxy of old nor a secular conceit of modernity; he offers us instead an "alternative modernity" (Carlisle, 2021, p. 10). This transcendental immanence that Jung and Spinoza share is both cause and consequence of the affective knowledge that both thinkers demand as well: hence why Jung writes that if God is not an immediate psychic experience, then God may well as not exist (CW. 7, 1916/1966, par. 402).

In any event the point is not to argue that Spinoza somehow presaged the struggle for reenchantment, centuries before the fact. Rather, Main's analysis of how Jung offers a response to disenchantment, both in his psychotherapeutic practice and in his study of alchemy, can also be used to determine if a similar response is available in Spinoza's thought. The answer is that, yes, Spinoza follows the same pattern: he commences what he sees as a necessary process of disenchantment, both in the broad goals of his philosophical project, as well as through his epistemology.

On Prophets

What are Spinoza's theological criticisms, his dismantling of the anthropo-morphic and transcendent image of God, other than something tantamount to breaking the spell of naive enchantment? Spinoza himself vehemently denied that his project was a covert endorsement of atheism, instead arguing that he was attempting to rescue knowledge of the Divine from what he saw as misuse from theologians (Ep. 30, CWS II, pp. 14–15). This misuse is nothing else than the propping of a creator atop a ladder of ontological scaf-folding conceived through inadequate ideas, a position that is a non-starter for both Jung and Spinoza (see Ch. 3, pp. 75–79). When Spinoza japes that if a triangle could speak, it would say that God is eminently triangular, he is joining Jung in a criticism of projective identification (Ep. 56, CWS II, pp. 420–424). And when the Dutch philosopher condemns the mind's feeble ability to make sense of the random affections that afflict the body, as well as the fictions and superstitions that invariably result from such an effort, he is attempting to sever one's belief in a sort of naive relationship with the world, to instead accept the harsh reality that the natural state of humanity is to be enthralled to the passions (E IIP18S, CWS I, pp. 465–466; E IV Preface, pp. 543–546).

That both thinkers agree about the dangers of the unconscious var-iety of enchantment becomes clear in their writings on prophecy. In the *Theological–Political Treatise*, Spinoza dismisses the idea that the Biblical prophets were directly informed by a supernatural spirit. He attacks the view held by Maimonides and other medieval philosophers that the Biblical prophets had a knowledge of the Divine equal or greater to that obtainable by philosophers due to their ability to render their findings into intuitive images. While Spinoza allows that the prophets were people of moral character whose vivid imagery allowed them to convey their messages to the public admittedly more effectively than the abstractions and rationalizations of a philosopher typically can do, there is nevertheless no reason to think the prophets had the intellect to discern the true nature of what they prophesied about. Moreover, Spinoza takes time to demonstrate that the particular backgrounds and biases of each respective prophet tends to inform the content of their prophecies—in other words, all the trappings of overreliance on the imagination, which becomes detrimental toward the ability to glean adequate ideas (TTP Ch. 2, CWS II, pp. 93–110; Nadler, 2011, pp. 62–73; 1999/2018, pp. 317–318). At worst, this expresses the kind of superstition that Spinoza blames not just on a lack of understanding about the world but moreover a lack of knowledge about oneself; as demonstrated by a person imagining that "the whole of nature were as crazy as they are" (TTP Preface 2–3, CWS II, p. 66). This echoes Jung's critique of an individual's attempt to free themselves from the collective psyche by *identifying* with it. Jung does not deny the existence of genuine prophets, but he stresses that one should be doubtful of each individual case, for all too often a supposed prophet is consumed by unconscious projections and in "psychic disequilibrium"; essentially they identify with the collective psyche and compound the problem by making a system of it to proclaim that they alone possess "eschatological knowledge" (CW. 7, 1916/1966, pars. 260–262).

When Spinoza analyzes the various ways scripture makes use of the word 'spirit', such as the Hebrew word *raugh*, he does so to point out such a word, charged with the meaning of 'wind' or 'breath' or, even 'heart', demonstrates that the prophets perceived God's revelations only with the aid of the imagination; that they needed such vivid *symbolism* in lieu of actually having direct communication with God. Spinoza does not dismiss that, somehow, the prophets may have implicitly apprehended something through the laws of nature; but he aims to eliminate any *supernatural* or eminent source for such revelation (TTP Ch. 1 26–44, CWS II, pp. 85–92). When Jung does a very similar analysis of the etymology of spirit in 'The Phenomenology of the Spirit in Fairytales', his aim is very much the same: to condemn an animistic identification with spirit just as much as a transcendent projection of it (CW. 9i, 1948/1969b, pars. 385–395). That he incorrectly accuses Spinoza of this latter error does not change the fact that both thinkers treat animistic beliefs, projective identification, and all other fallacies that might fall under the definition of naive enchantment in the same way. Once again, we arrive at the issue of unconscious projections and inflations left unchecked; once again we are left with knowledge that has not been properly routed through an understanding of oneself.

Reenchantment and Imagination

In the process of individuation, the ego must eventually face the unconscious—and, assuming one has undergone healthy development, not to again be subsumed by the unconscious, but rather to become "a unique self through the ongoing synthesis of consciousness and the unconscious." It is in this new interaction where Jung puts a premium on spontaneous psychic contents, such as dreams, fantasies, and synchronistic experiences, as well the use of a discerning, 'active imagination' that can further amplify the affectivity of those spontaneous contents in order to discover their meaning (CW. 8, 1916/1969a). It is through this confrontation that a new center of the psyche between the conscious and unconscious can be forged: the archetypal self (CW. 7, 1916/1966, pars. 399–406). Main identifies the discovery of the self as Jung's psychotherapeutic attempt at *reenchantment*, a restoration of mystery and meaning to the world, but in a way that maintains the discriminatory powers of a differentiated consciousness. In the alchemical analogy, reenchantment is equivalent to the second conjunction, where the *unio mentalis* unites with the body to produce the *caelum*, or "heaven on earth" (Main, 2022, pp. 30–39). In Jung's own life, the beginning of the process of reenchantment is said to come at his 'confrontation with the unconscious' following his fallout with Freud, where Jung underwent an "enantiodromic swing" from the Number 1 Personality back toward the mythical, timeless Number 2. Afterward, at least in theory, Jung could then continue his psychology practice from a balanced perspective between the two personalities (Saban, 2019, p. 136).

Now clearly Spinoza joins Jung in critiquing the first kind of enchantment. And no doubt Spinoza could be cast as an author of disenchantment, for not only does he take to task the superstitions and projections typical of religion and general ignorance alike; he summarily dismisses concepts like free will as they are typically discussed, arguing that the average person deceives themselves into believing they can even choose to "either do a thing or forbear doing it" (E IIP35S, CWS I, pp. 472–473). In Spinoza's view, there is no possibility of reaching a vacuum where one has a reprieve from the endless bombardment of affections, so that one can select which affection one prefers. *Freedom* only comes from transforming passions into actions (E VP3, CWS I, p. 598). This, again, is not at all different from Jung's view on unconscious complexes that affect us, and extracting the archetypal core within them (see Ch. 3, pp. 85–89). But for Jung, active imagination and the construction of unconscious fantasies are vital for this rapprochement with the unconscious (CW. 7, 1916/1966, pars. 342, 358, 366). It is the production of symbolic content teeming with irreducible meaning, a process that is contrary to a merely reductive intellect, that restores a 'magic' or 'mystery' to the world while still preserving a psyche that differentiates itself from its surroundings—this reinvigoration is a core aspect of Jung's championing for *reenchantment* (Main, 2022, Ch. 2). To master this technique of differentiation is also no easy task; it is no "plaything for children" (CW. 8, 1916/1969a, Prefatory Note). Yet as we have already seen, Jung sees this approach as the only safeguard against the very real dangers of the unconscious—and spirit (see Ch. 3, pp. 93–99). Only by paying heed to the symbol, by tracing the causes of things back to the plane of psychic reality, can one truly ascertain what affects oneself (CW. 9ii, 1959/1969c, par. 85). This is why, as he more or less explains to Pauli in their 1953 dialog, psychology *must* be the neutral language of the unascertainable (see Ch. 1, pp. 31–36). Nothing else will suffice.

Spinoza also sees the achievement of what he calls virtue—the deliberate transformation of passions into actions—as no easy feat. This is, after all, why he ends his masterwork with the statement "all things excellent are difficult as they are rare" (E VP42S, CWS I, pp. 616–617). But if Jung sees fantasy thinking as a vital tool for individuation, Spinoza does not hold the same faculty, at least in of itself, in such high esteem. Strictly speaking, he casts imagination into the realm of inadequate ideas; indeed, he defines it as the *very production* of those confused images from the affections that overwhelm us (E IIP17S, CWS I, pp. 463–465)! *Reason*, on the other hand, is the very apprehension of common notions, as well as the effort that *then* becomes possible to select affects that agree with us, that then allow us to form more common notions and greater active joys that follow (E IIP40S2, CWS I, p. 478; E VP10S, pp. 601–603). In this respect imagination seems decidedly *lesser* than reason—if not an outright hindrance to its power.

This brings us back to the problem of symbols, and the apparent gulf that separates Jung and Spinoza on this issue.

In the same passage where Spinoza defines the imagination as the conjuring of confused images, he also stresses that the imagination, considered in of itself, "contains no error," that the mind "does not err from the fact it imagines," but rather that it does not understand that things it imagines to be present are in fact not really there. Spinoza even goes as far as to say that if the mind *did* understand that what it often imagined as present were just trace affections from some other cause entirely, the power of imagination would no longer be a vice, but instead a virtue—*especially if what is imagined depends on the nature of the individual's mind alone* (E IIP17S, CWS I, pp. 463–465). This is another refrain of the postulate that within inadequate ideas there is always something adequate, that in all random affections there are common notions, those elements equally common to us and that which affects us, and thus can be explained by our nature or essence alone. Spinoza gives the example of someone who imagines the sun is 200 feet away from them. While it is true that this is nowhere near the correct distance of the sun from the earth, it is at the same time also true that *there is some sort of affection of the sun against one's body that causes them to believe the sun is only 200 feet away* (E IIP35S, CWS I, pp. 472–473). In other words, the imagining of the sun being that close, while expressly false, nevertheless implies some lineament of affectivity that really exists and is still yet to be discovered.

When the imagination is swept up with the passions, it produces inconsistent, contradictory, and unstable fictions; but when it is coupled with common notions, which are always explained by our nature alone, the imagination produces affects that we can reliably imagine as "present"— and are thus created by our nature alone (E VP7, CWS I, p. 600). Curley finds it strange that Spinoza uses the word 'imagine' in the context of producing active joys, given the faculty's role in the fabrication of inadequate thought. However, this is precisely why philosophers such as Christopher Norris and Antonio Negri have written at length about how the imagination and reason enjoy an intricate partnership in Spinoza's philosophy, how both powers blend together at the border of fiction and truth—and in tandem can be used to extract truths (ibid.; Norris, 1991; Negri, 1991).[3] Spinoza tacitly endorses the use of a discriminating imagination in order to excavate common notions—to imagine, for instance, the ability of one's own body to form rotations just as a circle rotates (see Ch. 3, pp. 79–82). When Spinoza cautions against *indiscriminate* use of imagination, it is to prevent someone from, say, literally imagining themselves to be a circle, rather than understanding that the ability to rotate simply expresses something true about their essence, as well as the essence of a circle. In other words, the coupling of the imagination *with* reason allows one to parse out projection, inadequate thoughts, and passions—in our current framework, the brew of naive enchantment—from adequate ideas. Spinoza is essentially providing a "regulatory principle" for the exploration of the unconscious (Deleuze, 1970/1988, p. 60).

Let there be no doubt that Jung follows this same demarcation between an indiscriminate and discriminate imagination. The way Spinoza describes the former, and how it is used by an individual completely lost in the madness of their passions is really no different than Jung's warnings on projection, projective identification, and *participation mystique* (see Ch. 3, pp. 75–79). Spinoza has no use for equivocation, for those who confuse "the dog that is a heavenly constellation and the dog that is a barking animal" (E IP17S, CWS I, p. 427)—but this is not what Jung prescribes as part of a healthy intellect either! Jung would heartily agree with Spinoza that it is no good if any person believes they are the circle, or that the sun is only 200 feet away; but, like Spinoza, he would certainly want to know *why* a person believes that they are the circle, or that the sun is so close. Moreover Jung's use of the symbolic, his language of the unconscious, is *his* own version of a discriminating imagination, his own way of *extracting what is true from what is false*. Consider Jung's example of a patient who had a fantasy of his fiancée who throws herself into a frozen river while the patient stands watching, helpless. It would be an error, Jung says, to interpret this vision as witnessing a literal suicide; rather, the image of the fiancée represents the patient's anima, which of course is projected onto his lover. The anima's drowning represents the patient's own psychic imbalance and inattentiveness to his feeling function; his passivity to stop the anima from throwing herself into the river exemplified his own inability, to that point, to value himself on an emotional level (CW. 7, 1916/1966, pars. 343–357). Just as the priest Abbé Oegger would have been mistaken to believe his fantasy had revealed himself to be Judas reincarnate, rather than nudging him toward an overdue sectarian leap, the fantasy image is not to be taken as absolute reality, but rather as a symbol that nevertheless expresses something *affective and true* (CW. 5, 1956/1967, pars. 41–45). Nor is this truth mere allegory or analogy—which, as Jung notes, are just means of para-phrasing, condensing, and ultimately reifying a truth that is already known. A true symbol is the most *exact* way of describing something *inexactly*, a way of depicting a reality that cannot be captured in any clearer way. Hence a symbol is *living* and not an abstraction of any sort (CW. 6, 1921/1971, pars. 815–816). And also hence why Spinoza sees truth in falsity, why one's belief that the sun is merely 200 feet away still implies something profound. For both Jung and Spinoza, the imagination and an *intrinsic type of reason* are companions that produce symbols in one case, the common notion in the other. The symbol is what differentiates the ego from the unconscious, the personal from the archetypal—yet it is also an element that both sides of the ledger share equally. And in this sense, the symbol and the common notion are discovered in the exact same fashion.

Beyond Opposites

Can Spinoza's common notions really be viewed as isomorphic with Jung's symbols? Although the common notion is the connection between the inner and outer for Spinoza, and despite its function as a middle third that super-sedes the conflicting passions caused by our affections, it may still seem like a leap to grant it the same numinous quality that Jung does for the symbol. Jacobi makes a similar point in her comparison of the archetype with the concept of the *Gestalt*; like the archetype, the *Gestalt* shares a fundamental structure between itself and specific variations, just as how a simple melody retains its form regardless of the key it is played in. Yet this is a purely formal concept that lacks "the richness of meaning" and affect-ivity that constitutes the archetype. Meaning in the sense of *Gestalt* simply refers to a structural pattern, nothing in terms of a connotation that arouses an emotional charge (1959, pp. 54–55). Why should Spinoza's conceptions be viewed differently?

Of course, we know that Spinoza treats knowledge and affectivity as inseparable, that the formation of common notions also produces active joys (see Ch. 3, pp. 83–85). Furthermore, the common notion is what allows one to apprehend the intrinsic "agreement, differences, and oppos-itions" between things (E IIP29S, CWS I, pp. 470–471). For Jung, the symbol acts as a neutral third that resolves contradiction, a "middle ground on which the opposites can be united" (CW. 6, 1921/1971, par. 825). And while Spinoza never speaks of paradox or opposition in this way, adequate ideas and the active joys that accompany them nevertheless supersede the passions and inadequate thought in a very similar fashion. For Spinoza the two most elemental affects are joy and sadness: joy being the passage from a lesser to a greater perfection, or our power to act; sadness, from a greater to lesser power (E IIIDef II–III, CWS I, p. 531). All the other emotions that Spinoza defines in his typology of affects are derived from these two most fundamental—and opposing—movements (E IIIP57, CWS I, pp. 528–529). Love, for instance, is nothing else than joy accompanied by the idea of an external cause for that joy; hate, predictably, is sadness also accompanied by the idea of an external cause of that sadness (E IIIDef VI–VII, CWS I, p. 533). And indeed, it's quite possible to be affected by both love and hate, or joy and sadness, simultaneously, even from the same external cause (E IIIP17, CWS I, p. 504; E IVP34, pp. 562–563). Those "torn by contrary affects do not know what they want" and are thrashed about in the madness of the passions (E IIIP2S, CWS I, p. 497). Spinoza is critical of any philosopher that denies this, of any philosophy that pretends that the human being is a "dominion within a dominion" exempt from the vicissitudes of nature (E III Preface, CWS I, pp. 491–492). The purpose of reason is to not deny this state of affairs but rather to understand it—and to find a way to transcend it.

Now Spinoza understands that joy and sadness are opposites, that the passions inevitably and violently conflict with one another. He in fact simply defines 'good' as that which increases our power, and 'evil' as all that diminishes it (E IVP38–41, CWS I, pp. 568–570). But the passage of joy and sadness, and therefore also of what is good and evil, are literally the transitions an individual goes through from one state of existence to the next. The passage of affects, or *affectus*, is what defines a mode's existence, and it is in fact how Spinoza defines duration: time is nothing but the passage of one affect to the next (E IIIP6–8, CWS I, pp. 498–499). And it is for this reason that Spinoza says that knowledge of good and evil is nothing more than an affect of joy or sadness that we are conscious of (E IVP8, CWS I, pp. 550–551). Consequently, he argues that everyone judges what is good and what is evil according to their temperament, or what increases or diminishes their power. While reason dictates humankind should live harmoniously together, since for most people solidarity fosters a greater power individually and collectively, Spinoza stresses that this dictate does not come from a hypostatized notion of good and evil (E IVP37S2, CWS I, pp. 566–567). As Deleuze notes, Spinoza, like Nietzsche after him, is rejecting a transcendent morality of good and evil in favor of an immanent ethic of good and bad (1970/1988, pp. 71–73).

Because of this, Spinoza insists that we view joy and sadness, good and evil, as those literal passages or movements in opposing directions, rather than reified oppositions, because this reification tears our sense of good and evil away from its immanent affectivity. This is also why he problematizes transcendental categories, such as Being, and warns not to juxtapose such a fictional category with its presumed opposite, such as perfection to imperfection (E IIP40S, CWS I, p. 477; E IV Preface, pp. 544–545). Now in the final analysis it is true that Jung may entertain the equivocal, paradox, and fantasy to greater lengths than Spinoza tolerates. Nevertheless, Jung is attentive to this very same error Spinoza describes of making opposites transcendent: it is what Jung cautions Pauli against in regards to fashioning binaries as absolute, metaphysical categories, such as with the dichotomy being versus non-being. The reason Jung prefers the pairing of ascertainable and non-ascertainable is because it keeps the opposition *immanent to the psyche* (Meier, 2001, p. 100). More pertinently, in his correspondence with Father White, Jung echoes Spinoza's plea to keep good and evil immanent to our existence, to understand that good cannot just be a lone title granted to a transcendent God but rather that both good and evil are tangible parts of our experience (Letters, Vol. 2, 1975, pp. 58–61). Elsewhere Jung writes that good and evil belong "to the category of human values, and we are the authors of moral value judgments, but only to a limited degree are we authors of the facts submitted to our moral judgment." Who knows what freewill we truly have in the choice of what affects us, Jung writes; instead, we can merely deem if what affects us is good for us or bad for us, and this judgment will vary from person to person. The psychologist cannot, and must not, say what is absolutely good and what is absolutely evil; all that can be said is that evil enjoys just as much existence in the psyche as good does, because both pertain to our relationships with the world and the unconscious (CW. 9ii., 1959/1969c, pars. 84, 97).

A key tenant as to why the psyche must be seen as a neutral medium through which all our knowledge passes is to avoid projecting psychic processes into spirit or matter (see Ch. 1, pp. 24–26). Jung explains to Pauli that such projection has historically led to the elevation of spirit to divinity and the absolute good—and therefore matter becomes depicted as wholly evil (Meier, 2001, p. 125). It is this scale of eminence, where evil is depicted merely as a diminution of what is good, a temperature nearing absolute zero, that Jung wishes to avoid. Instead of appealing to a universal, greater good that all things strive for, as the Church Fathers were wont to do, Jung suggests we instead simply acknowledge that every being "works for the sake of what suits it," and accept all the troubling implications that come from such a conclusion. Through words and intent that are unmistakably Spinozist, Jung says that clearly the devil has an "appetite" or desire, that *even Satan* "strives after perfection"—but the devil's judgment of what is good and what is evil is not an opinion most of us would countenance (CW. 9ii., 1959/1969c, pars. 93–94).

If a symbol is truly living, it is also because the opposites that it resolves are not eminent categories but our part of our lived experience. Jung himself acknowledges that the goal of individuation is essentially to "free" oneself from the confusion that opposites can generate (CW. 7, 1916/1966, par. 367). In a way Jung seems to understand that antimony is really just a necessary use of what is inadequate to glean what is adequate, to truly understand the problem our conception of good and evil poses to find a third that makes such a dichotomy obsolete—where joys and sorrows become transformed into passions and actions. And in turn, Spinoza does not deny contradiction, but rather casts it as the very passage of our existence.

Virtue and Blessedness

What then of meaning? This is a topic that will be treated more fully in the next chapter, but for now it will suffice to focus on two of the ways in which Main depicts Jung's use of meaning via reenchantment: *personal* and *collective* meaning.[4] Personal meaning encompasses affectivity related to one's "developmental needs and goals, unconscious as well as conscious— in Jungian terms, their individuation." Collective meaning meanwhile is the "expression of archetypal meaning that is transcendental to human consciousness" (2022, pp. 109–111). So for instance, in Jung's story of the reluctant patient and the synchronistic encounter of the scarab beetle, the arrival of the insect at Jung's window caused a transmutation of the client's attitude toward therapy, and thereafter her "process of transformation could at last begin to move." At the same time, the scarab beetle represents a meaning that is beyond the specific situation in which it manifests—per Jung, the "scarab is a classic example of a rebirth symbol" (CW. 8, 1952/1969a, par. 845). Within the personal meaning for Jung's client was a collective meaning that was both transcendent yet immanent to her own experience.

A consequence of this, and in Jung's mission for reenchantment, is that the tandem of personal and collective meaning found in synchronicity restores meaning as an inherent feature of the world, something that disenchantment has stripped away (Main, 2022, pp. 99–100). The word 'meaning' plays no special role in Spinoza's writing—but for the final time, will we find that he has the bandwidth for such a concept, or expresses the same thing but with different words?

Spinoza lists a third elemental affect along with joy and sadness: the conscious striving to persevere in one's being, or what he calls appetite or desire (E IIIP9, CWS I, pp. 499–500). This striving to persevere defines the actualized essence of an individual (E IIIP7, CWS I, p. 499). Nietzsche is scornful of what he sees as Spinoza covertly introducing a sort of teleology into his philosophy, even though what Spinoza is describing here is clearly localized and unique to each singular essence—in other words, essence as haecceity (Schact, 1999; E IIIP57, CWS I, p. 528).[5] But for Jung a 'local determinism' is no issue: he similarly describes the attainment or "entelechy" of the self as the very goal of individuation (CW. 7, 1916/1966, par. 405; CW. 9i, 1940/1969b, par. 278). According to Spinoza, typically one desires only what they know to be good through inadequate ideas—a tenuous state of affairs, since the fulfillment of such desires so often proves to be fleeting, contradictory, or diminishing (E IIIP51S, CWS I, pp. 522–523). To live a life of *virtue*, however, is to seek things that can be explained by one's power or essence alone (E IVD8, CWS I, p. 547). The creation of active joys not only surpasses but *transforms* the passions from whence they came; a transmutation of our affects takes place the moment a confused idea becomes distinct and clear (E VP3, CWS I, p. 598). And while an individual can be torn by conflicting passions, active affects are *always joyful* (E IVP34, CWS I, p. 562). To live a life of virtue is to no longer seek joyful passions over sad passions but rather to transform our passions into actions (E VPI-10, CWS I, pp. 597–603). Just as the self becomes the center between the ego and the unconscious, the virtuous individual becomes a conduit between the affections of existence and the power of their own essence. *Virtue, then, is Spinoza's version of personal meaning.*

But to seek virtue, to perpetually form common notions from our inadequate encounters, also grants one the ability to see how all things in fact compound with one another, to understand that there are common notions to find even between us and modes that do not agree with us. These notions become greater and multiply in scope, like rhizomatic roots that shoot in all directions, transcending the modular Spinozist landscape of compositions and decompositions until one truly sees that there are notions common to all things: for instance, one apprehends that all bodies, even a poison that may destroy oneself, are made of the same matter that composes the infinity of the universe; or, one realizes that all minds and ideas, including thoughts that would otherwise sadden oneself, must be part of an infinite intellect (E IIP38C, CWS I, p. 474). And these infinite modes could only have been produced by an absolutely infinite power. Hence one reaches the idea of a God who has an absolutely infinite power to conceive and create. And when one reaches the Idea of God, when they consider that God's Infinite Intellect must contain an idea of every singular thing God ever can and will create, that is when one passes into the third kind of knowledge, the intuitive intellect, which apprehends the eternal essences of all things as they are contained in the mind of God (E VP15–33, CWS I, pp. 603–611). This results in Blessedness, a Love of God where the experience of being eternal is refracted and resounds through us just as it does through God (E VP42, CWS I, pp. 616–617). If the achievement of virtue is Spinoza's version of personal meaning, then *collective meaning comes from the outcome of virtue: we rejoice that we are within God.* And likewise, for Jung, the self is the Divine within us, the most immanent psychological experience we can have of God (CW. 7, 1916/1966, pars. 399–402). Hence in the alchemical metaphor for reenchantment, Main points out that there is an extra step in the process, the realization that the self is part of an *unus mundus* (2022, pp. 40–41). This 'one world' is, as Jung writes in *Mysterium Coniunctionis*, the "eternal Ground of all empirical being" (CW. 14, 1963/1970, par. 760). Jung and Spinoza endorse a divine immanence where both we and the world inhere within God (see Ch. 2, pp. 61–63). This view is consonant with the restoration of God to the world—a chief goal of reenchantment (Main, 2022, Ch. 4).

The point of framing Spinoza under the lens of reenchantment was merely to demonstrate that his philosophy can in fact interface with a symbolic language of the unconscious, that Spinoza does treat the dangers of the unascertainable in a way that is not so irreconcilable with Jung's demands. Nevertheless, the argument may have merit in its own right. Why else did the German Romantics and Idealists, a movement that ran counter to the rationalist triumph of the Enlightenment, find so much inspiration in Spinoza's work (Förster & Melamed, 2012)? Why, a century later in France, did intellectuals who fought and died in the resistance against fascism turn to Spinoza as their elixir against the espousers of phenomenology and Cartesian idealism whom they felt stood idly by when the Nazis came to power—if not outright joined in the salutes (Peden, 2014)? Similarly, postwar socialists found solace in Spinoza's thought when they were eager to free their politics from the orthodoxy of Hegelian dialectics—an orthodoxy that had, in their bleak estimate, resulted only in Stalinism (Macherey, 1979/2011). It was Einstein who insisted that he was no atheist, but instead that he believed in the God of Spinoza who reveals himself through the harmony of nature (Katz, 2007). Spinoza's influence on philosophers, writers, scientists, and poets alike is manifold—whether one is looking to restore God to the world or to fashion weapons to combat the horrors of the state, his inspiration to those looking for meaning in the world is clear. Among those thinkers who may have found such meaning in Spinoza, whether they even know it or not, is Jung.

Inner versus Outer

In many respects Spinoza's entire metaphysics rests on an even deeper fundamental opposition than what has been said thus far: not the attributes of thought and extension, which are really just two of an infinity of formal ways to express God's absolute power; nor is it a dichotomy of inner and outer, which we have seen is more correctly posed as an expression of passions versus actions. Even the division of actions and passions is underwritten by a deeper difference, the true paradox at the heart of Spinozism: the very tension between existence and essence, or between duration and eternity (E VP22–23, CWS I, p. 607). As we have seen, durational existence is the very lived passage of affects that all modes experience in their perseverance to affect and be affected, the reality that one exists as a composition of external parts that come together under a specific ratio of relations that can eventually decompose; that is, death (E IVP39, CWS I, pp. 568–570; see Ch. 3, pp. 93–99). But beyond this extrinsic modal existence is an *intrinsic eternal essence*, or simply the eternal essence which durational existence expresses. The singular essences enjoy an *eternal* existence in God, both as singular expressions of his absolute power and in his intellect as unique ideas of everything he can and must create (E IP16, CWS I, pp. 424–425; IVP4, pp. 548–549). And it is from one's singular essence or nature—*the part of oneself that can neither be nor be conceived without also being oneself or conceiving oneself*—that one can form common notions and active joys, can transform the passions and inadequate ideas that characterize modal existence and instead maximize one's affections with one's own power (E IID2, CWS I, p. 447; IIP10S, pp. 454–456).

At first glance, the tension between existence and eternity resembles the formative opposition at the core of Jung's psychology, both professionally and personally: his Number 1 and Number 2 personalities. If personality Number 1 is concerned with the every day and the actual world, that is, the personal sphere or 'the spirit of the times', then it is also prey to disenchantment and a loss of meaning in the world on the one hand, and also the deleterious effects of the unconscious complexes that elude reductive explanation on the other. It was Jung's confrontation with the unconscious that allowed him to draw upon the atemporal powers of the universal personality, the Number 2, 'the spirit of the depths', and it is the goal of actualizing the self that allows the same kind of transformation of affective knowledge that Spinoza describes: projections are withdrawn, the archetypal causes of complexes are discovered, and a balance between the conscious and unconscious is established. Therefore, the resonance between Jung's two personalities and Spinozist essence and existence is also expressed in the way in which the conjunction of the actual and the eternal is used by both thinkers to uncover truths about oneself and the world at large, to ultimately view things 'from the eye of eternity'. But despite the clear similarity between these two processes, there is also a significant divergence, a disparity that is best highlighted by summarizing each process as has been articulated thus far.

In Spinoza's philosophy, modal existence is defined by affects, which come from our encounters with other modes that impact us. This results in (1) the thrall of inadequate ideas and passions. However, by discovering parts of ourselves that exist equally in ourselves and the modes that affect us, and thus can be explained by our nature alone, we can (2) form common notions, intrinsic connections between other things that also give us active joys, because we act from our own essence. The ramification of common notions and the practice of virtue leads us to a sense of the infinity that we are all compounded within, and thus a knowledge of the absolute power that creates this infinity. This leads to (3) an intuitive idea of singular essences, including ourselves, as they exist eternally in the Idea of God, and thus a Love of God or blessedness results (see Figure 4.1).

In Jung's psychology, the ego is swayed by complexes, the unconscious clusters of ideas and affectivity. In the personal sphere, this results

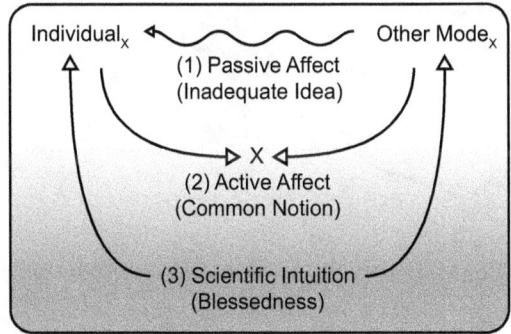

Figure 4.1 Spinoza's system of knowledge and affects. The passage to active joys and blessedness is visualized by the darker shading further down the figure.

in (a) projecting what remains in our unconscious onto other people and objects around us, as well as other maladies that ensue from complexes effectively 'possessing' us. However, attentiveness to the affective content of our psyche allows us to (b) apprehend symbolic content that is common to both the personal layer of the complex as well as its nuclear core. The archetypal meaning at the core of all complexes is discovered. This enables us to withdraw our projections, to dissolve the complexes' magnetic pull, and for the ego to come to grips with the unconscious, to engage in individuation and the fount of personal meaning that flows from it. (c) The realization of the self bridges the gap between the personal and the collective—and lets one glimpse the Divine within, or know the collective meaning of the 'one world' which we are all immersed in (see Figure 4.2).

The issue concerns the prioritization of inner and outer. It is clear that the Spinozist model begins with the conflict between oneself and other modes, as stated by (1), just as it is manifest that the common notions act as a bridge between inner and outer, as cited in (2). And certainly, as we have demonstrated there is at the very least a nominal relationship between inner and outer on the one hand, and actions and passions on the other. Nonetheless, it must be stressed that for Spinoza *all adequate ideas are predicated upon actual relations between us and other modes*. Our singular essence is of course internal to us in that it is uniquely our own, and it is from our essence that we can act from our own power and enjoy our own place in eternity (3). But Spinoza's adherence to the principle that all adequate knowledge is properly refracted through oneself does not mean

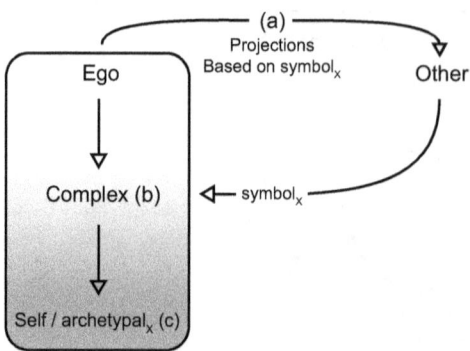

Figure 4.2 Jung's model of psychic development. Note that the shading representing a gradual approach to the collective is restricted to the side of the figure concerning one's inner world. The external other is a mere receptable for projections.

he also believes withdrawal from the world is a key to virtue—on the contrary, Spinoza insists that we experiment with our affects (E IIIP2S, CWS I, pp. 494–497), that one who has a body capable of a great many things will have a mind that knows eternity. Spinoza is not suggesting that only world-class athletes enjoy the benefits of the intuitive intellect; rather, he is reinforcing his notion that duration involves constant affectation, and therefore constant change, and an individual willing to experiment and discover the power of virtue in these changes will reap the rewards of their essence (E VP39S, CWS I, p. 614). The realization of one's own power does not diminish the existence of other modes, but rather enhances them: the common notions we form of our own nature help us also understand the ratio of relations that define other modes; the intuitive intellect gives us insight not only to our eternal essence but the eternal essences of other things (3). And to live a life of virtue may encourage others to do the same (E IVP37S, CWS I, pp. 564–568).

In Jung's outline, the outer and the personal as well as the inner and the collective are much stricter couplets. As we have seen, the struggle Jung conveys against the projections and affects of unconscious complexes (a) accords well with Spinoza's battle against the bondage of passions and inadequate thought (1). Similarly, both the common notion and the symbol act as a bridge that exists equally in both oneself and another (2)(b). But whereas the common notion is a connection between us and at least one other mode, which also implies some deeper composition (3), the symbol draws a route chiefly from the personal psyche 'down' into the collective unconscious. Now the symbol may also manifest, or be projected onto, the outside world. In the example of the patient whose anima appeared in a vision as the patient's fiancée and drowned herself, Jung notes that in real life, the patient's fiancée was certainly a symbol for his anima (CW. 7, 1916/1966, par. 355). But in Jung's account, to encounter the unconscious means that such projections must be withdrawn, so that meaning and comprehension come from a relationship that is enjoyed exclusively within. Eternal knowledge belongs to the inner world, as seen in Jung's Number 2 personality; relations formed with the outside, and the 'mundane' of Number 1, are diminished and can be explained entirely by the archetypes experienced within individuation. Therefore knowledge of the divine diminishes the outer world's relevance (c) and is at odds with the equal valence that Spinoza affords inner and outer at this stage (3).

Introverted Bias?

Certainly Jung might bristle at the suggestion that the goal of individuation is a hermitage. He does state that individuation "does not shut one out from the world," but rather "gathers the world to oneself" (CW. 8, 1946/1969a, par. 432). However, even this image of drawing the world within calls to mind the *inward* flow of psychic energy—how Jung defines the psychological attitude of introversion (CW. 6, 1921/1971, par. 769). Saban explores how Jung grants introversion certain powers that he denies to the outbound flow of libido, or the extraverted attitude—namely, the access to the archetypal and the 'spirit of the depths' that he also associates with his inward-facing, Number 2 personality (Saban, 2019, Ch. 5). So in the example of the patient with the drowning anima, Jung states that had the patient been an extravert, he would have focused on the patient's relationship with his fiancée, since the extravert "is governed primarily by his relationship with human beings," whereas the introvert is concerned more with the idea within—in this case, the anima (CW. 7, 1916/1966, pars. 355–356). Jung states that the introvert is someone who is primarily concerned with inner ideas because they shield "him from external reality" and give "him the feeling of inner freedom" (CW. 6, 1921/1971, par. 535). The idea, as Jung defines it here, is nothing less than the primordial image, that is, an archetype (ibid., par. 732). The extravert meanwhile craves the external object, is voluntarily dependent upon it (ibid., 535). The rendering of libidinal attitudes to such stark extremes leads to some confusion when the attitudes are applied to specific psychological functions. The American personality theorist David Keirsey, while professing admiration for Jung and acknowledging the debt his theory of temperament owes to Jung's typology, nevertheless highlights how Jung often confuses introversion with the function that is chiefly concerned with perception of the unconscious, intuition (1998, pp. 29–31).

In fairness, Jung cannot be blamed that the archetypes that he focuses on—such as the shadow, the anima and animus, and the self—are all involved with the development of the individual, which to some extent is necessarily an internal affair. Such is the task of his professional occupation. Nor is it entirely clear at this stage how Spinoza's version of archetypes would appear. If, however, one were to apply Spinoza's second kind of knowledge to psychiatric practice, Spinoza might demand that the fiancée be depicted as more than just a passive holder for the patient's anima projection, a mere carrier for a symbol that is later withdrawn, and instead insist that the anima symbolism represents a real, intrinsic connection between client and fiancée, a composition that involves them both. This call for bilateral dialog, a belief that outer relationships can lead to psychological understanding, is precisely what Jung's friend and former client Hans Schmid Guisan argues for in his letters with Jung, when Jung was formulating his typological theory around 1915. Schmid Guisan reminds Jung that there is life not only in oneself but also "in the object," and that anyone who takes Jung's phrase 'life flows from ourselves, not from objects' too literally might come to believe they can replace real experience with inner analysis alone (2013, p. 97). After this correspondence terminated in disagreement, Saban observes that Jung does in fact incorporate the importance of dialog into his theory as Schmid Guisan petitioned for—but only in the form of *an inner dialog between inner figures, rather than other people and the outer world* (2019, pp. 165–167). Thus intrinsic connections are twisted inward—and in a sense, the common notion is corrupted into a symbol that communicates only from within.

The Jungian typologist John Beebe grasps the amount of nuance needed on the topic of introversion and extraversion through his own typological model, where he suggests that one's dominant ego function, regardless of its libidinal direction, is associated with one's conception of a hero archetype and thus is very much related to a classic, inward hero's journey. This is in contradistinction to one's secondary function, which is displayed outward—again, regardless of whether or not it is an introverted or extraverted variant. By example Beebe notes that Jung's own dominant or 'hero' function was likely *introverted intuition*, or rather the introverted variant of intuition (2017). Introverted intuition "perceives all the background processes" of the psyche; it is the direct apprehension of the archetypal images of the collective unconscious (CW. 7, 1921/1971, pars. 657–659). In contrast, extraverted intuition, as Jung describes it, is primarily concerned with potentialities laden throughout the outer world; as with all of Jung's definitions of extraverted functions, the connection to the archetypal is less evident (ibid., pars. 613–615). In this respect it is noteworthy that Spinoza's intellectual intuition, which we've seen Jung directly cites in his general definition of intuition, gives one a sense not only of one's eternal essence—and all the *potential actualizations* that this essence affords—but insight into the eternal essences of other modes as well, via the outbound connections common to all things. Is Spinoza's conception of intuition the *extraverted variant*, contrary to Jung's premium on introverted intuition? Is this ultimately a clash between two thinkers who draw upon the same psychological function but with opposite attitudes? Or is Spinoza's third kind of knowledge simply less bound by these restrictions of inner and outer altogether?

For Spinoza the inner must never be conflated with the intrinsic, and the introverted never with the intensive—or intuition. Such moves would be to risk making man 'dominion within a dominion'. We should all strive to live by our own nature, but this does not necessarily mean it pertains to our essence to withdraw—to *introvert*. Of course, in some cases such an inward attitude may indeed be what pertains to one's essence, or precisely the affectivity one ought to experiment with. Each essence is singularly unique, and what is good for one's own perseverance to exist will not apply in all cases (E IIIP57, CWS I, p. 528).

The dominant function of one's personality is also tied to the Jungian notion of the persona (Beebe, 2017, p. 155). The persona, Jung notes, is in many respects an arbitrary 'cut' of one's unconscious psyche, fashioned into a mask and donned by the ego for purposes of adaptation and survival. The persona can become a sort of reification of one's personality that inevitably gets challenged by unconscious contents (CW. 7, 1916/1966, pars. 243–253). Is this fashioning—if not outright reification—of a persona not, in a sense, what Jung does with his mythical personality, by rendering all of its preoccupation with the safety of the inner world as an absolute? And is this, as we will see later, related to Jung forming a 'secret complex' around the 'timeless' side of himself, a 'secret' that is nonetheless *the underpinning of his entire psychological theory*—that his psychological theory is arguably an attempt to bring this 'secret' to the world (Saban, 2019, p. 65)? And is this partially why Jung cannot separate his introverted intuition from *any* apprehension of the unconscious, nor his theories from his own hero's journey? If so, why?

Secret, Spirit, and Spinoza

Saban challenges the narrative that Jung was serving solely his Number 1 personality during his ill-fated alliance with Freud. Instead he argues that Jung was attempting to achieve a kind of 'binocular vision' where both sides of himself worked in tandem, and where he could express the introverted, mythical side of himself through his extraverted, scientific attitude (2019, Ch. 3). Such a potential combination is, after all, what attracted Jung to psychiatry to begin with (1963/1989, p. 109). However, in many respects Jung was simply replaying the same experience he had with his father, when Jung failed to explain some of his early 'spiritual' experiences, which left him deeply frustrated. Jung should not have expected anything different from the wary Freud, who despite his own covert curiosities in the supernatural was fiercely protective of his fledgling psychoanalytic movement and refused to let it be bogged down by conjecture over the occult (Saban, 2019, Ch. 3).

After falling out with Freud, Saban argues that Jung never again honestly attempted to achieve this balance of his inner and outer selves, instead restricting the conversation to a purely internal dialog between the ego and the unconscious. This introverted bias permeated into the misleading narrative Jung and some of his followers have set around his subsequent 'confrontation with the unconscious', which is often depicted as a purely solitary affair. Saban points out that Jung was still fulfilling many professional obligations during this time; more pertinently, colleagues were directly helping him with the aforementioned confrontation, productive dialogs that Jung minimized in later retellings of the experience. Such behavior is exemplified in Jung's formulation of the anima archetype, and how he mitigates any and all involvement of the various women in his life who actively helped him discover the concept, to instead depict himself as having one-on-one, internalized conversations with his anima and that any outer correspondences were simply projections to be dissolved (ibid., Ch. 3, 4). Hence Schmid Guisan's lament to Jung, at the end of their increasingly acrimonious correspondence, that Jung's vision of the psyche had essentially become a lone tower surrounded by water, alone unto itself, and here and there upon the water would be other towers, other *introverts* "each in their own tower, loving humankind" but from a distance (Beebe & Falzeder, 2013, p. 154). One might even picture these towers as lighthouses, and the beams they cast as projections, which are, of course, ultimately extinguished.

This contradictory attitude in Jung, this need to protect his mythical personality yet at the same time his desperate wish to be understood, is what Saban identifies as Jung's 'secret complex' (2019, pp. 59–66). Now this secret complex encompasses the dreams and visions that occupied Jung from his childhood onwards, that later as a psychiatrist he became convinced could not be reduced to material explanation. In other words, the secret complex concerns ideas and experiences that have no obvious basis in the physical world—*precisely how Jung defines 'spirit' to Pauli in their 1953 exchange* (Meier, 2001, p. 125). Jung's secret complex, therefore, is tied directly to his conviction about the reality of spirit—both its glories and its dangers. But if Jung's Number 2 personality, the perception of "God's world," is linked to his conviction about spirit, then by interiorizing the mythical side of himself Jung is effectively interiorizing spirit as well. Experience of the archetypal images, the symbolic and the numinous, becomes an intrapsychic affair. And indeed, in his own writing Jung is ambivalent about the status of spirit, its autonomy from the psyche, until he unveils his tripartite spectrum in 'On the Nature of the Psyche', where he concludes that he has "no alternative" but to designate the archetypal images as belonging to something beyond the psyche, that is, spirit (CW. 8, 1946/1969a, par. 420). And it is only after this express declaration of spirit's autonomy that Jung more definitively speaks of the archetypes in ways that no longer restrict them to the psyche proper, but rather as potentialities that exist out in the world (Roesler, 2022; Atmanspacher & Fach, 2013, p. 226; Maxwell, 2022, pp. 175–176).

Now Jung's *explicit distinction between psyche and spirit is what facilitates this 'opening up'*—this relocation, or perhaps *dislocation*—of the archetype; yet it is a distinction that, as we noted in Chapter 1, has gone largely unheeded in Jungian studies (pp. 41–44). And *if*, hypothetically, Jung had in fact never dared to free spirit from the intrapsychic, *if* he had never actually committed to his tripartite monism—*if*, in other words, he had remained 'arrested' at the first conjunction, the union of psyche and spirit—then wouldn't many of his subsequent concepts become, at best, ambiguous? Does the psychoid, the term that Jung uses to designate the archetype's expression in *both* matter and spirit, become just a way to coin the archetype's mere emergence from biological instinct, since spirit is not given equal valence—if any right to exist at all (CW. 8, 1946/1969a, par. 439)? *If* synchronicity is simply a correspondence between mind and matter, rather than *spirit* and matter, how can justice be done to explain cases where a one-to-one description of mind-to-matter correspondence doesn't seem sufficient? Main and Saban point out how the symbol of the scarab was of great interest to Jung before he ever encountered his recalcitrant patient who had a breakthrough upon experiencing the same symbol herself (Main, 2013, pp. 137–140; Saban, 2019, p. 189). Far from suggesting that Jung had colored the incident with his own interpretation, it can instead be posited that both Jung and his client were at that specific moment enveloped by the same *idea*—the same *phenomena of spirit*—that is, the scarab symbol, which manifested itself in both the spiritual and material, which they were both separate witnesses to. This explanation is only possible, of course, *if* spirit is indeed freed from the psyche. And in this instance, Jung removes his own personal meaning in his account of the story, thus eliminating the possibility of discussing such an *interpsychic* experience, instead choosing to focus only on the one-to-one correspondence between his client's dream and the beetle at the window (CW. 8, 1952/1969a, par. 982). It is as if even as Jung began to form *outbound connections*, his hesitancy to fully unveil the contents of his Number 2 personality remained. This is why Saban argues Jung was implicitly forming *two* different models of psychotherapy—one that was beginning to treat inner and outer equally in his mature work, and another that obstinately continued to protect his 'secret' (Saban, 2019, Ch. 6).

If there is only psyche and matter, with spirit folded into either, then Pauli is entirely correct to challenge Jung, to question if Jung is indeed making too much of the psychic factor (Meier, 2001, pp. 100–101, 105–106). And if psyche and matter are the two aspects of the monist whole, with *no* neutral medium to speak of, then clearly Jung's collaboration with Pauli risks inflating the psyche with the ideal, the same kind of projective identification that Jung vehemently denounces (see Ch. 1). Then Jung's metaphysics could be construed to imply that the world is *dependent* on the mind to furnish it. This is an *anti-realist* perspective that quickly becomes untenable (Langan, 2020). If the archetypal, the numinous and the eternal remain confined to the interior, and if what is exterior is implicitly deemed inferior, then it is small wonder that some Jungian scholars have become disaffected with what they perceive as Jung's diminishment of the *real world*, and that they demand a critical reassessment of how Jung defines the self—perhaps to strip it of its 'eternal' qualities altogether (McCoy Brooks, 2019, Ch. 5). It is in this same sense of settling the score, or of addressing this imbalance between inner and outer, that some Jungian scholars have considered if the archetype should be conceived more in the vein of cultural phenomena or social constructs (Roesler, 2012, 2022). Others have diminished the importance of synchronicity—if not suggested that it be eliminated altogether (Knox, 2003, pp. 36–37; Brooke, 2015, pp. 70–71). Yet doesn't this justifiable desire to bring Jung 'back to earth' come at a cost? By diminishing the radical ideas of Jung's *oeuvre* to balance the scales between inner and outer, does that not also eliminate the very 'enchanting' aspects of his theories that draw so many to Jungian psychology to begin with? By making Jung fit for purpose so that he can plausibly exist in the halls of academia or as a marketable psychotherapeutic brand, does this not also rob Jung of the very aim of his psychology? Does this not, ironically, render him a figure of 'disenchantment'?[6]

There is an alternative. Instead of diminishing those numinous or radical ideas that Jung associates with his inner world, the other possibility would be to simply unmoor the archetypal from the interior—in other words, to render the inner and outer into intrinsic and extrinsic, or essence and existence—and to free spirit from the psyche. Now Jung's respect for spirit is very real; he refuses to engage it without his psychological method (see Ch. 3, pp. 93–99). At the same time, the concept of spirit also seems to be what he is protecting, due to its close association with his 'secret complex'. Because of this, Jung cannot free spirit from psyche without also, on some level, "betraying" his need to keep it a secret—a pact that Saban illustrates Jung was very keen to never break (2019, pp. 59–66). As we have seen, the risk that Spinoza represents for Jung initially is that, despite all their similarity, Spinoza would force Jung to treat spirit in a way he deems too dangerous (see Ch. 3, pp. 93–99). However, even if Spinoza can, in fact, furbish a 'method of psychology' similar to Jung's own, Jung would *still* resist Spinoza at this juncture—because to accept Spinozism is to break his vow and let spirit 'free'. The threat of Spinoza is that he summons the rhizomatic roots within Jung that will tear him inside-out; he abolishes the 'closed' monad in the name of forming outbound connections; he breaks the spell of disenchantment by *also breaking the spell of interiority*, so that divine immanence may be enjoyed by inner and outer alike. Here, at last, we can address the question Joseph Cambray posed when he first explored the perplexing way in which Jung treats Spinoza: what is the source of Jung's 'Spinoza Complex' (2014, pp. 45–48)? The answer is found within a miasma of potential complexes, or perhaps a single complex that could be aptly named *Secret*, *Spirit*, or *Spinoza*. Jung fears the unmooring that Spinoza demands of him. Yet at the same time, Spinozism—or specifically, the distinction of psyche and spirit, and the allegiance to a tripartite monism where the psyche is a neutral third that inheres within God—provides the 'Eternal Ground' that Jung's psychology requires to put an end to the ambiguities listed earlier. Therefore, in order to finally achieve the balance of opposites within his psychology—*and his own psyche*—Jung must reevaluate his opinion of this Dutch philosopher who, despite his name only taking up seven words within Jung's *Collected Works*, seems to appear behind so many more.

The Outbound Jung

Of course, we know that Jung ultimately does what Hegel, as seen in the previous chapter (Ch. 3, pp. 93–99), could not—he makes a concession toward Spinoza. Not only does Jung distinguish psyche from spirit; but like Spinoza, he demands that all knowledge be refracted through the self. Furthermore, he commits to a metaphysics where we 'move' within a transcendental immanence. The essay in which Jung first openly declares the psyche–spirit distinction, 'On the Nature of the Psyche', coincides with his curious treatment of Spinoza in 'The Phenomenology of the Spirit in Fairytales', where Jung critiques how Spinoza allegedly depicts spirit—before arriving at a conception of the Divine *that is quintessentially Spinozist* (see Ch. 1, 2).

This shift also occurs around the same time Jung writes 'Psychology of the Transference', which, as Saban notes, accounts for bilateral transferences and countertransferences between individuals that occur on multiple levels (2019, pp. 180–185). In this work, Jung constructs a pattern that overwrites his previous description of projections merely being withdrawn to seek purely interiorized knowledge, in favor of a framework that allows, and even seeks, exteriority.

For instance, not only do a husband and wife (i) have a personal relationship, but (ii) *both* husband and wife have a relationship with the other's unconscious; in this case, the anima and animus figures, which in turn can only be understood by (iii) understanding *their own respective unconscious*; at the same time, the anima of the wife and the animus of the husband (iv) have a relationship that both husband and wife are wholly unconscious of. Jung is clear that this "counter-crossing" pattern is a push and pull involving both persons, as well as the unconscious that encompasses them both (CW. 16, 1946/1967, par. 422–425). The personal relationship (i) and potential projections and introjections (ii) that may result echo Spinoza's inadequate ideas that result from passive affects and extrinsic encounters (1). Improving the relationship one has with one's own unconscious material (iii), which in turn is part of an unconscious substrate that other person—*all persons*—shares in (iv) is a discovery of intrinsic connections shared between individuals, that is, (2) common notions and adequate ideas. That all things are compounded by intrinsic connections, of course, leads to (3) knowledge of things as they are in eternity (see Figure 4.3). Suddenly, the withdrawal of projections and the gleaning of archetypal meaning behind personal complexes need *not* be a purely intrapsychic affair—rather, the symbol becomes a means to understand the *connection not just between oneself*

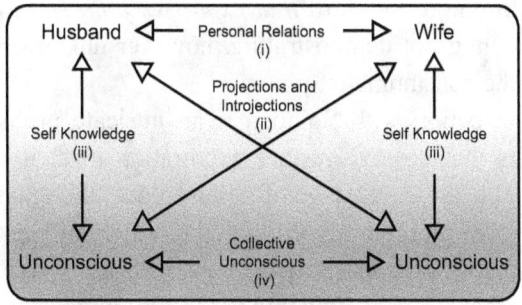

Figure 4.3 Here Jung allows for eternity to be enjoyed by inner and outer alike.

and a particular archetype but also with other people and indeed whatever else in existence is also constellated around that archetype. What in effect happens, as Jung insists to Pauli in their 1953 exchange, is that the hermetically sealed monad is indeed unfolded, so that outbound connections—or transversal connections, as McMillan calls them—can freely occur (Meier, 2001, p. 115; McMillan, 2018).

Jung, notwithstanding how aware he was of the choice he was forced to make, and regardless of how much he would undoubtedly protest at being told as much, takes a Spinozist position with his metaphysics. By doing this he secures the proverbial 'fourth' for his tripartite monism of matter, psyche, and spirit to be grounded in. Furthermore, by fashioning his psychology as capable of identifying those intrinsic, outbound connections between things, Jung is adapting something that is functionally resonant with Spinoza's second form of knowledge, but in the psychologist's case, specific to study the relation of psyche and spirit. Spinoza's discourse on common notions almost exclusively concerns how they manifest under extension, or matter— but as the order and connection of things is the same as the order and connection of ideas, it stands to reason that a whole theory of 'psychic' and 'ideal' common notions, considered exclusively under the attribute of thought, ought to exist as well (E II, CWS I, pp. 446–491). Is this not exactly what Jung does—excavate common notions, or symbols, that explain our intrinsic connections between our psyche and the "irruptions of the unconscious," that is, spirit? When Jung insists that he is only sticking to psychic facts, and that he must proceed from the psyche to spirit, or—in those instances when he *does* concern himself with the physical world—from the psyche to matter, is he not adhering to the principles of a tripartite monism? When he says that one must never mix these routes up, that one must never leap from spirit to matter so hastily, that to ignore the third *that expresses both spirit and matter* is the key error, is Jung not demonstrating, however unknowingly and grudgingly, that he is the consummate Spinozist?

Interrogating Jung's connection with Spinoza is an intricate problem, with many different facets that deserve further exploration in their own right. One could further delineate the lineage of philosophical thought that bridges the two thinkers, most prominently through the writers of German Romanticism and Idealism but also via philosophers such as Nietzsche. One could also explore further the debt Jung and psychiatry in general had to Spinoza in terms of the notion of affectivity. It would also be understandable if one lingered longer on the fears and prejudices that thwarted Jung from openly acknowledging any debt he owed Spinoza. However, what this theoretical analysis of 'Jung the Unlikely Spinozist' intends to demonstrate is not just that Jung is, indeed, a Spinozist, but also that within Spinoza there is a foreshadowing of Jung to be found as well. Perhaps the concepts that concern both thinkers—namely, transcendental immanence, a union of knowledge and affectivity, and ultimately the distinction of psyche and spirit—irrevocably bind them together, and so in spite of the chasm of centuries, culture, and lineages of thought that separate Jung and Spinoza, their affinity strengthens the metaphysics that they jointly champion.

Notes

1   Other writers who have discussed Jung as a thinker of reenchantment include Berman (1981), Tarnas (1996), and Asprem (2014).
2   Spinoza was in fact deeply engaged with the 'redintegration' experiments of Robert Boyle (see Ep. V–VII, CWS I pp. 172–190; also see Duffy, 2006).
3   Negri goes further on this point than Norris. While Norris maintains that Spinoza places the intellect as higher than imagination, their cooperation notwithstanding, Negri believes that Spinoza's writing on the affects betrays an "ambivalence" he holds toward both reason and the imagination, and that he in fact grants the imagination a "savage power" in terms of ability to create and destroy affections (Norris, 1991; Negri, 1984; also see Lloyd, 1996, Ch. 2). An example of this imaginal 'savage power' Negri describes will be provided in the next chapter.
4   Main actually draws four different levels of meaning concerning synchronicity, based on the work of Robert Aziz (1990). These levels include a simple level of two events sharing content; the experience of affectivity or numonisity; and then personal and collective meaning.
5   Haecceity is a term that Deleuze borrows from the medieval philosopher Duns Scotus to describe the "thisness" of a thing, or rather its singular essence (Deleuze and Guattari, 1987, pp. 408–409). While the positing of universal essences leads to reification, haecceities avoid this problem since they are not *a priori* forms that sweepingly apply to many or all things, but rather the essences of individual things—hence, they are singular (see DeLanda & Harman, 2017, pp. 51–53).
6   Following Weber, Main notes that the university is the place where the "concomitants of disenchantment" tend to flourish (2022, pp. 7–8).

References

Adler, G. & Jaffe, A. (1975). *C.G. Jung Letters 2: 1951–1961*. Translated by R. Hull. Princeton: Princeton University Press.

Asprem, E. (2014). *The Problem of Disenchantment: Scientific Naturalism and Esoteric Discourse 1900–1939*. Leiden, Netherlands: Brill.

Atmanspacher, H. & Fach, W. (2013). "A structural–phenomenological typology of mind–matter correlations." *Journal of Analytical Psychology*, 58, 219–244.

Aziz, R. (1990). *C.G. Jung's Psychology of Religion and Synchronicity*. Albany, NY: State University of New York Press.

Beebe, J. (2017). *Energies and Patterns in Psychological Types: The reservoir of consciousness*. New York: Routledge.

Beebe, J. & Falzeder, E. (2013). *The Question of Psychological Types: The Correspondence of C.G. Jung and Hans Schmid Guisan, 1915–1916*. Princeton: Princeton University Press.

Berman, M. (1981). *The Reenchantment of the World*. Ithaca, NY: Cornell University Press.

Brooke, R. (2015). *Jung and Phenomenology*. London & New York: Routledge.

Cambray, J. (2014). "The Influence of German Romantic Science on Jung and Pauli," in *The Pauli–Jung Conjecture and its Impact Today*, edited by H. Atmanspacher & C. Fuchs. Exeter: Imprint Academic.

Carlisle, C. (2021). *Spinoza's Religion: A New Reading of The Ethics*. Princeton: Princeton University Press.

DeLanda, M. & Harman, G. (2017). *The Rise of Realism*. Cambridge, UK & Malden, MA: Polity Press.

Deleuze, G. (1970/1988). *Spinoza: Practical Philosophy*. Translated by R. Hurley. San Francisco: City Light Books.

Deleuze, G. & Guattari, F. (1987). *A Thousand Plateaus: Capitalism and Schizophrenia*. Translated by Brian Massumi. Minneapolis: University of Minnesota Press.

Duffy, S. (2006). "The difference between science and philosophy: The Spinoza–Boyle controversy revisited." *Deleuze and Science*, 29(2), 115–138.

Förster, E. & Melamed, Y. (eds.) (2012). *Spinoza and German Idealism*. Cambridge: Cambridge University Press.

Israel, J. (2002). *Radical Enlightenment: Philosophy and the Making of Modernity*, 1st ed. Oxford: Oxford University Press.

Jacobi, J. (1959). *Complex, Archetype, Symbol in the Psychology of C.G. Jung*. Translated by Ralph Manheim. Princeton: Princeton University Press.

Jung, C.G. (1916). *Two Essays on Analytical Psychology*, 2nd ed. Translated by R. Hull. Collected Works of C.G. Jung, Vol. 7. Princeton: Princeton University Press, 1966.

Jung, C.G. (1916). "The Transcendent Function," in *The Structure and Dynamics of the Psyche*, 2nd ed. Translated by R. Hull. Collected Works of C.G. Jung, Vol. 8. Princeton: Princeton University Press, 1969a.

Jung, C.G. (1921). *Psychological Types*, 2nd ed. Translated by R. Hull. Collected Works of C.G. Jung, Vol. 6. Princeton: Princeton University Press, 1971.

Jung, C.G. (1940). 'The Psychology of the Child Archetype', in *The Archetypes and the Collective Unconscious*, 2nd ed. Translated by R. Hull. Collected Works of C.G. Jung, Vol. 9i. Princeton: Princeton University Press, 1969b.

Jung, C.G. (1946). "On the Nature of the Psyche," in *The Structure and Dynamics of the Psyche*, 2nd ed. Translated by R. Hull. Collected Works of C.G. Jung, Vol. 8. Princeton: Princeton University Press, 1969a.

Jung, C.G. (1946). "Psychology of the Transference," in *The Practice of Psychotherapy*, 2nd ed. Translated by R. Hull. Collected Works of C.G. Jung, Vol. 16. Princeton: Princeton University Press, 1967.

Jung, C.G. (1948). "The Phenomenology of the Spirit in Fairytales," in *The Archetypes and the Collective Unconscious*, 2nd ed. Translated by R. Hull. Collected Works of C.G. Jung, Vol. 9i. Princeton: Princeton University Press, 1969.

Jung, C.G. (1952). "Synchronicity: An Acausal Connecting Principle," in *The Structure and Dynamics of the Psyche*, 2nd ed. Translated by R. Hull. Collected Works of C.G. Jung, Vol. 8. Princeton: Princeton University Press, 1969a.

Jung, C.G. (1956). *Symbols of Transformation*, 2nd ed. Translated by R. Hull. Collected Works of C.G. Jung, Vol. 5. Princeton: Princeton University Press, 1967.

Jung, C.G. (1959). *Aion: Researches into the Phenomenology of the Self*, 2nd ed. Translated by R. Hull. Collected Works of C.G. Jung, Vol. 9ii. Princeton: Princeton University Press, 1969c.

Jung, C.G. (1963). *Mysterium Coniunctionis*, 2nd ed. Translated by R. Hull. Collected Works of C.G. Jung, Vol. 14. Princeton: Princeton University Press, 1970.

Jung, C.G. (1963/1989). *Memories. Dreams, Reflections*. Edited by A. Jaffe, Translated by R. Winston and C. Winston. New York: Vintage Books.

Katz, M. (2007). "Einstein and His God." *Moment*. https://momentmag.com/einstein-and-his-god/ (Accessed March 2023).

Keirsey, D. (1998). *Please Understand Me II: Temperature, Character, Intelligence*. Del Mar, CA: Prometheus Nemesis Book Company.

Knox, J. (2003). *Archetype, Attachment, Analysis: Jungian Psychology and the Emergent Mind*. London & New York: Routledge.

Langan, R. (2020). "Jung, Spinoza, Deleuze: A Move Towards Realism" (Ch. 10), in *Holism: Possibilities and Problems*. Edited by C. McMillan, R. Main & D. Henderson. London: Routledge.

Lloyd, G. (1996). *Routledge Philosophy Guidebook to Spinoza and the Ethics*. London: Routledge.

Macherey, P. (1979/2011). *Hegel or Spinoza*. Translated by S. Ruddick. Minnesota: University of Minnesota Press.

Main, R. (2013). "Myth, Synchronicity, and Re-enchantment," in *Myth, Literature and the Unconscious*, edited by L. Burnett, S. Bahun, & R. Main. London: Karnac Books.

Main, R. (2022). *Breaking the Spell of Disenchantment: Mystery, Meaning, and Metaphysics in the Work of C.G. Jung*. The Zurich Lecture Series: Volume 8. Asheville, NC: Chiron Publications.

Maxwell, G. (2022). *Integration and Difference: Constructing a Mythical Dialectic.* London & New York: Routledge.

McCoy Brooks, R. (2019). "A Critique of C.G. Jung's Theoretical basis for Selfhood: Theory Vexed by an Incorporeal Ontology" (Ch. 5), in *Jung and Philosophy*, edited by J. Mills. London & New York: Routledge.

McMillan, C. (2018). "Jung and Deleuze: Enchanted Openings to the Other: A Philosophical Contribution." *International Journal of Jungian Studies*, 10(3), 184–198.

Meier, C.A. (ed.) (2001). *Atom and Archetype: The Pauli/Jung Letters 1932–1958.* London: Routledge.

Nadler, S. (1999/2018). *Spinoza: A Life*, 2nd ed. Cambridge: Cambridge University Press.

Nadler, S. (2011). *A Book Forged in Hell: Spinoza's Scandalous Treatise and the Birth of the Secular Age.* Princeton: Princeton University Press.

Negri, A. (1991). *The Savage Anomaly: The Power of Spinoza's Metaphysics and Politics.* Translated by Michael Hardt. Minneapolis: University of Minnesota Press.

Newman, W. (2018). *Newton the Alchemist: Science, Enigma, and the Quest for Nature's "Secret Fire".* Princeton: Princeton University Press.

Norris, C. (1991). *Spinoza and the Origins of Modern Critical Theory.* Oxford: Blackwell.

Papadopoulos, R. (1991). "Jung and the Concept of the Other," in *Jung in Modern Perspective*, pp. 54–88. Bridgeport, CN: Prism.

Peden, K. (2014). *Spinoza Contra Phenomenology.* Stanford: Stanford University Press.

Roesler, C. (2012). "Are Archetypes Transmitted More by Culture than Biology? Questions Arising from Conceptualizations of the Archetype." *The Journal of Analytical Psychology*, 57, 223–246.

Roesler, C. (2022). *C.G. Jung's Archetype Concept: Theory, Research, and Applications.* Translated by A. Ulyet & C. Roesler. London & New York: Routledge.

Saban, M. (2019). *'Two Souls Alas': Jung's Two Personalities and the Making of Analytical Psychology.* The Zurich Lecture Series: Volume 2. Asheville, NC: Chiron Publications.

Schact, R. (1999). 'The Spinoza-Nietzsche Problem', in *Desire and Affect: Spinoza as Psychologist.* Edited by Y. Yovel. New York: Little Room Press.

Spinoza, B. (1985). *The Collected Works of Spinoza*, Vol. I, Edited and translated by Edwin Curley. Princeton: Princeton University Press.

Spinoza, B. (2016). *The Collected Works of Spinoza*, Vol. II, Edited and translated by Edwin Curley. Princeton: Princeton University Press.

Stewart, M. (2006). *The Courtier and the Heretic: Leibniz, Spinoza, and the Fate of God in the Modern World.* New York & London: Norton & Company.

Tarnas, R. (1996). *The Passion of the Western Mind: Understanding the Ideas that Have Shaped Our World View.* London: Pimlico.

Chapter 5

Archetypal Compositions

Psyche and spirit. The mind and thought. This distinction of the mind (or *psyche*) from the attribute of thought (or *spirit*) is what distinguishes the monism of Jung and Spinoza from those dual-aspect approaches where the psyche as 'middle third' remains unspoken for. By declaring that the archetypes are not truly of the psyche, Jung is assuring that the great "stumbling block" that he warns Pauli of, the error of reducing spirit to the psyche so that the aspects of existence become "physis versus psyche," is avoided. Instead one understands the aspects are "physis versus pneuma with the psyche the medium between the two" (Meier, 2001, pp. 116–117). Consequently, the archetypes are no longer to be thought of as 'inborn' or 'internal' psychic processes; instead, they have a psychoid factor, an "unascertainable" aspect that, like the psyche itself, sits between spirit and matter. Hence why the archetypes are *attractors of ideas* on the one hand, affecting the psyche through symbolic manifestations that have no clear object in the physical world, that is, archetypes as manifestations of *spirit*; while on the other hand they are also "directly connected with physiological processes" of the body and even arrange *outer material circumstances* in cases of synchronicity, that is, manifestations in *matter* (CW. 8, 1952/1969a, par. 840; ibid., pp. 100–101, 112–113, 125–126). It is this double actualization of "archetypal conceptions and instinctual perceptions" where "spirit and matter confront one another" in the psyche as two expressions of the same world (CW. 8, 1946/1969a, par. 420).

What is Spinoza's version of an archetype? Not that Spinoza speaks of such a concept—but how might we extrapolate it from his philosophy, if we wished to do so? For Spinoza only two things truly exist: substance and modes, or rather that which is and that which is in another—or, more specifically, that which is conceived through itself, 'naturing nature', and

DOI: 10.4324/9781003516996-6

that which must be conceived *through* something else, 'nurtured nature' (E IA1, D3, D5, IP29S, CWS I, pp. 408–410, 434). It may be tempting to classify the archetypes as substance itself, or 'naturing nature', so that they might be cast as a grand set of metaphysical laws equivalent to God himself, and that give shape and order to the modes. Yet with Spinoza there is always this demarcation between the infinity of modes and the absolutely infinite power that creates this infinity, or, rather, between everything that God necessarily produces and his absolute power to necessarily produce anything that he conceives—which is, of course, *everything that is conceivable* (E IP16, CWS I, pp. 424–425). Anything that can conceivably exist, *will* exist—even if something stops it *extrinsically* from existing in this moment of duration (Matheron, 2020, pp. 33–35). When Spinoza denies God has freewill, it is not to diminish him; rather, it is to make clear that *God is beyond the concept of choice*. Hence Spinoza dismisses the notion that God could produce things in any other way than the order that he does—because to speak of things as contingent, and therefore possible to alternatives, reflects only a defect in our knowledge and betrays our ignorance of how God's perfection is expressed in what he produces (E IP33, CWS I, pp. 436–439). Jung conveys the same thing in 'Answer to Job' when he writes that God could not have helped but create the world in the way that he did, but that this does not "imply any limitation on his omnipotence; on the contrary, it is an acknowledgment that all possibilities are contained in him, and that there are in consequence no other possibilities than those which express him" (CW. 11, 1952/1969a, par. 630). If *any* laws can be ascribed intelligibly to God, it is only the laws of *his* nature, that is, his absolute power to produce everything, and the fact that no other substance exists that could compel God to do anything else (E IP17, CWS I, pp. 425–428).

The consequence of this is that if one were to try and seriously articulate the laws of *God's* nature, one would have to account for *all potential worlds and histories that have ever existed, currently exist, and will exist*—and therefore, one would have to be able to explain all the possibly divergent laws of nature specific to each of those worlds and times. In Matheron's opinion, Spinoza's fledgling awareness of this problem is why he balks at detailing a theory of physics beyond his exposition on the composition and decomposition of individuals. Instead, Spinoza arrives at the position that physics is ontologically grounded yet also not foundational; he is, on some level, presaging a modern conception of science (Matheron, 2020, Ch. 3). And it is in this sense that if the archetypes are analogous to physical laws of nature, then they cannot be considered substance *proper*.

The archetypes must be modes then. Remember that for Spinoza all modes are individual compositions made up of extrinsic individuals, who are in turn made of other extrinsic individuals, a chain that goes on and on until one must speak of an infinite mode, such as "the face" of the entire universe.[1] Each composite is defined by its specific ratio of relations, what Spinoza calls (under extension) 'motion and rest'. And so long as an individual's specific ratio of relations is not compromised, the extrinsic parts can freely enter and leave the composition (E IIP13SL6–7; CWS I, pp. 461–462). And so it goes: an organism replaces its cells, doctors transplant organs, a transplant leaves her home state, states cede from unions. In many cases the composition remains intact. In a sense, *every* mode is a composite of other modes, and can be called a compound mode—our bodies are made of flesh, blood, and bones, which are made of tissues that can be broken all the way down to organic molecules, which could be broken down to atoms, which can be broken down into increasingly unstable subatomic particles, and so forth. Some compound modes come and go, others readily recur. Every time an athlete gets on a road bike and attempts to break the record on their local climb, they become a compound mode: a cyclist. Every night an aspiring writer crouches over their keyboard and hammers out their novel, they *are* a writer, a composite of aspiring writer and keyboard. Unless something that already exists prevents a mode from existing, it will exist. Put another way, unless a mode thwarts essence B's ratio of relations from gaining the external parts it needs to be actualized, mode B will exist. Therefore, recurrence is possible, just not guaranteed. The cast of the American sitcom *Seinfeld* reunited after a decade of not seeing one another, yet personal and professional differences were swept away when the 'magic' of the ensemble subsumed them all once again; it was as if Jerry, George, Elaine, and Kramer had never left (FoundationINTERVIEWS, 2014). On the other hand, anyone who has tried in vain to rekindle an old romance can attest to how old arguments arise all too easily, how the drama resumes right where it was paused, and how it becomes evident that, despite a mirage of hope, the relationship was still very much dead. For any number of reasons, some modes more readily recur than others. And some modes not only return; they have multiple actualizations. *Homo sapiens* is presently actualized in billions of places at once, and will recur so long as the species perseveres to exist.

There are viruses that one cannot see, but they can still cause great harm to one's body; there are political movements that someone who professes to be apolitical nonetheless declares for by how they conduct their life and how they ignore certain injustices. With compound modes moving like tectonic plates that slide over and under one another at scales well beyond our existence, one may never even be conscious of the assemblages that they become enveloped by. Spinoza captures this limited scope of what we can perceive in the example he raises of a hypothetical "little worm" that lives in blood and is capable of distinguishing the various parts that make up blood: "lymph, chyle, etc." And this worm would "live in this blood as we do in this part of the universe, and would consider" everything else around it to be separate parts, and oblivious as to how "all the parts of the blood are regulated by the universal nature of the blood"—in other words, that blood is an individual whole in its own right. And the worm would be doubly oblivious to blood itself being a part within an even greater whole, such as a human being—which in turn is a part within a society or state, and so forth (Ep. 32, CWS II, pp. 18–20). This example is redolent of Jung's depiction of a hypothetically conscious eye that would be oblivious to how it was affected by the body it was in, how it would not understand the light that affects it is not randomly changing, but rather is caused by the movements of the head that it is part of (CW. 8, 1926/1969a, pars. 637–641). And Spinoza himself notes that his example of the worm and blood applies to the realm of thought as well, that all ideas and minds are equally parts of greater ideas (Ep. 32, CWS II, p. 20). Since beyond substance there is nothing but modes, and since Spinoza is explicit that all modes, considered under any attribute, are composites, we must stretch this notion to even to things we ordinarily would not think of as an 'individual'. *Everything conceivable*, whether a corporeal individual, a complex idea, an atom or a planet, a passing affair or an intermittent event, are nothing but compounding modes with their own unique composition, affective powers, and actualizations.[2] It may be strange to think of an event like the Battle of Midway, for instance, as a mode on the exact same ontological footing as the human beings, battleships, and bombs that composed the battle—to say nothing of the ocean, atolls, ideologies, and histories that set the stage for the conflict—but all that exists is nothing more than composites upon composites, assemblages that interlock and diverge, subsume and are subsumed, cohere or destroy, and this is exactly what Spinoza's metaphysics demands.

Archetypes are compound modes of recurring human events. All modes are brought into existence by other modes that already exist, even though the essences of those modes are conceived by God (E IP28, CWS I, p. 432; E VP22, p. 607). And clearly some modes share a certain kind of affinity, and the existence of one begets the existence of another: the ocean, the tropics, and the jet stream beget the potential of hurricanes; people who live according to reason sufficiently enough to cooperate will do what is best for the common essence of humanity: the formation of a civil state, or the use of animals for livestock that produces food, clothing, etc. Remember, all these things must be seen as modes in their own right (E IVP36S, CWS I, pp. 564–568). And the common essence of humanity must beget certain inevitable compound relations: every person has a mother, falls in love, or has parts of themselves and the world that they fear and do not understand, and therefore deny (see Ch. 3, pp. 85–89). The archetypes are these recurring compositions. They are brought into existence because, just as Spinoza's God must express everything conceivable, Jung contends that the unconscious has "an innate drive toward expressing itself" entirely and, just as modes beget the formation of other modes, the attitude of the conscious individual begets the interjection of unconscious material that demands recognition and integration (Main, 2022, pp. 30–32). Jung's client who dreamt of his fiancée throwing herself into a river while he helplessly watched on was forced to understand that the dream deployed his partner as a symbol to represent his anima, to whom his attention was long overdue (CW. 7, 1916/1966, pars. 355–356). Like any essence that comes into existence, the archetype is like an assemblage that is constructed of individuals external to itself, but which are nevertheless compatible with 'the ratio of relations' that the archetype expresses: concerning the anima, one can imagine how actual situations (such as one having a fiancée), or one's personal complexes (someone who unknowingly seeks or avoids the same things from different romantic partners), or cultural and mythological motifs (the image of a woman drowning herself, or the implications of suicide), as well as biological instinct (the desire to have a partner), are pressed into the service of the archetype's actualization. And an archetype must be as indiscriminate about *where* these parts come from as evolutionary forces are when they blindly press into their service disparate genomic material from unrelated species, such as bat, bird, insect, or pterosaur, into the same convergent need: namely, wings. Inner and outer, intrapersonal and inter-personal, body and the world, the personal and the universal—these distinctions mean *nothing* to a compounding mode. So long as the parts agree with the archetype's characteristic relations, they can and will be used to express its essence.[3]

Now it is the abolition of the strict couplet of *inner* with the divine that allows for these archetypal compositions. That is to say, it is the very distinction of "all the phenomena" of an individual's inner world, that is, the psyche, from things of an ideal nature that it encounters, that is, spirit, that lets us dispense with a dichotomy of inner and outer in favor of a tension between essence and existence which in many respects is the foundation of Spinoza's philosophy (Meier, 2001, p. 125; see Ch. 4). Abolishing the primacy of the interior is what Spinoza demands, and what Jung ultimately concedes. Yet how does this differ *in practice* from a dual-aspect monism where the inward prerogative remains intact? How does Jung's 'tripartite monism' of matter, psyche, and spirit—in other words, Jung the Spinozist—differ from a dual-aspect monism where there are simply two aspects, mind and matter, and the psyche remains unspoken for?

Spirit or Subject

In Harald Atmanspacher's reconstruction of Jung and Pauli's dual-aspect monism, what he calls the 'Pauli–Jung conjecture', mind and matter *alone* are taken to be complementary aspects of an underlying, psychophysically neutral whole (Atmanspacher, 2012; Atmanspacher & Fach, 2013, 2014). Spiritual experiences and the very psyche that has those spiritual experiences are compressed into the same entity: the aspect of mind. Thus, the mind plays a double role by being both the host of mental representations that decompose from the psychophysically neutral whole, as well as the very subject that can trace correlations between those mental representations and matter (Atmanspacher & Rickles, 2022, pp. 50–51). The psyche's role as the middle third is absent.

As we saw in the previous chapter, the conflation of psyche with spirit invariably necessitates an emphasis of the inner over the outer, of subject against object (see Ch. 4, pp. 121–128). In *Dual-Aspect Monism and the Deep Structure of Meaning*, Atmanspacher and co-author Dean Rickles survey some theories analogous to Atmanspacher's work which actually make this emphasis explicit. Physicists Arthur Eddington and John Wheeler arrive at the idea that the individual's participation in the world, the experience of the subject, is key to forming objective reality as we know it, and therefore, in order to recognize what they see as the most important partition, in their respective frameworks the twin aspects are not simply deemed mind and matter, but indeed subject and object (Atmanspacher & Rickles, 2022, Ch. 4). In Atmanspacher's reconstruction of the Pauli–Jung conjecture, the two aspects are termed mind and matter, not subject and object; nevertheless, Atmanspacher permits that the two binaries are closely related (ibid., pp. 152, 167). And clearly within Atmanspacher's dual-aspect system the aspects are not merely a distinction between ideal and physical things. Rather the mental aspect is intimately tied to the subject and their inner experiences, while the material aspect is tantamount to the object and external events. This is most evident in Atmanspacher's reliance on the work of German philosopher of mind Thomas Metzinger. Metzinger argues that the mind is a set of phenomenological processes created by the brain. These processes create two different models of reality: a self model and a world model (2003, Ch. 3, 6). As Atmanspacher and his colleague Wolfgang Fach explain, the self model entails 'inner experience', not just as the source of ideation, but as the vessel it is forever bound to. 'Inner experience' is not synonymous with thought or spirit, nor is it even a mere conflation of spirit and psyche. Rather, it is the hermetic enclosure of one's internal "sensations, cognitions, volitions, affects, motivations" and "inner images," which are all deemed necessarily first-person and exclusively private. "As a rule," Atmanspacher and Fach write, these representations "can be experienced only by the subject itself." In contrast, any representation that can actually be communicated must necessarily be of the world model. This severe restriction notwithstanding, Atmanspacher and Fach find it "evident" that the self model is identical to the aspect of mind, and the world model to the aspect of matter (2013, p. 234; 2019, pp. 13–15). Therefore, not only is the mind both the source of all ideal phenomena while also being what experiences such phenomena, but additionally this entire process is restricted to the intrapsychic to such an extreme that what the aspect of mind expresses is an entirely private language.

Needless to say this move leaves us with an especially strict version of the psyche–spirit couplet. Jung's 'secret complex', as discussed in Chapter 4, needn't even be treated as a sacred vow any longer—its discretion is metaphysically secured. From Spinoza's perspective, the objection is clear: since the attribute of thought (or spirit) is an expression of God's power, not only must the individual mind never be rendered equivalent to it, but the attribute of thought must also *precede* any notion of subjectivity or consciousness altogether. For this reason it is entirely incorrect to conceive this correspondence as an even partition of subject and object, or inner experience and the outer world. Ideas are not contained in the finite subject, but rather in the Infinite Intellect (E IIP3, CWS I, p. 449; IIP8, pp. 452–453). And surely Jung would agree with Spinoza, since any move to elevate the subject to such a rarified position is an act of projective identification with *either* aspect of existence, which enables us to "project great truths out of the subjective sphere into a cosmos" that the individual alone fabricated—what Jung considers 'bad' metaphysics (CW. 8, 1946/1969a, par. 358; see Ch. 1, pp. 24–26). The human mind, and any sense of subjectivity or consciousness that may follow from it, is not anterior or equivalent to thought, but rather a product of it. To pose the aspects of existence as *self* and *world* can only lead to error.

The danger of giving the human mind dominion over existence is that one invariably diminishes the external in favor of the internal, to render reality dependent on the subject's intervention (see Ch. 4, pp. 121–128). This danger is certainly manifest in the respective works of Eddington and Wheeler. Eddington's 'selective subjectivism' states that the very act of observing by a subject is what gives rise to empirical phenomena, that all we truly know is the subject's understanding of physical reality; however that understanding, that shared structural knowledge between perceiving subject and perceived object, implicates the mind in the construction of the outer world itself. This move is parallel with the notion that mind and matter are simply phenomenological models as seen with Metzinger. Atmanspacher concedes that this approach evokes a certain kind of idealism; however, because this method depicts subject and object emerging from a neutral whole, and because it unmoors matter from its place as ontological bedrock, he views this as a permissible, perhaps even necessary, step. This countervailing move against physicalism is, according to Atmanspacher, "the port of entry to the monist position" (Atmanspacher & Rickles, 2022, p. 91). Wheeler takes this line of thought even further with his 'participatory universe', where the act of measurement or action by a participant determines the entire history of the system measured or acted upon; so that the universe, prior to the existence of participators, was pure, invariant potentiality. The measurement of the Big

Bang, for example, is the cause of the Big Bang itself. It is the decisions of the subject that determine the history of the material universe, what causes the subject and object to emerge out of what was hitherto a neutral, invariant domain, what Wheeler calls 'pregeometry' or what Eddington refers to as a 'spiritual world' (ibid., Ch. 4). The subject therefore becomes the arbiter of existence, since by giving the inner world such a privileged position, the mind's interjection becomes necessary for mental representations, and therefore also their physical correlates, to even exist. Another example of this direction is given by Atmanspacher's colleague Hans Primas, who conjectures that it is the mind that causes the forward movement of time; that is to say, the very *movement* of the observable universe is activated by the mental aspect (2003, 2017).

Now for Spinoza this entire route, irrespective of how far it is taken, is entirely unacceptable. Finite things indeed beget the existence of other finite things, and in this sense there is *participation* in the actualization of what God produces (E IP28, CWS I, p. 432). And it is also true that the affective existence of a finite mode is the same thing as its duration—in other words, the passage from one affect to the next is the very passage of time (E IIIP6–8, CWS I, pp. 498–499). But this pair of stipulations applies for *every mode that God produces*. To feign that there can be a subject that exists *outside* nature, whether that subject is deemed the human mind or a demigod, is to pose a "dominion within a dominion." To go on to propose that this subject is not only exempt from the vicissitudes of nature, but even disrupts or manipulates that natural order, is contrary to all Spinozism (E III Preface, CWS I, p. 491). Such a position treats relations between the human and non-human as privileged compared with relations between the non-human and non-human. As Della Rocca puts it, Spinoza demands that we all "play by the same rules," human or otherwise (2008, p. 5). Not only is this the true meaning of Spinoza's naturalism, but as we will see in the next chapter, it is the source of his 'univocity' that is crucial to the status of singular essences. To declare that all of existence can be evenly bifurcated between subject and object is the hallmark of *anti-realist* philosophy, where reality itself becomes dependent on the human mind's intervention (Langan, 2020). This is the inevitable outcome of conflating psyche with spirit, to confuse the mind with its ideas. Anti-realism champions the fiction that all ideas are generated within the mind that has them, rather than through the relationships that both mind and body have with other modes.

Yet all that this attempt to hoist the mind beyond nature has accomplished is to confuse the essence of humankind with the essence of God (E IVP4, CWS I, pp. 548–549). "What happens when man introjects God?" asks Jung. "A superman psychosis" (Letters, Vol. 2, 1975, p. 407).

No Such Thing as Selves

Atmanspacher could rightfully point out that he does not go as far as Eddington or Wheeler in their joint march to a sort of renewed idealism, that in his model the archetypes are neutral factors that govern *both* mind and matter. Furthermore, he allows for the subject to be affected by something greater than itself. To illustrate, Atmanspacher asks us to consider someone who has just experienced a grave personal loss, and the case of synchronicity that follows:

> In Jungian terms, this situation may activate an archetypal pattern of loss manifesting itself in grief. The corresponding state [psychophysically neutral *loss*] will manifest itself in states [mental *grief*] and [*physical* grief] and correlations [mental *grief* ~ physical *grief*] between them (representing a synchronistic event). These correlations are experienced as meaningful by the subject insofar as it attributes grief-related content to them in its state [mental *grief*]. Likewise, any other archetypal pattern would manifest other kinds of synchronistic events related to its content and, thus, limit the range of possible subjective experiences […] the attribution of meaning is always subjective—but it is never arbitrary.
> (Atmanspacher & Rickles, 2022, p. 55)

Here the archetypes act as governing patterns that regulate the parallel mental and physical phenomena. Synchronicity here is treated as a one-to-one correspondence between an inner mental state and an outer physical state. Furthermore, as soon as the mental *grief* state becomes conscious, it has a "backreaction" onto the psychophysically neutral whole, which causes perturbations in the archetype that is manifesting, and in turn could lead to a new physical state of *grief* that correlates with the changed *mental* state (ibid.). Moreover, the same label may be conferred upon both the subject and the 'mental' experiences of that subject—but both functions are nevertheless implicitly present: there is mental content, as well as some sort of subject that designates the mental content to a physical correlation.

Jung and Spinoza can protest all they want about the need for keeping the psyche separate from spirit, they can warn Atmanspacher of all the dangers that come with combining them, but Atmanspacher could ask what difference any of those concerns make to his theory if, despite being packaged together, psyche and spirit are still *de facto* accounted for.

Yet possessing a faculty that designates meaning to different states is not the same thing as an embodied psyche that experiences. And not only is the psyche in this sense absent in Atmanspacher's model—in one source he draws heavily upon, it is outright rejected. Metzinger claims that one errs by confusing an identity or sense of one's self with the "content of the self-model currently activated by" one's brain. There are "no such things as selves," writes Metzinger. "Nobody ever *was* or *had* a self." There are only phenomenological models that the brain creates in its role as an "ontological machine." Therefore we do not have direct access to reality, limited as we are to this "autoepistemic enclosure" within our heads (2003, p. 1). The brain "constantly hallucinates the world," Metzinger declares, "vigorously dreaming of the world and thereby generating the content of phenomenal experience" (ibid., p. 52). There does not seem to be much place in Metzinger's philosophy for the psyche, much less an *unus mundus* that it moves within.

Unlike Metzinger, Atmanspacher subscribes to an underlying monist whole; nonetheless he and Fach otherwise agree with Metzinger's position, stating that "the notion of the self in the sense of a 'mediator' of first-person experience should not be given ontological significance." Mistaking one's self model for individuality is akin to "the Jungian notion of an ego that fails to realize its status as being purely epistemic" (2019, p. 17). In other words, the notion of a psyche that is the source of raw experience is illusory and thus dispensed with. But if there is no psyche that moves within the world, paradoxically it then becomes difficult to explain our knowledge of the world without resorting to a construct that is purely intrapsychic, like Metzinger's 'autoepistemic enclosure'. Therefore the dual aspects of mind and matter become intrapsychic simulations—in a sense, *both aspects could be collapsed into the mind alone.* This is a consequence that Atmanspacher gladly affirms, since it reserves the purely ontological for the underlying monist whole (Atmanspacher & Rickles, 2022, p. 23).

As should be obvious at this stage, just as Jung and Spinoza refuse to conflate spirit with psyche, so too would they strongly object to the outright elimination of the psyche as our source for raw experience. Not that our awareness of our own psyche is a given; on the contrary, we are usually blithely ignorant of our true causes. Yet the adequate idea of ourselves must exist as surely as a composite that forms our body exists; otherwise we would be disembodied, reduced to hollow knowledge, and there would be no affectivity, and therefore no true knowledge to even speak of (see Ch. 3). But another point that Jung and Spinoza would reject is this reduction of spirit and matter to intrapsychic processes. Thought and extension are indeed different ways in which we conceive the same thing, but that is not because they are merely faculties our brain uses to make sense of the world, but rather because our very existence involves those two attributes, and the attributes are not fictions, but rather the very expressions of God's power (E IIP1–2, CWS I, pp. 448–449). Spirit and matter are forms of the same transcendental being (CW. 9i, 1948/1969b, par. 392). To suggest that thought and extension are mere mental categories, even if through evolutionary adaptations, is to essentially restate Hegel's interpretation of Spinoza, where any sense of singular existence is an illusion, and that the underlying monism is nothing but a barren featureless substance which we all inevitably collapse back into (Ch. 2, pp. 57–61). This is in fact what Atmanspacher's model risks endorsing—so long as it relies on the logic exemplified by Metzinger.

Immediate problems also arise from binding the aspects of the monist whole to the intrapsychic. Metzinger repeatedly claims that these models are all we really have in terms of knowledge, a position that Atmanspacher endorses by labeling the aspects of mind and matter as *epistemic* (Atmanspacher & Rickles, 2022, p. 55; Atmanspacher & Fach, 2019). Our knowledge of things is always an approximation (Metzinger, 2003, p. 59). Our only recourse is to refine our understanding of the cognitive and neurological processes that give rise to our phenomenological models of existence (ibid., p. 83). But if all we have are our simulations of inner and worldly existence, how does one guarantee any sort of "correlationism" between the simulations in our head and reality?[4] Metzinger essentially claims that our models are often accurate approximations because evolution guarantees their precision (ibid., pp. 1, 57, 198). As speculative realist philosopher Graham Harman notes, this plea to Darwinism is a standard trope of 'hardcore' naturalist philosophers, and it skirts around the fact that it seems difficult and altogether contradictory to try and explain how representations of real things are gleaned from "mere simulations," despite that according to Metzinger's theory we shouldn't be able to do any better than those simulations. What Metzinger's neurophenomenology leaves us with is nothing more than a very familiar dualism: a physical reality upon which everything is predicated, and yet which we have no access to; and a closed mental reality where all our knowledge occurs, and yet nothing really happens (Harman, 2011, pp. 14, 30).

Now unlike Metzinger, Atmanspacher claims that our mental and physical knowledge of things decomposes from an underlying whole, and that correlations between mental and physical processes can be studied to make sense of their shared origin. Yet this does nothing to solve the deeper problem of *correlationism*—not correlations between mind and matter, but instead between what we know and what really is. Atmanspacher speaks of how fMRI experiments have demonstrated the complementary ways in which certain brain patterns are activated during specific mental tasks as an example of correlations between mind and matter, where one aspect cannot be reduced to the other (Atmanspacher & Rickles, 2022, p. 47). Yet such epistemological parallelism does not address an ontological source for both aspects. Atmanspacher suggests, as Pauli did to Jung at the onset of their 1953 exchange, that it is at the fringes of both physics and psychology where the two approaches would meet: that is to say, it is where the study of subatomic particles becomes so volatile that it has been conjectured the very psyche of the observer directly affects what is observed that matter meets the mind; similarly, it is the study of unconscious patterns, which go from personal to progressively more universal until perhaps one reaches a level where physiology must play its part, that the mind meets matter (Meier, 2001, pp. 84–97). This is precisely what Atmanspacher envisions: two parallel lines of existence that become increasingly blurred with one another as we trace them back toward the monist whole. If the archetypes are ordering factors of mind and matter, then as we near the underlying psychophysical reality they would appear neutral (Atmanspacher & Rickles, 2022, p. 44). But when does one *know* they've reached this neutral starting point? One can claim, as Pauli did, that the influence of the observer at the level of microphysics is proof of a neutral domain; or, similarly, one can attribute the psychoid quality of the archetype to physiology (Addison, 2019). Yet from the perspective of the individual, one is still observing a material manifestation while simultaneously having an idea of that same manifestation—in other words, our experience is still bifurcated into two separate aspects. In this respect the 'fringe' of physics and psyche is really not much different than mental and neural correlations on the level of everyday life, just at an infinitely smaller and less stable scale. Is there an infinitesimal point where one at last reaches the moment of collapse? Or do the psychophysical parallel lines go on forever, with the 'first cause' perpetually on the horizon?

Atmanspacher tries to head off this issue by introducing the notion of 'relative onticity', where the ontic becomes whatever is most appropriate for a given context: for instance, when trying to understand mental illness from a purely psychological perspective, behavioral and psychoanalytic descriptions of schizophrenia, depression, or obsessive-compulsive disorder would suffice as an ontology; yet if one were seeking the neurobiological genesis of such diseases, the psychological explanations become 'merely' epistemological (Atmanspacher & Kronz, 1999; Atmanspacher & Rickles, 2022, pp. 129–131). Yet this explanation bears resemblance to Metzinger's appeal to Darwinism: it dresses the problem as its own solution, without ever really solving it. In Metzinger's case, the question of, "Why is it that we just so happen to have developed the ability to hallucinate simulations that, for the most part, 'get it right'?," is answered by simply restating: *we just so happen to have developed the ability to hallucinate simulations that, for the most part, 'get it right'!* With Atmanspacher, the puzzle of, "When can I start speaking of the ontic rather than the epistemic?," is solved by simply declaring: *whenever I need to speak of the ontic rather than the epistemic.*

Both Metzinger and Atmanspacher seem to realize that this state of affairs will not suffice, that they have essentially written themselves into corners. Both try to find other means of escape from the 'autoepistemic enclosure'. For Metzinger, this comes in the form of a rather astonishing concession. In spite of his declaration that all knowledge is but useful hallucinations, he permits that our phenomenological models are capable of "transgressing their physical boundaries" and extracting information from the real world, a process that he calls "pulsation" (2003, p. 21). Echoing Jung's revision of Leibniz's monadology, where monads are not closed microcosms but have windows into the cosmos, Metzinger declares that, as it turns out, our phenomenological models are also capable of forming windows into the world (ibid., p. 585). Atmanspacher forges a similar fracture in the epistemic by offering a conjecture regarding moments of immanence, such as in religious experiences, where our perceptions of mind and matter collapse and we are left with only a feeling of unity (Atmanspacher & Rickles, 2022, pp. 77–80). This sense of an *unus mundus* evokes Jung's collective version of meaning (see Ch. 4, pp. 118–121). But it is not entirely clear how these moments of immanence are achieved, or if we have any control over engaging them. Metzinger is similarly vague about how "pulsation" works, and the sheer contradiction of its existence in his philosophy is what leads Harman to disparage it as an apparent ontological miracle (2011, p. 33). So aside from some fleeting and irreproducible hiccups, what we know of things is forever sealed off from what things truly are. If so, then not only is the ontic permanently separate from the epistemic, but suddenly it is hard to differentiate the epistemic aspects of mind and matter from any other sort of Cartesian dualism, save the promise of a source that is always out of reach.

Parallelism versus Equality

Even the idea of bidirectional traffic does not bridge the gulf between the ontic and epistemic as Atmanspacher might hope. After all, if the archetypes are really nothing but regulators for the simulations in our head, then whatever changes in the whole that they convey to us will still always keep us at arms' length from wherever they emanate from. One can forever ask *"Why this simulation and not another? Why this set of laws and not another?"* These are the very questions one is left with when one conceives of a God who rules by decree, rather than a God who is beyond the notion of choice. But the very inability to explain why we do, indeed, have the set of experiences we have, or why we are in this world and not another, is precisely the quandary one is left with when one projects the psyche into either aspect of existence. And since these projections are inherently untenable, one's viewpoint confusingly and unconsciously flips between the extreme ends of the metaphysical spectrum, in subliminal yet desperate attempts to find firm footing (CW. 8, 1946/1969a, par. 407). Metzinger's appeal to neurobiology as the source for our mental simulations is contradicted by the fact that our mental simulations are all we really have; Atmanspacher's deployment of quantum theory to color much of his dual-aspect monism is contrasted with a theory of knowledge that teeters on a totalizing subject. Ultimately, the elimination of the psyche as middle third does not lead strictly to either idealism or materialism, but rather an *anti-realism* that oscillates between both.

This failure to hold the middle and instead be thrashed between dead materialism and grandiose idealism is precisely what Jung accuses Spinoza of (CW. 9i, 1948/1969b, pars. 385, 390–391). While we have deemed Jung's assessment of Spinoza to be erroneous, the demand of being able to hold a neutral ground between the physical and ideal nonetheless remains the chief standard by which Jung judges metaphysical ideas (see, Ch. 1, pp. 24–26; Ch. 2, pp. 52–57). The fact that anti-realism can apply to either idealist or materialist philosophies is why Harman and neo-materialist philosopher Manuel DeLanda ascribe anti-realism not only to the phenomenologies of Edmund Husserl and Martin Heidegger as well as the postructuralism of Jacques Derrida, but also to any form of materialism without realism, such as the mathematical philosophy of Alain Badiou or the 'agential realism' of Karen Barad (2017, pp. 37–39). Barad's agential realism, where consciousness is the catalyst for the emergence of reality, is a pertinent example (2007). Barad's work is derived from the Copenhagen School of quantum mechanics, which places acute emphasis on how observation of quantum systems affects the very system being measured. Pauli was a key figure in this school, and crucial in his motives to collaborate with Jung was Pauli's belief that the problem with quantum measurement did not just involve the instrumentation being used but also the internal or psychic state of the observer (Gieser, 2005, p. 71; Atmanspacher and Fach, 2013, p. 224). Does Pauli's position inevitably give way to anti-realism? Atmanspacher claims that it does not, that the idea that consciousness acts directly upon quantum states is an "unfounded fantasy" that he or past proponents of dual-aspect monism reject—even though Wheeler, at the very least, seems to go quite far in this direction (Atmanspacher & Rickles, 2022, p. 4). Yet as DeLanda and Harman note, it is often not a question of whether or not a philosopher truly believes the mind creates reality, but whether or not they have done a sufficient job in forming a philosophy that sufficiently balances these extreme positions (2017, p. 31). If this is not achieved, then one way or the other, the subject becomes a guarantor, filter, and arbiter of existence.

But how is this 'autoepistemic' knowledge cut off from true ontology inferior or any different to the psyche as middle third? After all, when we say that the psyche is that through which our knowledge of spirit and matter must pass, doesn't this effectively mean the same thing? Why should we be certain that thought and extension truly pertain to God's essence, when we are merely relying on our experience of the attributes? Is this still not just another type of correlationism, albeit better disguised? Why should we believe that the division of essence and existence is immune to the problems encountered with the split of inner and outer?

The answer lies with how we typically conceive of psychophysical parallelism, where the mental has no place in the physical, nor the physical in the mental, but they are related to one another through their shared neutral origin. In dual-aspect monism, the positing of an undivided source from which both aspects arise is supposed to deflate the issue of how psychophysical correlations arise to begin with—assuming, of course, the undivided origin is indeed guaranteed (Atmanspacher & Rickles, 2022, p. 4). Atmanspacher credits Spinoza as the originator of such a dual-aspect monism, where the aspects of existence run epistemologically parallel to one another yet emerge from an ontological whole (ibid., p. 8). And the investigation of complementary yet non-causal links between the parallel branches of mind and matter is not only a key application of the Pauli–Jung conjecture; it is also generally how synchronicity is defined (ibid., Ch. 3).

Despite this, it is actually not evident that Jung would agree with this form of parallelism.[5] Sometimes Jung speaks of the mind and body as being two ways of thinking about the same unity; or more explicitly, that the mind and body are probably one and the same thing, but we have great difficulty conceiving this (CW. 18, 1935/1977, pars. 69–70). On the surface this does not seem too different from what Atmanspacher proposes. More perplexing are passages where Jung states that the psyche is dependent on the body, that psychic processes have "intimate connections" with physical processes and therefore we cannot deny the materiality of the psyche (CW. 9i, 1948/1969b, par. 392). And even very late in his work, in the same passages where Jung writes of an *unus mundus* from which both ideal and physical things spring, he writes of *causal connections between the psyche and the body* (CW. 14, 1963/1970, par. 768)! Now certainly any causality between mind and body, at least in a straightforward sense, goes against the demands of dual-aspect monism—but it would also seem to diminish the primacy of the psyche as well, which hitherto was seemingly the point of Jung's entire project. Is this Jung simply being careless with his words? Or is even Jung, who elsewhere demands that the psyche be treated as irreducible, conceding that the psyche can be reduced to brain and physiology?

Can we once again turn to Spinoza to find an analogous question—and an answer? Although Spinoza is often associated with parallelism, he never uses the word in his philosophy. Spinoza would in fact reject the proposition that there is a multitude of non-secant lines that, as we have already witnessed, only meet beyond an ever-receding horizon. There is not an order and connection of things that is separate from an order and connection of ideas, and which nevertheless correspond with one another. Rather, the order and connection of things is the *same* whether one considers those things as ideas or as matter (E IIP7, CWS I, pp. 451–452). And this union of mind and body is immediate because the attributes are not trajectories that decompose from a remote cause and which yield correlating yet separate states, as it is with Atmanspacher's monism or Hegel's version of Spinoza. Instead, the attributes are what render modes utterly immanent to substance, because although modes and substance have different essences, the capacity to think and to act is what pertains to both (IP29S, CWS I, p. 434).

French Spinozist Chantal Jaquet has argued the word 'parallelism' should be dispensed with from Spinozist scholarship entirely, as it does nothing to "recreate the idea of unity" that Spinoza had in mind, instead introducing "a form of irreducible dualism and plurality" (Jaquet, 2019, pp. 13–14). While other approaches to the psychophysical union treat it as a "juxtaposition of two monologues that echo each other word for word, without there ever being a key phrase in one register without a matching counterpart in the other," Jaquet argues that Spinoza freely allows that "certain events are better or more strongly expressed in one register than another," that instead of seeking uniformity between thought and extension he instead views it as an equality that does not exclude alterity. The equality between "the body's power of acting and the mind's power of thinking is in reality an equality of aptitudes to express all the diversity contained in each person's nature" (ibid., pp. 11, 17–26). For example, Spinoza depicts some affects having a greater register in the body than in the mind, such as pleasure and pain (E IIIP11S, CWS I, pp. 500–501). And affectivity itself necessarily expresses the mind and the body in asymmetrical ways. The object of true ideas is nothing else than the *affections upon the body*, even if those affections are from ideas rather than other bodies. Therefore all of our affects, and our ideas of those affects, necessarily involve our body's power of acting (E IIP13S, CWS I, pp. 457–458; IVP52, p. 575). Yet at the same time, the ability to perceive actions from passions falls squarely to the mind and the common notions that it alone can construct (E IIIP3, CWS I, pp. 497–498). Similarly, Genevieve Lloyd describes how desire manifests in the body as the maintenance of one's ratio of relations, while in the mind it becomes the idea of affections that bring us joy (1996, pp. 14–25). In many respects, this can be seen as the two ways in which thought and extension are expressed in an individual. Jaquet contends that Spinoza seeks a mixed discourse for discussing the affects—and therefore all knowledge. This discourse does not reduce thought to extension, or vice versa, nor does it seek uniformity and symmetry. Instead, Spinoza describes equality of powers between the attributes, which are expressed in diverse and asymmetrical ways within a given context (Jaquet, 2019, pp. 153–156).

Affective Knowledge Revisited

What Jung seems to be wrestling with in his perplexing comments on the psyche's dependency on the body is this same mixed discourse and how intimate the connections between psyche and body are. Even if one aspect cannot be reduced to the other, there is an intricacy in their union that cannot be done justice by a vision of non-secant lines. The psyche is indeed of spirit insofar as it consists of thoughts and ideas. But unlike that broader realm of spirit, which we can easily conceive of as immaterial, the psyche exists in a "narrower sense," clearly concentrated within a specific materiality, that is, the body. Hence it seems "dependent" on it (CW. 9i, 1948/1969b, par. 392). Not only is the psyche a microcosm of spirit, and the body a microcosm of matter; but they are folds of the same thing (see Ch. 1, pp. 37–41). Now these folds of existence are nothing else than those individual compositions that define the actualization of all things (see Ch. 3, pp. 93–99). Rather than illusory emanations that decompose from a whole that has no particularity, Spinoza emphasizes how each union of mind and body constitutes a singular and unique individual, that is, *a middle third*.

Psyche, spirit, and matter all play unique roles that can't be reduced to one another. Spirit is what catalyzes the soul, awakens it; at the same time, the *unio mentalis* must descend back into the material world to truly *live* (CW. 14, 1963/1970, pars. 681, 696, 704). There is no such thing as knowledge that does not involve the body. Moreover, there is no such thing as knowledge that is not related to what *affects* the body. The mind of course is the idea of the body, and so nothing happens in the body that does not also happen in the mind. *Therefore there are no ideas the mind has that do not come from other ideas* (E IIP11–12, CWS I, pp. 456–457). The workings of the psyche and how the affects change its power of acting, that is, the *affectus*, must always be differentiated from *what* affects it, that is, the *affectio*. In other words, the affects of the psyche must be distinguished from the affections of matter and spirit. The failure to acknowledge the psyche as middle third, whether by outright elimination or by compressing it together with spirit, leads to a kind of epistemological confusion, since the fact the psyche is that through which our knowledge of spirit and matter passes is really to say that *the psyche is embedded in a greater reality that affects it*. Without that acknowledgment, one is essentially in a vacuum. If we do have faculties that developed to see the world a certain way, we are at least owed an explanation as to what caused us to evolve them in the first place. This is why Jung and Spinoza reject the autoepistemic enclosure; because their entire theory of knowledge is based on lineaments that must exist before and beyond the psyche. Unlike the insoluble gap between knowing subject and unknown object, essence and existence are never truly separate, *because essence is always found within existence*. This is proved by our very ability to transform passions into actions, as actions are explained by our essence alone (see Ch. 3). And this is exactly why psychic health is inseparable from adequate knowledge of what the psyche is and what it experiences (CW. 8, 1952/1969a, par. 429). There is no existence to speak of if the individual is not embedded within a whole; the infinite cartography a mode navigates is the very source of our passions and actions—or, once more, the source of all knowledge.

We have dispensed with an epistemology predicated upon seeking symmetries and uniformity between the two aspects of reality in favor of a theory of knowledge that expresses only the diverse powers of individual things, which is achieved by understanding how other modes intrinsically relate to us, relations that inevitably involve both ideas and matter. As we discussed at the outset of this chapter, archetypes themselves are modes, so our understanding of archetypes also comes from these intrinsic relations. Rather than being emanations that put arbitrary limits on our existence, the actualized, constellated archetype is a living thing, both as a symbol that expresses meaning and as the corporeal elements involved in its existence (CW. 6, 1921/1971, par. 816). But how do we conceive this? How are we to understand an encounter with an archetype in the same way that Spinoza discusses the way a poison or an elixir affects the body's composition? And how must we rethink the archetype's emergence in both psyche and the world, that is, synchronicity, which is usually depicted as a one-to-one correspondence between an *inner* mental state and an *outer* psychic state?

A Father's Love

In 1664, Spinoza wrote a letter to a friend of his named Pieter Balling. Balling's son had recently died, probably from the plague, which was surging through Northern Europe at the time; Balling himself likely died from the disease not long after this correspondence. Spinoza's friend was convinced that he had experienced a premonition of his son's death—namely, that while his child was still healthy, Balling had heard sickly sighs in the middle of the night, just like those the son later made when he became ill and passed away. Balling wrote to Spinoza seeking an explanation (Nadler, 1999/2018, pp. 246–250).

Rather incredibly, Spinoza agrees—he thinks his friend did experience an omen. Spinoza is quick to point out that he does not believe Balling literally heard his son's future breath, or that corporeal affects could somehow violate time. What Balling heard was the work of the imagination—but images that have their origin in the mind *can* glean omens of a future thing, "because the Mind can confusedly be aware, beforehand, of something which is future. Hence it can imagine it as firmly and vividly as if a thing of that kind were present." How is this possible? For Spinoza it simply comes down to a father's love for his son. To love one's son so that a union is formed allows one to have an idea of the son's essence, and "necessarily participate in the son's ideal essence," to have an idea of that essence's potential "affections, and consequences." Under certain conditions, this allows the father to "imagine something of what follows from [the son's] essence as vividly" as if it were occurring in the present (Ep. 17, CWS I, pp. 352–354).

One might be quick to suggest that Spinoza was merely writing comforting words for a grieving friend.[6] But if this is the case, it is surely odd that Spinoza makes intricate use of his metaphysics—specifically the eternal nature of essences, the experience of which is in many ways the aim of his entire philosophy—to simply offer his sympathies. Spinoza even gives four conditions for how these 'omens from essence' can occur. In the case of Balling and his son, the omen was possible because: (1) the incident that happened to his son was remarkable; (2) it was a distinct event that could be readily imagined; (3) the time that the incident occurred was not far off from the omen itself; and (4) Balling was "well constituted as regards health," and free of anything that might "disturb the senses externally" (ibid.).

What we are left with is a powerful demonstration of just what Spinoza thinks a discriminating imagination can do, by distinguishing between the fiction of imagined supernatural effects versus the real intermingling of essences (Lloyd, 1996, pp. 64–65). Here an adequate idea is formed not even with something that exists in extension but rather with the idea of something eternal, that is, the son's essence. The idea of a person's essence allows another to glean what may happen to that person in their lifetime, so long as the event is imminent enough, and so long as the other person who experiences the omen is of sound mind and constitution. For Spinoza, it seems omens are possible in the same way that one may experience a static charge before the thunderbolt, a 'dark precursor' before the flash of actualization.[7] This is also an example of what Spinoza thinks compounding modes are capable of. For surely the love between Balling and his son, this intermingling of essences, forms a doubly powerful individual (E IVP18S, CWS I, p. 556). And being involved in such a compound is what allows one to have affections that the mind or body would ordinarily never possess—even ideas that eclipse our own duration.[8]

Now Spinoza considers the first event in this episode, Balling's hallucination, exactly that: a product of the imagination. There is no way a corporeal cause could have an effect that precedes it; there's no way that the sound of the son's breath could have traveled back in time. Spinoza permits that hallucinations can have material causes, that the imagination can be affected by "fevers and other corporeal changes that are causes of madness." But in this case, the cause had to have been ideal. Why is this so? Balling's imagination was affected by his unconscious apprehension of what might happen to his son in the near future, and this apprehension could come from no corporeal source. It had to have originated from a sense of all the potential ways in which his son's affective power could be increased or diminished—in other words, the idea of his son's essence (Ep. 17, CWS I, pp. 352–354). Any singular essence is eternal, and the idea of each singular essence is held within the Infinite Intellect. The second and third kinds of knowledge are what let us have an idea of things as they are in the Idea of God—in other words, to view things from the eye of eternity (E IIP40S2, CWS I, p. 478). Therefore to view things from the eye of eternity is, by its necessity, an ability of the intellect (E VP15–33, CWS I, pp. 603–611).

We only know that Balling had gleaned something eternal because of what subsequently happened—his son's illness and subsequent death rattle that echoed the breathing Balling had previously imagined. If his son had never gotten sick, Balling would presumably have interpreted his hallucination as strange, but meaningless. Nor is the second event, in and of itself, extraordinary. It has a perfectly corporeal, if traumatic cause: the son's death from the plague. It is the juxtaposition of the two events together, within the otherwise seemingly random flow of nature, that causes the idea that Balling is swept up in something that exceeds him. And according to Spinoza, this idea can only be a compound mode that was forged by the love between Balling and his son.

What Spinoza describes here is a synchronicity: two disparate events are connected by a meaning that surpasses them both, and this connection cannot be explained by a corporeal cause. But what Spinoza explains is not a mere point of symmetry between mind and matter. It is true that, at first glance, there is an ideal event with the hallucination and a corporeal event in the death of the son. But Spinoza's definition would apply even if the events could not be so neatly categorized. Consider a story Jung relays from the wife of one of his patients, who had told him that, upon the respective deaths of her mother and grandmother, a flock of birds had congregated outside the windows of the rooms where they had died. Later on, the woman's husband unexpectedly collapsed and soon died thereafter—but as it happened, the wife had already been quite anxious, because birds had alighted their house (CW. 8, 1952/1969a, par. 844). Just like Balling's case, if only one event had occurred, if birds were only present at the death of *either* the mother or grandmother, but not both, and certainly not her husband as well, the woman may have just thought it was just a fitting but unremarkable addition to a mournful occasion. Instead the way each event stacks upon the other is what generates an affect that engulfs each individual occurrence. But unlike Balling's story, in this case a corporeal explanation could likely be given in each and every instance. Perhaps it just so happened that in each instance the birds were drawn to the house for random but intelligible reasons: the presence of food or shelter, a stopover during migration, and so forth. Physicist and Jungian scholar Victor Mansfield makes a similar example with the story of the recalcitrant patient and the scarab beetle—the beetle very well could have been drawn to Jung's window due to warmth or light. But that cause cannot also explain the dream the client had of the scarab the night before, or the meaning that encompasses both experiences (1995, p. 24). The *meaning* that these cases express—whether it be the scarab as a symbol of rebirth, or birds as a messenger of death, or a father's love for his son—presses into its service a mix of ideal and corporeal parts, no different than how Jung explains that the *meaning* of a leaf-cutting ant contains the ant's interaction with tree, leaf, and the ability to transport the foliage it cuts back to its home (CW. 8, 1946/1969a, pars. 398, 402). If we could somehow prove that Balling had a lingering memory of hearing the sickly breath of a random stranger who was ill while he was going about his business through plague-ridden Amsterdam, and if we proceeded to argue that his imagined hearing was but a product of cryptomnesia, it would not change the fact that the imagined hearing and the subsequent death of the son can only be connected by meaning.

The notion that meaning itself recruits into its actualization unrelated elements that otherwise might seem ordinary squares with an alternative definition to synchronicity that Jung provides, where synchronicity is the *simultaneous occurrence of two different psychic states*, where one experience seems normal and could be explained causally—the presence of birds, or hearing a cough—but the other, the *critical experience*, defies all causal explanation—in these cases, omens of death (CW. 8, 1952/1969a, par. 855). Each synchronicity seems to compound a previous one, so the meaning becomes clearer yet more improbable until it forms an idea that eclipses each specific coincidence—such as the association of birds and death. What seems at first like an ordinary, if odd, coincidence to the psyche later becomes, by the second or third synchronicity, extraordinary and unsettling. The claim that a correspondence between the ideal and physical is much less important than the way a series of experiences stack upon one another is resonant is similar to Main's proposal that synchronicity can be defined as simply two corresponding events that pertain to any combination of inner and outer, so long as no causal explanation can be given (2007, p. 19). This would certainly make it easier to account for exceptional experiences where the correspondence between the ideal and the physical is not so clear. Main points out that Jung himself struggled to explain exceptional experiences that did not conform to such a clear partition (2022, pp. 80–83). It is one thing when a person, say, dreams of honeybees and then has a bee fly through their car window while driving to work the very next morning. The correspondence is obvious. Instead, consider Jung's tale from 1916 when his house became haunted, wherein his eldest daughter claimed to have seen a ghost, his second daughter had her blanket snatched from her in the middle of the night, and his son had an anxiety dream; later, the front doorbell began ringing over and over without explanation. The hauntings ceased when Jung started to write a work that concerned departed spirits, the *Seven Sermons to the Dead*. Before that there had been a "restlessness" in Jung to compose something inspired by one of the fantasy figures that he conversed with in his process of active imagination, the 'ghostly guru' Philemon (1963/1989, pp. 189–192). Assuming this all occurred as Jung recounts it, how can we even possibly explain this occurrence in terms of psychophysical parallelism? How does the framing of correspondences between mind and matter explain a phantom of spirit demanding that Jung produce a finished work, or the hauntings that subsequently besieged the entire Jung household? Do we need to first determine if each event was either a physical or a mental anomaly, and then try and match one to the other? Or should we only deem an event synchronistic if it involves a clear correlation between a psychic state and a material state?

Perhaps it was due to these difficulties that Jung himself acknowledged there could be an alternative hypothesis to synchronicity. Main (2022, p. 82) observes that this was expressed in a conversation Jung had with American psychologist and psychical researcher James Hyslop. Jung later wrote of the discussion he had with Hyslop, who told Jung that in his opinion "all these metaphysical phenomena could be better explained by the hypothesis of spirits than by the qualities and peculiarities of the unconscious." And, Jung, based on his own experience, ultimately agrees with Hyslop, that although he must be skeptical of each and every case of exceptional anomalies, he nevertheless concedes "that the spirit hypothesis yields better results in practice than any other" (Letters, Vol. 1, 1973, p. 431).

It is difficult to see how the notion of objective spirits coincides with the theory of synchronicity. Is it a competing hypothesis, or a complementary one (Main, 2022, p. 82)? Jung himself notes that it would be an extraordinarily difficult theory to furnish proof for (Letters, Vol. 1, 1973, p. 431). And no doubt Jung was wary of utilizing spirit in this way, a concept he is so protective of, a notion so central to his 'secret complex' (see Ch. 4, pp. 128–132). Yet Jung does supply the foundation for such a hypothesis; what is more, it is a theory not contrary to synchronicity, but rather accords with it and affirms it. For spirit, that aspect of the Divine which is distinct from the psyche is in truth no different than objective meaning itself.

Spirit (or Meaning) Revisited

An identity between meaning and our personal affectivity should not be assumed. It is true that the ability to see intrinsic connections and the archetype that constellates them is the hallmark of virtue, that is, personal meaning (see Ch. 4, pp. 118–121). Nevertheless, meaning is *not* synonymous with, nor restricted to, the way in which it affects a subject. In two notable passages, Jung actually depicts meaning as something in *contradistinction* to both affectivity as well as the psychological function one uses to assess the 'value' of what affects them—feeling. In his argument for the importance of affective knowledge, Jung states that while intellectual understanding may grasp the *meaning* of a thing, it is only feeling that can grasp the *intensity* of the thing; that is to say, feeling judges how the thing affects an individual and whether that thing is good or bad for them. Intellectual judgment tells us what a thing is, that is, what it means; but value judgments give us the complete picture of what a thing is (CW. 9ii, 1959/1969c, pars. 52–53). Or, as Jung says more plainly in *Psychological Types*, it is thinking that tells us what a thing means, and feeling that tells us what its value is (CW. 6, 1921/1971, par. 983). Therefore, meaning is *not* necessarily consonant with the personal impact it has upon someone.

As we saw in Chapter 1, in multiple instances Jung uses the phrase 'spirit or meaning', which suggests he sees the terms as interchangeable. Meaning in this sense differs from personal meaning, which is precisely what Jung is referring to when he tells Pauli that a purely mythological study of dreams would tell him the *spirit or meaning* of a dream, or even an "archetypal physics," but not the personal or psychological value of what the dream expressed (Meier, 2001, p. 124; see Ch. 1, pp. 26–31). The scarab beetle as a symbol of *rebirth* is the objective 'spirit or meaning' of the synchronicity it manifests in, irrespective of the impact it had on the recalcitrant patient herself. *Birds and death* bring to light motifs that have mantic significance, an objective meaning that exists independently of the woman whose husband dropped dead (CW. 8, 1952/1969a, par. 850). And *a* father's love for his son has repeated and recurred countless times before, during, and after the life of Peter Balling. According to Jung, these are all examples of an *objective meaning* that exists beyond the psyche, an objective meaning that implicates the existence of archetypes (ibid., par. 915). But because this type of meaning is no different than spirit itself, then in this context *spirit must be the ideal expression of archetypal compositions.*

Now this notion of objective meaning accomplishes several things. First, it accounts for synchronicities where multiple people are involved, such as the scarab beetle story. This symbol was of great interest to Jung before his dealings with his reluctant client, and the appearance of the insect at his office window was in many ways a synchronicity for him as well (Main, 2013, pp. 137–140; Saban, 2019, p. 189). Rather than wonder if Jung's interests influenced his client, we can instead propose that both of them were affected by and caught up within the same composition of spirit. Another example would be with the woman whose husband collapsed. Recall that the husband was a patient of Jung's. As it so happened, Jung had noted some of the husband's physical symptoms might have been a sign of serious cardiac issues (CW. 8, 1952/1969a, par. 850). What was a very conscious concern for Jung was an unconscious fear in the patient's wife, which suggests that objective meaning involves people at differing proximities and depths, which would complement Jung's supposition about an 'archetypal physics'.

Second, objective meaning does not discount the existence of affective or personal meaning; on the contrary, it guarantees it. The value or intensity of a thing, which Jung contrasts with objective meaning, *is precisely what personal meaning is*. Archetypal compositions affect individuals who become involved in them. For Jung's patient, this forced a complete change in her attitude. Peter Balling perhaps found peace, or even rejoiced, in the love he still shared with his son's essence, a complete transformation of his grief. It is the excavation of intrinsic connections of the unconscious, the apprehension of common notions and symbols, and the following of those leads to archetypal or essential causes that allow one to apprehend the objective meaning of the situation they become mired in (see Ch. 3). The apprehension of these archetypal compositions, which one is otherwise unaware that they are within the spell of, is the wellspring for psychic growth, that is, individuation, which we have demonstrated is Jung's *personal meaning*, as well as Spinoza's idea of virtue (see Ch. 4, pp. 121–118). It is the very navigation of the archetypes that we are compounded by that in turn affords a chance for our psychic development. This is why synchronicity and individuation are so closely linked.[9] When Jung claims the unconscious seems to transgress space and time during synchronicity, it cannot be because the psyche literally bends spacetime to its will. Rather, one becomes aware of being compounded by something at a scale much larger than oneself, that passes through time in a way wildly different than one's own affectivity.

What then of *collective meaning*, the awareness that one is immersed in something larger than oneself, that one is implicated within a transcendental immanence (ibid.)? This notion overlaps with objective meaning, but it also implies a *numinous* affect that acts as a bridge with personal meaning. Therefore, arguably *three* types of meaning can be found in Jung's writing: first, the personal meaning of psychic growth; next, an objective meaning that, as Jung explains it to Pauli, is purely metaphysical and *not* psychological, and therefore is a sort of archetypal physics, the ideal expression of an archetype with no personal consideration taken into account (Meier, 2001, pp. 114–115); and, finally, a collective meaning that connects the personal with the objective, such as when one uncovers the archetypal core at the heart of a complex affecting them. To consider an archetype on its own is to describe its objective meaning, but when describing the archetype's effect on an individual, one then speaks of collective meaning.

Since meaning is of spirit—if not spirit itself—it is inherently ideal. In other words, *the idea of something corporeal is also its meaning*. This is in contrast to a depiction of meaning where it acts as a bridge *between* the mental and physical, between "a representation and what it represents." This is one way in which Atmanspacher deploys meaning, stressing that he prefers not to assign meaning to a mental state, but rather, as a 'meta-representation' between mental and physical states (Atmanspacher & Rickles, 2022, p. 52). For Spinoza this is a redundant step. After all, *all ideas are representations*; what matters is the quality of the idea one has. If it is inadequate, the idea will represent a confused mix of oneself and the thing one is affected by; if it is adequate, it will be the idea of a thing's essence (E IIP16C2, CWS I, p. 463; E IIP40S2, pp. 477–478). If the idea of something is properly posed, it requires no further explanation; once it is known, it cannot be expressed in any better way. This reflexive nature of an idea is simply due to the fact that an idea and its object share the same *formal* essence (E IIP13S, CWS I, pp. 457–458). To postulate anything else is an unnecessary step. Therefore, to conceive something intelligibly is to also explain its essence—and therefore also the cause of its existence (Della Rocca, 2008, pp. 92–98). And so to have an adequate idea of an archetypal composition one becomes involved in is to also apprehend its *meaning*. Again, as Jung says about the image of the leaf-cutting ant and all the components it incorporates—the ant, its ability to cut and carry, the tree and leaf, etc.—the meaning of a situation becomes self-evident (CW. 8, 1946/1969a, pars. 398, 402). For Balling, to understand his hallucination and his son's death were interlinked was to understand the loving bond he shared with his son. For the recalcitrant patient, to understand the importance of the scarab symbol was to understand the importance of her rebirth. *If meaning is also the cause of a thing, then meaning is also the cause of synchronicity.* To be sure this does not point to a reductive or corporeal cause, but rather an explanation that eclipses our normal scale of affectivity. Birds were not deliberately seeking out the woman whose husband, mother, and grandmother all passed in the presence of birds; nevertheless, the entire story can only be explained—and therefore was precipitated—by the symbolism of birds witnessing death. When ghosts made their editorial demands to Jung, there was no linear chain of causality that can explain each episode in the haunting of the Jung household; but the ghostly demands *are* the cause of the entire situation because they express the necessity for Jung to write the *Seven Sermons to the Dead*—and this need, and the transformation it caused, is therefore the meaning of the entire story. The reason for this is because just as we have a singular essence that is expressed both as mind and body, so too does an archetypal composition. The psychoid factor is what designates this *middle third* of the archetype, between spirit and matter. The psychoid aspect of the archetype refers to its singular essence, which exists within the same spectrum as any other essence conceived by God.

Now just as meaning is not simply a referent between mind and matter, neither should it be depicted as a fleeting glimpse into a remote cause of our synchronicities, to which we never have true access—an ontological miracle of immanence as some effervescent sense of our psychophysically neutral origin (Atmanspacher & Rickles, 2022, pp. 77–80). Such a scheme is only necessary when the middle third is not accounted for, when psyche and archetypes are not seen as individuals among other individuals on the same plane and thereby the psyche is affected by things that transcend yet remain immediate to it. Emanation or decomposition will always be too slow, too many steps behind, to truly grasp a synchronicity's actualization, to fully comprehend how spirit or meaning constellates itself with greater and greater clarity, until the 'critical events' in which it actualizes become manifest to even the most skeptical of observers. Consider the account Main gives of the synchronistic experiences of former British Chess Champion

James Plaskett, or of mystic Edward Thornton, where coincidences with varying motifs and images seemed to converge and ramify atop one another, even involving other people with whom they shared the experiences with, as if multiple compositions collided and converged, until the meaning could only be expressed plainly, bluntly—even violently (Main, 2007, Ch. 4–6). To trace the intrinsic connections of such compositions, to follow these lines of flight, is to follow ideas as they occur in the mind of God. For methodologies that prioritize identifying correspondences or backtracking along lines of emanation, this dynamism will likely remain elusive.

Fields of Sense and Affordances

It must be acknowledged that Atmanspacher provides alternate ways in which meaning might be deployed in his model, including directions that would seem contrary to the mental representations and correlationism found in Metzinger. For instance, his recent work has focused on the "New Ontological Realism" of speculative realist Markus Gabriel, where reality is defined by "fields of sense" and their relations with one another. To give an example of his ontology, Gabriel asks us to imagine we are standing in front of Mount Etna in Sicily. While a metaphysics that attempts to explain things with absolute objectivity might argue that one can describe the volcano in a way that voids how we think of it, and while an *anti-realist* approach would insist it is our perspective that creates the volcano, Gabriel instead posits that our sense of the volcano is what is grounded in reality, and this sense varies from perspective to perspective: we may see Mount Etna as a mountain, but from the perspective of a Martian with a completely inverted spatial orientation to our own, it may see Mount Etna as a valley. In Gabriel's estimation, both perspectives or *senses* are ontologically valid (2015, Loc 359). In this framework, as Atmanspacher observes, the human mind "does not stand detached face-to-face to a perceived external reality but is always already embedded in a field of sense" and each "situation establishes its own field of sense as its own reality" (Atmanspacher & Rickles, 2022, p. 36). Here we find affinity to an *objective meaning* that is immanent to the world. Atmanspacher also draws upon the work of ecological psychologist James Gibson (1979), whose notion of 'affordances' describes the capacities of an organism to act and be acted upon by its environment. Gibson's work is utilized by Manuel DeLanda to expand the way in which Deleuze discusses how an individual should not be defined by what it *is*, but rather by its capacity to affect and be affected (2002, pp. 63–64). And in turn Deleuze draws this priority of 'what a thing can do' over 'what a thing is' from his reading of Spinoza's affective powers (1970/1988, pp. 48–51). In other words, the affordance of an organism can be related to its affectivity, and therefore also its ability to act from its own power, that is, *personal meaning*.

This alternate route that Atmanspacher proposes suggests several things. First, meaning as a *sense* is emphasized over meaning as *reference*. For Gabriel in fact, no distinction should be made between an object and its concept (2015, Loc 112). This reflexive nature of meaning or ideas is precisely what we find with Spinoza and Jung described previously. Therefore, this direction demands a certain concession from Atmanspacher: both the theory of affordances as well as 'fields of sense' point him in the direction of realism, because both theories emphasize the relations between all individuals, where the human and non-human alike play by the same rules. For Gabriel this is an ontological pluralism, where reality is constituted by a multiplicity of perspectives that interlock and complicate one another (ibid., Loc 3811–12). Atmanspacher is grasping this issue when, in regards to Gabriel's theory, he asks just how one is to articulate relations between varying fields of sense (Atmanspacher & Rickles, 2022, p. 36). To reconcile this approach with his decompositional monism, Atmanspacher again appeals to relative onticity, where any scope of description can be treated as ontological, if necessary. Yet if this is the case, it is not simply due to choosing what explanation is practical for a given context, but rather because every individual or 'field of sense' must be seen as ontologically valid. Individuals cannot be treated as corrupted fragments that decay from a hidden one. The fringes of atomic physics or the depths of the unconscious may indeed be where we glimpse a scale infinitely beyond our own place in the universe, but such an infinity merely implies the existence of an absolute power that contains *all scales and all existences*. Essence, whether God's or an individual's, is always ontological.

Yet this leaves us with an outstanding question. If what we are ultimately describing is not an interplay of mind and body, but rather the actualization of eternal essences that are expressed both as ideas and as bodies, then what exactly does this mean for the psyche as the middle third? Is not the psyche, though not the same as spirit, still of an *ideal* existence? Has its role as our neutral medium been usurped? What, precisely, is the psyche's relation to essence?

Notes

1   In addition to the finite modes of singular things, Spinoza also writes of 'infinite modes' that are produced immediately by God (E IP21, CWS I pp. 429–430). What does this mean? Under the attribute of thought, for example, the immediate infinite mode is none other than God's Infinite Intellect, or rather the eternal ideas of everything that God can and must create. Under extension, Spinoza states that the immediate infinite mode is "motion and rest," or rather the potential of all 'ratio of relations' that, we have seen, defines the composition of any potential mode; in other words, eternal, physical essences (Ep. 64, CWS II pp. 438–439; see Ch. 3, pp. 93–99). Therefore the immediate infinite modes, whether conceived under thought or extension, contain the infinity of singular essences that God produces (E VP22, CWS I p. 607). In addition, there are also infinite modes that are mediated by, or rather follow from, these immediate infinite modes (E IP22, CWS I, p. 430). Spinoza gives only one example of a mediate infinite mode, specifically for the attribute of extension: "the face of the whole Universe, which, however much as it may vary in infinite ways, nevertheless always remains the same" (Ep. 64, CWS II, pp. 438–439).

It may seem reasonable to ascribe archetypes to either of these infinite kinds of modes; so, when considered under spirit (or thought), either the Infinite Intellect or whatever the mediate infinite mode might entail. And certainly one might find an affinity between an Infinite Intellect that contains all eternal ideas that endlessly actualize in duration on the one hand, and on the other a collective unconscious that holds all the primordial thoughts or "images" that repeat in varying manifestations throughout history (E IP16, CWS I, pp. 424–425; CW. 7, 1916/1966, pars. 106–109). But while the archetypes are contained in the collective unconscious, they are not really equivalent to it. Rather they are distinct eternal ideas that are contained within this timeless reservoir. The archetypes may indeed mesh, blend, and entwine with one another, or they may reveal themselves within one another, such as how the archetype of the shadow leads one to their anima or animus, and then to the wise old sage—but they are distinct ideas, and one of the objectives of Jung's work is to describe them as such (CW. 9i, 1954a/1969b, pars. 45–86). What is more, Spinoza is explicitly clear that the infinite modes cannot be reduced to specific modes (E IP28, CWS I, pp. 432–433). The whole can never be reduced to its parts, which may vary in infinite ways within it, without any change to the whole (E IIP13SL7, CWS I, pp. 461–462). To suggest otherwise would again suggest that the Divine creates certain finite modes at expense of others. The introduction of the infinite modes, which all finite modes are essentially included within as "part of a package" that God produces wholesale, is in fact Spinoza's way of avoiding this problem (Della Rocca, 2008, pp. 70–71). Therefore, it seems that the archetypes are best conceived of as finite modes.

2   An issue left unspoken here is that by saying archetypes are just another kind of individual mode, one is putting them on the same plane as people, rocks,

and stars, among anything else imaginable. One might object that this approach glosses over any difference between things that are universal or common to many, such as an archetype or a species like *Homo sapiens* versus particular things with singular existences, like a specific person, or *this* rock or *that* star. Is this not some sort of categorical error? The question comes down to how Spinoza defines the nature, or essence, of singular things, and whether or not they are universal or particular. In other words, is there just a general essence for say, *Homo sapiens*, or is there a unique essence for every person? There is little doubt Spinoza upholds the existence of *particular* essences, for example, an essence specific to Tim and a different essence specific to Dave; but despite classifying universals as inadequate ideas, he at times speaks of general essences too, such as an essence that is common to all humanity. Della Rocca suggests that Spinoza allows for both general and specific essences (2008, p. 95). Why this is the case, and how to explain it in a way that does not appeal to the kind of taxonomy that Spinoza otherwise rejects, is an outstanding problem in Spinozist literature. Also, see Hübner (2016).

3   That archetypes are entirely indifferent to the outmoded question of 'nature versus nurture' is captured in Erik B. Goodwyn's proposal that archetypes emerge from a 'middle third' between biology and culture, and that they deploy elements of both in their actualization. Goodwyn further mirrors the proposal given here by suggesting that the reason archetypes can constellate as such is because the thresholds that trigger their appearance are common to all humans (2023).

4   "Correlationism" in the sense used by Quentin Meillassoux in his book *After Finitude*, which essentially refers to the tendency of the human and the world always coming in a pair (2008, p. 5).

5   Brooke states that Jung never seemed entirely satisfied with explanations proffered by his associates, who suggested that the relationship between mind and body could be explained by meaningful correspondences in the same way that synchronicity is typically discussed (see Brooke, 2015, p. 70).

6   This is precisely what Steven Nadler suggests in his characteristically secular interpretation of Spinoza (1999/2018, p. 250). Aside from the fact that Spinoza does a lot of philosophy here to 'just be nice' to a grieving friend, it does not seem in Spinoza's character to simply 'make something up', especially when it concerns ideas of great importance to him. Spinoza was indeed cautious about fully explaining his philosophy to people he did not fully trust—a measure to protect himself from the authorities of his day. But nor was Spinoza ever hesitant to dismiss ideas he found absurd, such as his somewhat impatient dismissal of a correspondent's naive belief in ghosts (Ep. 54, CWS II, pp. 413–416).

7   'Dark precursor' is a term used by Deleuze to describe how the actualization of something is preceded by a constellation of intensities that presage it. "Thunderbolts explode between different intensities, but they are preceded by an invisible, imperceptible *dark precursor*, which determines their path in advance but in reverse, as though intagliated" (see Deleuze, 1968/1994, p. 119).

8 Jung cites a portion of this letter in his medical dissertation, specifically an example that Spinoza gives to Balling to explain why the breathing he heard could not have been from actual sounds. Balling had noted that when he sat up in bed and moved his head to better hear the noise, it faded. Spinoza notes that this is a sign it was but a hallucination and not something of a material cause. By example he proffers a vision of his own, concerning images from a dream Spinoza had in his sleep that lingered when he woke up, particularly the image of a "scabby Brazilian" stalking at his bedside. Yet as Spinoza diverted his attention to a book or some other object, the image eventually faded (Ep. 17, CWS I, p. 353). Jung, while discussing people who suffer from waking visions, notes that highly imaginative people are especially susceptible to them, and then mentions Spinoza's vision of the Brazilian as an example (CW. 1, 1957/1970, par. 100, n. 49). It is tempting to wonder what Jung thought about the rest of this letter, as he surely would have taken a great interest in Spinoza's argument for precognition. However, Jung cites this passage through a secondary source, *Zur Theorie der Hallucination* by German psychiatrist Freidrich Wilhelm Hagen (1868). Hagen only raises Spinoza's example of the lingering dream image. Therefore, there is no evidence that Jung was aware of the rest of the letter's contents.

9 The link between the process of individuation and the meaning expressed by a synchronicity is why physicist and Jungian scholar Victor Mansfield argues synchronicity should be distinguished from all other forms of anomalous experiences (1995, p. 29).

References

Addison, A. (2019). *Jung's Psychoid Concept Contexualised*. London: Routledge.

Adler, G. & Jaffe, A. (1973). *C.G. Jung Letters 1: 1906–1950*. Translated by R. Hull. Princeton: Princeton University Press.

Adler, G. & Jaffe, A. (1975). *C.G. Jung Letters 2: 1951–1961*. Translated by R. Hull. Princeton: Princeton University Press.

Atmanspacher, H. (2012). 'Dual-Aspect Monism à la Pauli and Jung', *Journal of Consciousness Studies*, 19(9–10), 96–120.

Atmanspacher, H. & Fach, W. (2013). "A Structural–Phenomenological Typology of Mind–Matter Correlations." *Journal of Analytical Psychology*, 58, 219–244.

Atmanspacher, H. & Fach, W. (2014). "Introduction," in *The Pauli–Jung Conjecture and its Impact Today*, edited by H. Atmanspacher & W. Fach. Exeter: Imprint Academic.

Atmanspacher, H. & Fach, W. (2019). "Exceptional Experiences of Stable and Unstable Mental States, Understood from a Dual-Aspect Point of View," *Philosophies*, 4(1), 7.

Atmanspacher, H. & Kronz, F. (1999). "Relative Onticity," in *On Quanta, Mind and Matter: Hans Primas in Context*, edited by H. Atmanspacher, A. Amann & U. Muller-Herold. Dordrecht: Springer.

Atmanspacher, H. & Rickles, D. (2022). *Dual-Aspect Monism and the Deep Structure of Meaning*. London & New York: Routledge.

Barad, K. (2007). *Meeting the Universe Halfway: Quantum Physics and the Entanglement of Matter and Meaning*. Durham: Duke University Press.

Brooke, R. (2015). *Jung and Phenomenology*. London & New York: Routledge.

DeLanda, M. (2002). *Intensive Science & Virtual Philosophy*. London & New York: Bloomsbury Academic.

DeLanda, M. & Harman, G (2017). *The Rise of Realism*. Cambridge, UK & Malden, Massachusetts: Polity Press.

Deleuze, G. (1968/1994). *Difference & Repetition*. Translated by Paul Patton. New York: Columbia University Press.

Deleuze, G. (1970/1988). *Spinoza: Practical Philosophy*. Translated by R. Hurley. San Francisco: City Light Books.

Della Rocca, M. (2008). *Spinoza*. London & New York: Routledge.

FoundationINTERVIEWS. (2014). "Jason Alexander Discusses the Seinfeld Reunion on 'Curb Your Enthusiasm' – EMMYTVLEGENDS.ORG." www.yout ube.com/watch?v=9spg6o-wIWU (Accessed April 2023).

Gabriel, M. (2015). *Fields of Sense: A New Realist Ontology (Speculative Realism)*. Edinburgh: Edinburgh University Press.

Gibson, J. (1979). *The Ecological Approach to Visual Perception*. Boston: Houghton Mifflin Company.

Gieser, S. (2005). *The Innermost Kernel: Depth Psychology and Quantum Physics. Wolfgang Pauli's dialogue with C.G. Jung*. Berlin: Springer.

Goodwyn, E. (2023). "Archetypal Origins: Biology vs Culture Is a False Dichotomy" (Ch. 2), in *Archetypal Ontology: New Directions in Analytical Psychology*, edited by J. Mills & E. Goodwyn. London & New York: Routledge.

Hagen, F.W. (1868). "Zur Theorie der Hallucinationen." *Allgemeine Zeitschrift Für Psychiatrie*, 25, 1–113.

Harman, G. (2011). "The Problem with Metzinger." *Cosmos and History: The Journal of Natural and Social Philosophy*, 7(1), 7–36.

Hübner, K. (2016). "Spinoza on Essences, Universals, and Beings of Reason." *Pacific Philosophical Quarterly*, 97(1), 1–155.

Jaquet, C. (2019). *Affects, Actions and Passions in Spinoza: The Unity of Body and Mind*. Translated by T. Reznichenko. Edinburgh: Edinburgh University Press.

Jung, C.G. (1916). *Two Essays on Analytical Psychology*, 2nd ed. Translated by R. Hull. Collected Works of C.G. Jung, Vol. 7. Princeton: Princeton University Press, 1966.

Jung, C.G. (1921). *Psychological Types*, 2nd ed. Translated by R. Hull. Collected Works of C.G. Jung, Vol. 6. Princeton: Princeton University Press, 1971.

Jung, C.G. (1926) "Spirit and Life," in *The Structure and Dynamics of the Psyche*, 2nd ed. Translated by R. Hull. Collected Works of C.G. Jung, Vol. 8. Princeton: Princeton University Press, 1969a.

Jung, C.G. (1935). "The Tavistock Lectures," in *The Symbolic Life*, 2nd ed. Translated by R. Hull. Collected Works of C.G. Jung, Vol. 18. Princeton: Princeton University Press, 1977.

Jung, C.G. (1946). "On the Nature of the Psyche," in *The Structure and Dynamics of the Psyche*, 2nd ed. Translated by R. Hull. Collected Works of C.G. Jung, Vol. 8. Princeton: Princeton University Press, 1969a.

Jung, C.G. (1948). "The Phenomenology of the Spirit in Fairytales," in *The Archetypes and the Collective Unconscious*, 2nd ed. Translated by R. Hull. Collected Works of C.G. Jung, Vol. 9i. Princeton: Princeotn University Press, 1969b.

Jung, C.G. (1952). "Synchronicity: An Acausal Connecting Principle," in *The Structure and Dynamics of the Psyche*, 2nd ed. Translated by R. Hull. Collected Works of C.G. Jung, Vol. 8. Princeton: Princeton University Press, 1969a.

Jung, C.G. (1954). "Archetypes of the Collective Unconscious," in *The Archetypes and the Collective Unconscious*, 2nd ed. Translated by R. Hull. Collected Works of C.G. Jung, Vol. 9i. Princeton: Princeton University Press, 1969b.

Jung, C.G. (1957). *Psychiatric Studies*. 2nd ed. Translated by R. Hull. Collected Works of C.G. Jung, Vol. 1. Princeton: Princeton University Press, 1970.

Jung, C.G. (1959). *Aion: Researches into the Phenomenology of the Self*, 2nd ed. Translated by R. Hull. Collected Works of C.G. Jung, Vol. 9ii. Princeton: Princeton University Press, 1969c.

Jung, C.G. (1963). *Mysterium Coniunctionis*, 2nd ed. Translated by R. Hull. Collected Works of C.G. Jung, Vol. 14. Princeton: Princeton University Press, 1970.

Jung, C.G. (1963/1989). *Memories. Dreams, Reflections*. Edited by A. Jaffe, Translated by R. Winston and C. Winston. New York: Vintage Books.

Langan, R. (2020). "Jung, Spinoza, Deleuze: A Move Towards Realism" (Ch. 10), in *Holism: Possibilities and Problems*, edited by C. McMillan, R. Main & D. Henderson. London: Routledge.

Lloyd, G. (1996). *Routledge Philosophy Guidebook to Spinoza and the Ethics*. London: Routledge.

Main, R. (2007). *Revelations of Chance: Synchronicity as Spiritual Experience*. New York: State University of New York.

Main, R. (2013). "Myth, Synchronicity, and Re-enchantment," in *Myth, Literature and the Unconscious*, edited by L. Burnett, S. Bahun, & R. Main. London: Karnac Books.

Main, R. (2022). *Breaking the Spell of Disenchantment: Mystery, Meaning, and Metaphysics in the Work of C.G. Jung*. The Zurich Lecture Series: Volume 8. Asheville, NC: Chiron Publications.

Mansfield, V. (1995). *Synchronicity, Science, and Soul-Making: Understanding Jungian Synchronicity through Physics, Buddhism, and Philosophy*. Chicago & La Salle, IL: Open Court.

Matheron, A. (2020). *Politics, Ontology, and Knowledge in Spinoza*. Translated by D. Maruzzella and G. Morejon. Edinburgh: Edinburgh University Press.

Meier, C.A. (ed.) (2001). *Atom and Archetype: The Pauli/Jung Letters 1932–1958*. London: Routledge.

Meillassoux, Q. (2008). *After Finitude: An Essay on the Necessity of Contingency*. Translated by Ray Brassier. London: Continuum.

Metzinger, T. (2003). *Being No One: The Self-Model Theory of Subjectivity*. Cambridge, MA: The MIT Press.

Nadler, S. (1999/2018). *Spinoza: A Life*, 2nd ed. Cambridge: Cambridge University Press.

Primas, H. (2003). "Time-entanglement between Mind and Matter," *Mind and Matter*, 1, 81–119.

Primas, H. (2017). *Knowledge and Time*. Edited and Annotated by H. Atmanspacher. Cham, Switzerland: Springer.

Saban, M. (2019). *'Two Souls Alas': Jung's Two Personalities and the Making of Analytical Psychology*. The Zurich Lecture Series: Volume 2. Asheville, NC: Chiron Publications.

Spinoza, B. (1985). *The Collected Works of Spinoza*, Vol. I, Edited and translated by Edwin Curley. Princeton: Princeton University Press.

Spinoza, B. (2016). *The Collected Works of Spinoza*, Vol. II, Edited and translated by Edwin Curley. Princeton: Princeton University Press.

Chapter 6

We Are the Third, God Is the Fourth

On the Univocal Psyche and the Blessed Self

While reading Jung, one sometimes has the fear that one's interpretations are groundless, that any conclusions about what Jung 'really meant' on some given topic are nothing but a kind of conceptual Rorschach test, where one conclusion is as good as any other. This is due in part to the multiple and at times contradictory definitions Jung gives for some of his most important ideas throughout the *Collected Works*. The archetype, for instance, has been the focus of multiple texts that attempt to wrangle and come to terms with the myriad explanations Jung gives for their existence (Knox, 2003; Roesler, 2022). Some of Jung's inconsistency is surely due to his theories developing throughout his life, which caused him to overwrite older conceptions—his gradual differentiation between instincts, archetypes, and spirit is one such example of this (see Ch. 1, pp. 26–31). Nevertheless, there are instances where the chronology does not support this, where Jung's inconsistencies appear both in his early and later work. His treatment of the psyche in relation to spirit and matter is such a case.

To review, in the 1953 correspondence with Pauli, Jung adamantly argues that the psyche must be seen as the middle third between spirit and matter. To highlight his point, Jung outlines a quaternity that places spirit and matter on the ends of the horizontal axis, with psyche at the bottom of the vertical axis, and a transcendental fourth on top of that vertical line (Meier, 2001, pp. 84–129). This scheme matches what Jung first introduced a few years earlier in 'On the Nature of the Psyche', a tripartite spectrum of matter, psyche, and spirit, as well as a fourth element, the psychoid, that both the ideal and physical emerge from (CW. 8, 1946/1969a, pars. 419–420). A true opposition between spirit and matter is much more evident than between the psyche and body, which feature some sort of undeniable interdependence; hence Jung speculates that spirit and matter may be two forms of the

DOI: 10.4324/9781003516996-7

same transcendental being (CW. 9i, 1948/1969b, pars. 391–392). Therefore the psyche moves within a transcendental immanence that is expressed both through spirit and matter. This was the initial meeting point between Jung and Spinoza, on which Jung's unlikely Spinozism is predicated (see Ch. 2).

Yet even after Jung formalizes his tripartite monism, there are instances where he still speaks of the fundamental opposition as if it were between the psyche and matter, not matter and spirit. This occurs in *Mysterium Coniunctionis*, where he discusses psyche and matter as being fundamental expressions of the *unus mundus* (CW. 14, 1963/1970, par. 766). It happens again in the final letter he writes to Pauli in 1957, where Jung states that "psychic" and "material" are the attributes of the psychoid (Meier, 2001, pp. 166–169). On the surface this completely disregards the very distinction of psyche and spirit that Jung so adamantly argued for to Pauli just four years prior!

Now as we have seen, an answer for these seeming contradictions can be gleaned from the fact that Jung sees the psyche as a microcosm of spirit, just as the body is a microcosm of matter (see Ch. 1, pp. 37–41). Similarly, when Jung speaks of intimate connections between psyche and body, he very well may simply be acknowledging that they are intricate expressions of the same thing (see Ch. 5, pp. 153–159). However, Jung continues to not only speak of an opposition between psyche and matter but also that of *inner and outer*. In a letter Jung writes to Pauli in 1956, again after the crucial 1953 correspondence, Jung speaks of "inner and outer opposites" that only the whole person can reconcile. In Chapter 4 we demonstrated that Jung's distinction between psyche and spirit was also effectively spirit's liberation from the intrapsychic (pp. 128–135). This portrayal of *inner and outer* as aspects of the world that only the individuated person can distinguish would seem to run contrary to any such liberation. Of course, Jung's highlighting of inside versus outside here comes from the context of Pauli's dreams, which, among other symbolic content, concerned forming 'eyes' into one's inner spiritual world in addition to the outer sensory world—and so arguably Jung is reaffirming his position that a whole person abolishes the distinction of inner and outer altogether (Meier, 2001, pp. 134–157). Yet it is also possible that all these contrary examples can be attributed to the fact that even after Jung declares the distinction between psyche and spirit, within his lifetime he never fully accepted the unmooring of spirit from the inner world, that even as he made his moves toward Spinozism, he was still holding onto his 'secret complex', and so in his mature work he was basically, as Mark Saban puts it, creating two different psychologies that reflected the crossroads he was at (2019, Ch. 6).

Even this concession does not explain the following passage from *Memories, Dreams, Reflections*, where Jung reminisces about his visit to the Athi Plains in Kenya. While observing the savanna, and herds of different animals moving about, heads nodding as they grazed, Jung was struck with the feeling that he was "the first human being to recognize that this was the world, but who did not know that in this moment he had first really created it." He goes on:

> There the cosmic meaning of consciousness became overwhelmingly clear to me. "What nature leaves imperfect, the art perfects," says the alchemists. Man, I, in an invisible act of creation put the stamp of perfection on the world by giving it objective existence. This act we usually ascribe to the Creator alone, without considering that in so doing we view life as a machine calculated down to the last detail, which, along with the human psyche, runs on senselessly, obeying foreknown and predetermined rules. In such a cheerless clockwork fantasy there is no drama of man, world, and God; there is no "new day" leading to "new shores," but only the dreariness of calculated processes. My old Pueblo friend came to my mind. He thought that the *raison d'etre* of his pueblo had been to help their father, the sun, to cross the sky each day. I had envied him for the fullness of meaning in that belief, and had been looking about without hope for a myth of our own. Now I knew what it was, and knew even more: that man is indispensable for the completion of creation; that, in fact, he himself is the second creator of the world, who alone has given to the world its objective existence—without which, unheard, unseen, silently eating, giving birth, dying, heads nodding through hundreds of millions of years, it would have gone on in the profoundest night of non-being down to its unknown end. Human consciousness created objective existence and meaning, and man found his indispensable place in the great process of being.
>
> (1963/1989, pp. 255–256)

It appears to stretch credulity to interpret this passage as Jung saying anything other than the world is dependent on the psyche—the *human* psyche—for its existence. This would be an undeniably anti-realist position; and

Atmanspacher in fact cites this same excerpt when discussing Wheeler's "participatory universe," claiming that Jung too believes that the universe can only come into existence from "observership" (Atmanspacher & Rickles, 2022, p. 107). Jung says something similar in 'On the Nature of the Psyche'—just three paragraphs after he formalizes the tripartite spectrum of matter, psyche, and spirit. Here, Jung writes that the "psyche is the world's pivot," and that "it is the one great condition for the existence of the world at all"; furthermore, the psyche is "an intervention in the existing natural order, and no one can say with certainty when this intervention will finally end" (CW. 8, 1946/1969a, par. 423). Not only is this another capitulation toward the universe's dependence on the psyche, but the psyche is described as a 'disruptor' of the natural order, rather than being a part of it. In other words, the psyche becomes a "dominion within a dominion," precisely what Spinoza cannot accept (E III Preface, CWS I, p. 491).[1] It is one thing to say that the psyche is the source of all experience and thus must be conceived as the neutral third. It is quite another to state that it is the *cause* of all existence. How do we reconcile this apparent identity of the psyche as creator, when the same man who makes this claim also says that to introject the role of God is to have a Superman psychosis (Letters, 1975, Vol. 2, p. 407)? In other words, how do we make sense of this cosmic valorization of the psyche when much of Jung's own thinking runs contrary to it?

An adjacent issue concerns the archetype of the self. In the previous chapter, we depicted archetypes as compound modes by which individuals become subsumed, and thus they actualize both within us and outside us (see Ch. 5, pp. 139–144). How does this theory of archetypal compositions relate to the self, which is supposed to be both the center and circumference of all psychic processes (CW. 12, 1953/1968, par. 44)? Atmanspacher suggests that the self is an overarching structure of the psychophysically neutral whole that is then projected into the personal conscious ego. Following the phenomenological model of Metzinger, the ego is nothing more than an epistemic fiction (Atmanspacher & Fach, 2019, p. 17). Pauli also held this line of thought, believing that the self could be conceived as the "superordinate organizing principle overarching psyche and the world" (Gieser, 2005, p. 281). When Jung speaks of the self as the "God within us," is he really capitulating to this anti-realist perspective and all its paradoxes, such as the belief that it is our perspective that creates the world, even though our very individuality on which this perspective is formed is illusory (CW.

7, 1916/1966, par. 399)? After all this, do we discover that this primacy of the psyche proves to be an irreconcilable difference between Jung and Spinoza?

Self, Other, God

The archetypal self seems replete with contradictions. How can the self be the totality of the psyche, including the archetypes, yet also an archetype in its own right? Of course, this question ignores Jung's declaration that the archetypes should no longer be considered of the psyche, which is what prompted our Spinozist construction of archetypes as modes; but how can this advancement apply to the self as well, when the self is the very potential of one's own personality, the "unconscious prefiguration" of the ego (CW. 11, 1954/1969d, pars. 390–391)? If the attainment or realization of the self is the goal of individuation, how can the archetypal self also be 'outside' of us (CW. 7, 1916/1966, par. 405; CW. 9i, 1940/1969b, par. 278)? Or, at the very least, if the ego is to be distinguished from the archetypes, how is it nonetheless that the ego is something that 'crystallizes' out of the unconscious depths (CW. 9i, 1939/1969b, par. 503)? In an attempt to clear up these issues, Jungian psychiatrist Michael Fordham proposes that the self should be seen not as an archetype, but beyond both archetypes and ego, which both "deintegrate" from the self (1963). Therefore the self becomes a "special transcendental concept" (Samuels, 1985, p. 106).

But does such a mapping do justice to the numinous power that the self is supposed to bestow upon the experiencing ego? This harkens directly back to Jung's critique of 'hollow' philosophical knowledge: a metaphysical idea that does not account for the *affect* something has upon an individual is worthless (CW. 9ii, 1959/1969c, pars. 50–61). Jungian scholar Lucy Huskinson suggests that this affectivity must be paramount in any discussion of the self, namely that the 'violence' the self has upon the ego, or rather its transformative and creative impact, must be fully depicted. To do this, Huskinson enlists the work of French philosopher Emmanuel Levinas (1906–1995), who argues that the ego can only exist in relation to an infinite 'Other' that the ego depends on for its very existence; but while the ego is dependent on this infinity, it is not equivalent to it, and every time the ego encounters the other it is reminded, painfully, of its own inadequacy. The crushing demands that the infinite Other makes upon the ego can be either our source of anguish, or psychic growth (Huskinson, 2002).

Huskinson notes that Levinas' dichotomy of the individual and the infinite was inspired by a proof of God's existence furbished by none other than Spinoza's intellectual predecessor, René Descartes. In his *a posteriori* proof for God's existence, Descartes claims that an effect cannot be greater than its cause, and therefore an individual cannot be the creator of ideas that exceed the individual itself. The idea of God would be such an idea; that we are capable of conceiving God, who certainly exceeds our finitude, suggests that God must exist (1911/1996, pp. 12–19). Huskinson proposes that the Cartesian God, Levinas' Other, and the Jungian Self refer to the same thing: an infinity that exceeds the finite ego and forcibly makes it aware of its own limitations (2002, p. 444).

Now, it must be said that Spinoza detests this particular proof for God's existence. In one of his early works, a commentary on Cartesian philosophy, Spinoza is mostly even-handed with how he handles his forbearer's thinking, even on topics where later Spinoza would radically diverge. Yet when Spinoza arrives at the *a posteriori* proof he cannot help but voice his displeasure with it. This proof comes in two stages. First, Descartes explains that the cause of something must have as much reality, or perfection, as its effect; therefore, the idea that we have of God is an effect that can only come from a cause greater than us. Second, only that which can bring about what is more difficult can also bring about what is easier; the fact that we, finite beings who do not have the power to produce ourselves, nevertheless exist, surely implies that there is an infinite being who has the more 'difficult' power to produce itself and also the 'easier' power to produce us.[2] Yet what exactly does Descartes mean, Spinoza asks, by what is difficult or what is easy? A spider easily weaves a web that a human would have the greatest difficulty spinning, just as a human can do many things that might be impossible for, say, an angel. What seems 'difficult' or 'easy' to us is always dependent on its context, that is, the nature of the cause. And so what task could possibly be 'difficult' for God? Does Descartes mean that God is capable of rendering things that we, in our limited existence, find miraculous and impossible? If so, *why* would accomplishing a difficult feat then guarantee God should be able to do things that are also 'easier'? If God can produce a square circle, that does not also suggest he can make a circle with equal radii—quite the contrary, it would only suggest that God is unintelligible!

How are we to understand what Descartes meant? The argument seems to come down to how much 'perfection', or reality, a thing has: God has infinite perfection whereas we, as finite beings, decidedly have *less* perfection. But Spinoza finds this explanation to be, at best, very obscure (PP IP6S, CWS I, pp. 247–251).[3] At worst, it suggests that existence is really a sliding scale of reality or perfection, where an infinite amount of perfection is reserved for God alone, while finite beings teeter on the brink of nothingness. Even in his very early writings, Spinoza had marked this notion of nothingness or "nonbeing" as a pernicious "being of reason," another abstract universal that fails to truly understand what a thing is, and instead juxtaposes it against a reified opposite—in this case, a supremely infinite being (CM I, CWS I, p. 301).[4] In other words, what Spinoza identifies in Descartes' proof is a logic of eminence, where finite beings can only be explained by the shadow cast from a being who is infinitely more perfect. Therefore finite existence is always a "degraded" form of what God possesses alone (Matheron, 2020, p. 59). Just as we found Atmanspacher's dual-aspect monism risks endorsing a metaphysics where, in comparison with a remote first cause, actual existence is always provisional, if not outright illusory (see Ch. 5), so too is this scheme of emanation present in the Cartesian God—and, by proxy, this notion of the self as an infinite 'other'.

Essence as Power

The thrust of Spinoza's attack on Descartes' *a posteriori* proof focuses on its second part, rather than the first portion where Descartes argues that the idea we have of God is an effect that suggests a cause greater than ourselves (i.e., God). But as Deleuze points out, Spinoza's criticism suggests he takes issue with the proof's first stage as well. Why is it that the idea of God must guarantee the existence of its object? It is as if Descartes moves too hastily from the idea of a thing to its presumed reality or perfection (Deleuze, 1968/1990, p. 86). It is not that Spinoza disagrees with the premise that an idea necessarily begets its object—we have seen that Spinoza considers a concept and its object to be one and the same (see Ch. 5, pp. 166–168). But this is only because a sufficient explanation must reveal the very cause and essence of the thing described, and so Spinoza requires a better explanation than what Descartes provides.

To achieve this, Spinoza dispenses with this comparison of nebulous quantities of reality in favor of an argument based on a thing's *power*—or essence. Remember once more that the essence of any thing is that which, being given or conceived, the thing is also given or conceived; and that, if taken away, the thing can neither be nor be conceived (E IID2, CWS I, p. 447). God's essence is that he creates everything that he conceives—which is everything conceivable (E IP16, CWS I, pp. 424–425). And so Spinoza's own *a posteriori* proof for God's existence that he gives in Part I Proposition 11 of the *Ethics* states that to "be able not to exist is to lack power, and conversely, to be able to exist is to have power," and if what exists is only finite beings, that would suggest finite beings are more powerful than an absolutely infinite being, which is absurd. Therefore, there is either nothing, or there is an absolutely infinite being; and since there can only be substance and modes, the absolutely infinite being must be substance, and finite beings its modes, which exist only through the absolute substance (E IP11, CWS I, pp. 417–418). In the scholium to this proposition, Spinoza clearly has Descartes in mind when he scolds those who contemplate this problem via an understanding of what is easy versus what is difficult—because such notions concern the evaluation of random factors, while essence is immutable and eternal (IP11S, pp. 418–419). Between the identity of something and its existence, there is always this *middle third:* its power or essence (Matheron, 2020, Ch. 4). The essence of something is precisely what is expressed both in thought as well as in extension (E IIP7, CWS I, pp. 451–452). Hence the Idea of God necessarily begets God's essence. One must pass through the essence of a thing to affirm its relationship with existence.

Now this identity of being and power transforms how we must consider particular things, because it frees individuals from being defined by their alleged imperfections. It is true that the essence of a particular thing does not involve existence as it does with God, since only God, as substance, has an essence that is the same as his existence (E IP20, CWS I, pp. 428–429; IP24, p. 431). And it is also true that, while God is the cause of a particular thing's essence, that particular thing's actual existence can only be determined by a second particular thing, whose essence is also determined by God, and that second particular thing's existence is caused by a *third* particular thing, whose essence is also determined by God, and that *third* particular thing's existence is caused by a fourth …so on, to infinity (E IP25, CWS I, p. 431; IP28, pp. 432–433). Yet the power of a singular thing is nonetheless part of God's infinite power; it is explained *through* the power of God. A singular essence and the essence of God of course differ, but this is because the essence of each singular thing is what God necessarily produces—*anything that God can conceive he will produce* (E IP16, CWS

I, pp. 424–425; IVP4, pp. 548–549). And so the essence of a finite thing is unique to it and it alone; hence its essence cannot be conjured or conceived without also conjuring or conceiving the very thing in question. Now, an essence corresponds to a mode's affective power—that is to say, while a mode exists, it can affect and be affected by other things (E IIIP6–7, CWS I, pp. 498–499). This affective power is defined either by how a mode is affected by other things—its *passions*—or by its essence alone—its *actions* (E IIIP58–59, CWS I, p. 529; see Ch. 3, pp. 83–89). Now God, as the absolutely infinite substance, is affected by nothing other than himself—and therefore God's affects are always active (E IP15, CWS I, pp. 420–424). Yet this also means that when we act from our essence—when we produce active affects—*we are acting from God's power to think and act through our specific essence.* We no longer need to vainly try and rank a hierarchy of perfection between a spider, a person, or an angel: rather, the spider weaves its web because this activity pertains to its essence; the person contemplates his or her existence because this is an expression of his or her essence; and the angel sings in a heavenly choir because this, too, involves the angel's essence. The singular power of each and every thing is what enables Spinoza to cast down a scheme of eminence between God and finite things and instead declare that finite things are immanent to and within God: our essence partakes in exactly the same powers that pertain to God's essence, the capacity to think and to act; that is, the attributes of thought and extension. And this is also why Deleuze identifies in Spinoza the medieval notion of univocity: the powers that constitute the essence of God are also common to God's modes, the essences of which are nothing less than particular and unique ways in which the Power of God is expressed (Deleuze, 1968/1990, pp. 48–49).

The True Middle Third

Just as there must be a medium between spirit and matter, so too must there be an intermediate term between reality and being. As it turns out, the middle third for both cases is actually the same thing. At the end of their 1953 dialog, Jung remarks to Paul that the problem is an age-old one: "How does one get from Three to Four?" (Meier, 2001, p. 129). That is to say, if the psyche is the middle third between spirit and matter, then how is one to describe the transcendental fourth that spirit and matter are different forms of, and that the psyche moves within? In Atmanspacher's dual-aspect monism, the answer is to designate the transcendental *itself* as the middle third, from which spirit and matter decompose (Atmanspacher & Rickles, 2022, p. xi). Just as we found with Descartes that finite existence is always degraded or diminished before God, so too does the mechanism of decomposition yield life that is but a shattered corruption of a perfect whole. Per Atmanspacher, while the self is indeed an "overarching archetypal structure" within the neutral third, our personal existence is but a "fragmented projection" of that third, an epistemic surface feature that should not be mistaken for anything substantial. Furthermore, Atmanspacher suggests that the ego is tantamount to Metzinger's self model, or what Atmanspacher has identified with the entire aspect of mind within his monist framework. Metzinger claims that the self model is mistakenly believed to be evidence of an individual when it is just a simulation; likewise, Atmanspacher states that the personal psyche works the same way, and that therefore the goal of individuation would be to deny the individual altogether, to instead accept the individual's provisional and illusory being before a cosmic whole (Atmanspacher & Fach, 2019, p. 17).

As demonstrated earlier, this elimination of the third between the ideal and physical causes considerable epistemological confusion (see Ch. 5, pp. 144–153). Spinoza demands finite modes must not be treated as 'decayed' correlates between mind and matter, but rather as ontologically valid compositions first and foremost (ibid., pp. 153–169). We can now see more clearly why this must be the case. One's mind and one's body are not at the end of infinitely long chains of being that slowly dissolve into one another as one traces them back to an eminent God, Self, or Other. Infinite chains do exist in Spinoza, but purely in terms of extrinsic reality: one mode affects another because it was affected by another mode, which was affected by *another* mode, and so on; similarly, the actualization of an individual mode depends purely upon other individual modes being subsumed by a specific ratio of relations, and those other individual modes also came into existence due to other individuals being subsumed by their relations, etc. But for every mode described, God is the immediate cause of their singular essence (E IP18, CWS I, p. 428; IP28, pp. 432–433). And in any event, since each composition is embedded within another composition, on and on to infinity, whether one plunges into the smallest crevices between atoms or gaps between galaxies, across civilizations or within the thoughts in one's own head, any direction leads us to an infinite composition that subsists even when the parts within it change, such as 'the face of the whole Universe', and so all things must be immanent to substance (Ep. 64, CWS II, pp. 438–439; also see Ch. 5, p. 170, footnote 1).

Isn't this focus on overcoming Cartesian dualism something of a red herring? We can declare that mind and matter are aspects of a monist whole, proudly proclaim that we have severed any causal links between the parallel lines, and yet clearly we can still encounter the same old problems—particularly if that monist whole is never truly present to us (see Ch. 5, pp. 148–153). To be sure, Spinoza does oppose Descartes' conception of the mind and body as two separate entities that causally interact. But for Spinoza the issue of dualism is a byproduct of Descartes trying to have it both ways: God is an infinite substance, says Descartes, since God can be explained through himself. Yet he says that finite things are substances too: the tree, the human body, and the human mind are all finite substances since they all could, conceivably, be explained through themselves. Descartes is particularly interested in designating the mind as a finite substance, separate from the body, since this protects the mind from the vicissitudes of nature—the mind is rendered immutable. Spinoza does away with this maneuver by declaring that minds and bodies are simply two ways of explaining the same modular essence (Della Rocca, 2008, p. 102). Now singular essences are *not* substances, because they are explained *through* God, who for Spinoza is the only substance. Yet the singular essences are nonetheless what God immediately produces (E IP16, CWS I, pp. 424–425; IP21, pp. 429–430; Ep. 64, CWS II, pp. 438–439). And the ideas of the singular essences do exist eternally in the Infinite Intellect (E VP22, CWS I, p. 607).[5] Therefore, Spinoza transfers the immutability that is ordinarily granted to the mind—that is, the *mind as the soul*—and *instead confers it upon essence.*

One might object and point out this appears similar to what Atmanspacher does in making the mind an epistemic manifestation of the psychophysically neutral whole. The difference is that when one dismisses the middle third, when one casts aside singular essences to get straight to the Divine fourth, one short circuits the entire process. As Jung warns, when one suppresses the middle third all they really have done is project it elsewhere into their metaphysics (see Ch. 1, pp. 24–26). Hence it seems Atmanspacher and Metzinger vacillate between the wholesale rejection of individuality on the one hand, and on the other a reality that depends entirely on the monstrous apparatus of a totalizing subject (see Ch. 5, pp. 148–153). Conversely, Atmanspacher's move toward the fields of sense described by Markus Gabriel is a step toward the multiplicity demanded by Spinoza's monism (ibid., pp. 168–169). There is not just one thing being expressed in two different ways; rather, there is an *infinity* of things that are expressed in (at least!) two different ways, because each part of that infinity is explained through the absolute power of thinking and creating. If Spinozism can be accused of causing claustrophobia, it is not because it implies every individual is an illusion and that there is only one thing; rather, *everything is a thing*, or has an essence. There is no exception, no metaphysical vacuum to be found.

But it is also at this very moment one might imagine Jung, forever leery of triggering his own fear of ontologically cramped spaces, pushing himself away from the table and accusing Spinoza of going too far. Yes, Spinoza, like Jung, emphasizes that an individual mind cannot be conflated with the entire attribute of thought. And Spinoza, like Jung, demands a 'middle third' that moves within the Divine (see Ch. 2, pp. 57–63). But under closer inspection, clearly for Spinoza this middle third is *not* the individual's mind. Rather, essence is what sits between thought and extension, whether one is talking about the singular essence of a person who has both a body and a mind, or the absolute power of God as it is expressed both in his Infinite Intellect and in the motions of the entire universe. *The true middle third for Spinoza is essence.*

Surely for Jung this might smack of betrayal. Why should he assume that this introduction of 'essence' is anything other than an imposition upon the psyche's territory, a covert introduction of a "neutral language" in the way Pauli sought (see Ch. 1, pp. 31–36)? How can knowledge of oneself be necessary to understand things beyond oneself if the middle third is no longer the psyche? Yet couldn't Spinoza simply shrug and point out that Jung's aforementioned declarations, of how the psyche is the 'world's pivot' and that consciousness has a privileged role as the 'second creator' of all existence, suggest that Jung is not so dedicated to the cause of transcendental immanence after all, that deep down Jung still covets total immunity for the subject—despite all the delusions of interiority, isolationism, and (by Jung's own estimate!) imbalance that comes with it? Spinoza might even produce a letter Jung wrote to Father White, where Jung goes as far as to say that he sees the psyche as nothing less than an 'ousia', a Greek word which can be translated to substance—in other words, the psyche is an irreducible being that exists totally in of itself (Lammers & Cunningham, 2007, p. 141). Jung could retort that 'ousia' just as easily translates to essence, and that despite Spinoza's qualifier that essences technically have God as their cause, they nonetheless are apparently immutable and eternal.

Spinoza might consider that, then ask Jung if he still considers the psyche as part of a whole; in other words, the psyche is not identical to what Jung calls the *unus mundus*. Jung would say of course they are not the same, that instead, the individual realizes they are within this one world, the "eternal Ground" for all potential existence. That does not mean they are identical; did he not just chastise such a belief as a "superman psychosis" (CW. 14, 1963/1970, pars. 664, 760; Letters, Vol. 2, 1975, p. 407)? Clearly, Jung agrees, there is a transcendental fourth beyond the psyche (Meier, 2001, p. 115). Spinoza might then ask Jung to clarify whether or not the idea that one has of oneself in existence, that is, what Jung calls the ego, is equivalent to the entire psyche. Of course not, Jung would scoff; he is very clear that the ego evolves out of the unconscious (CW. 11, 1954/1969d, par. 391). Spinoza then might smile, apologize for the misunderstanding, and offer Jung to again take a seat. For the question of whether the middle third is best called essence or psyche does not split Jung and Spinoza apart after all. Nor do Jung's comments about the primacy of the psyche and the self contradict his Spinozism. On the contrary, they affirm it.

Essence and Self

How are we to think of essence beyond Spinoza's claim that it is identical to a thing's power, and that the conception or production of a thing's essence necessarily conceives or produces the thing? Spinoza often speaks of things that 'pertain to', 'constitute', or 'express' one's essence: weaving a web pertains to the essence of a spider, just as the absolutely infinite power constitutes the essence of God (Deveaux, 2007, pp. 70, 106–111). When we conceive of a creature perfectly suited for weaving a 'spider's' web, we conceive a spider; when we conceive an absolutely infinite being, we conceive God. Again, essence is the same as power (E IP34, CWS I, p. 439; IIIP7, p. 499). So if we say that Power L constitutes the essence of Tim, then Power L is Tim's essence. One might object that this is a seemingly futile route to take. How are we to distinguish what *pertains* to one's essence versus what does not? It's all well and good to state that weaving a web expresses the essence of a spider; but what about the fact it has eight legs, or that it is related to other arachnids? At what point does our definition of essence become just another version of taxonomy and classification—what Spinoza says is the stuff of inadequate ideas (see Ch. 3, pp. 75–79)? How do we differentiate between ordinary traits and those that are significant? If a thing's power is all the ways it can affect and be affected, then it would seem the traits we must sort through are endless.

Yet for Spinoza, there is no mystery as to what our barometer must be: all thoughts and actions that pertain to an individual's essence must also produce active joys. Active joys can *only* be caused by affects that directly express an individual's essence (E IIIP58–59, CWS I, p. 529). Now, joy is any affect that increases an individual's perseverance to exist, or strengthens that individual's composition (E IIIDef II–III, CWS I, p. 531). One might readily conclude that, under this definition, web weaving is indeed joyful for a spider—the benefits it reaps from it are obvious. But how do we know it is an active joy and not a *passive* one? Passive joys can also increase our power, but since they come from affects outside us, this increase always comes on a haphazard and provisional basis (E IVP59, CWS I, pp. 579–580). How do we know the spider's web weaving is not a passive affect? Saying that this is an instinct with a genetic basis does us no good, since genes are individual modes in their own right, and they in no way constitute the singular essence of the compound mode that they are enlisted to help actualize, no more than the element of oxygen can express the essence of Earth's atmosphere. But for Spinoza this too has a very simple answer: it comes down to common notions. Remember that common notions express an intrinsic agreement between at least two modes, through some component that they share. The realization that this shared component can be explained by our essence alone is what gives us active joy, because it is our power that creates it, rather than waiting and hoping for an external, joy-giving mode to affect us. And it is the accumulation of common notions that allows us to see the eternal essence of something—including ourselves (see Ch. 3, pp. 79–89).

In Chapter 3, we discussed how an athlete's bodily relation to their craft is a prime example of a common notion. Similarly, the essence of Tiger Woods is not defined by genetics that may have predisposed him to have quick hands or explosive hips, admittedly all ideal components for a golf swing; nor is his essence explained by his demanding taskmaster of a father who molded him into a fierce competitor with proverbial "ice in his veins";

in a sense, these things all come from without Tiger, and while they no doubt molded his actualization, in some ways for better and some ways for worse, they are passive affects. Consider instead Tiger's return to form after devastating injuries and personal scandals that had many doubting he would ever again win a major championship. Tiger used his intrinsic understanding of the golf swing—his golf swing—in relation to his surgically rebuilt body to reconstruct his game in a way that he could use to get back into contention. Let us assume that Tiger's relation to his body and his golf swing are common notions, in the manner we discussed in Chapter 3. The use of common notions allows one to rearrange the affections of their body according to the order of the intellect: in other words, the formation of common notions allows one to form active joys (E VP-1–10, CWS I, pp. 597–601). Tiger's comeback demonstrated *his intrinsic understanding of himself, the game of golf, and how he was able to find new ways to assemble and express those relations in a sort of constellation of active affectivity*, which culminated in his historic win at the 2019 Masters, a decade after his last major championship (Sampson, 2019). For Spinoza, what a thing can do is much more important than trying to state what it is (E IIIP2S, CWS I, pp. 494–497). This story says something specific about *what Tiger Woods can do*. Sports anchors and talking heads might dub this as 'resilience' and 'determination'; a less succinct but more revealing explanation is that Tiger Woods' comeback demonstrated his ability to rearrange his affections based on common notions, so that they became wholly an expression of his own essence.

Essence reveals itself in adversity, in adaptation—in life and how we solve the problems it poses for us. The yucca moth, as Jung tells us, has only a single opportunity to lay its eggs: the one day of the year the flowers of the yucca plant open. Not only does the moth afford this opportunity to lay its eggs in the pistil of a flower that it cuts open; it takes pollen from another flower and rolls it into a pellet that it leaves with the eggs (CW. 8, 1919/1969a, par. 268). It is only in existence where the drama between actions and passions is given to us. Spiders were taken aboard the Skylab space station to see if they would weave webs in space; indeed they did, in slightly different styles than they did on Earth; eventually these spiders succumbed to this alien existence and died (Witt, Peakall, & Gause, 1977). But if death is a passive affect that removes a mode from durational existence, its essence is eternal, and so the opportunity to weaponize the laws of one's own nature, to see oneself from the eye of eternity, seems to loom at crucial junctures of an individual's existence in ways that the extrinsic causal chains of existence, the vicissitudes of nature, cannot explain. George Lucas once remarked that had he not gone into filmmaking, he might have pursued another interest, such as anthropology or illustrating. Yet Lucas believes had he taken one of these other routes, they would have ultimately been subsumed by the path he ended up taking: anthropology would have led to an interest in mythology and storytelling, and thus in the direction of *Star Wars*; illustrating could easily have tangentially piqued an interest in animation, and thus filmmaking, and therefore toward the direction, ultimately, of *Star Wars*. Lucas describes the choices that ultimately led him to *Star Wars* in tracing the connections between things he cared about and loved: in other words, the hallmarks of common notions and active joys (What It Takes, 2021). Small wonder that acting in accord with one's essence might evoke a feeling of destiny: how could living through the laws of one's own nature not conjure such a numinous affect? For Spinoza this is blessedness itself (see Ch. 4, pp. 118–121).

Previously we discovered how Jung and Spinoza agree on affective knowledge, that they both think understanding oneself is paramount to understanding the world, and consequently they even share similar definitions of meaning (see Ch. 3; Ch. 4, pp. 118–121). But now we see that their metaphysics of the individual is also consonant, that they both describe the dynamics between an actualized individual and an eternal essence. For it is during moments of hardship, of psychological upheaval, where the ego is afforded the chance to reckon with the self which it is but an exponent of. The self is a "more compendious personality" that is to the ego as the mover is to moved, or even subject to object. The ego, while a product of the unconscious, is but a fraction of it; the potential growth that the self offers is unlimited, even though it is in another respect limited because it is "individuality in the highest sense" (CW. 11, 1954/1969d, pars. 390–391). In other words, the self is both infinite yet particular. How can this be? Spinoza provides an explanation when he explains that a modal essence can still be infinite: picture a circle drawn within a larger circle, but slightly askew so that they are non-concentric. The sum of unequal distances between the two circles "exceeds any number," and is infinite. Yet there is nonetheless a minimum distance where the borders between the two circles are closest, and also a maximum distance where the two borders are furthest apart (Ep. 12, CWS I, p. 204). In other words, one is left with a bounded degree of power, a capacity that can be fulfilled in an infinity of different ways. Perhaps this is why Jung sees the self as a source of so much antimony, yet also where such oppositions are succeeded. For we become aware that we are "an actual, living something, poised between two world-pictures and their darkly discerned potencies." The self "is strange to us and yet so near, wholly ourselves and yet unknowable, a virtual centre of so mysterious a constitution that it can claim anything—kinship with beasts and gods, with crystals and with stars—without us" to dissent (CW. 7, 1916/1966, par. 398). It is both temporal and yet eternal, quite literally the very essence of individuality and yet also universal in the sense that it is an archetype at the very heart of individuation (CW. 9ii, 1959/1969c, par. 116). The ego is to the self as an existing mode is to their eternal essence.

It can again be asked, if the archetype is a compound mode of recurring human events, then how can the self—or *oneself*—be an archetype? Yet this question is not as perplexing as it first seemed. After all, is not one's very existence an event? Doesn't our story of Tiger Woods demonstrate that when one 'weaponizes' their affective powers, they necessarily involve other modes that affect them? More pertinently, doesn't individuation commence with our understanding of the other archetypal compositions we are embedded within—which inevitably involve the circumstances of one's actual life? One seldom deals with their anima or animus without also coming to grips with one's romantic relationships; the wise old man has something to say about the mentors in our own life, and so forth (CW. 7, 1916/1966, par. 355; see Ch. 4). Therefore, if the self is a compound mode, then it is the *very compound mode of an individual's existence*. If other archetypes govern the compositions that subsume us, then the self is what governs our very composition. This is why one experiences the self as both part of the whole and *as* the whole—it is where we sense that all these compositions exist on the same plane. If the self balances and patterns the archetypes we encounter in our existence, it is not because the self is a closed whole from which other archetypes 'deintegrate' as Fordham posits, a final appeal to a scheme of emanation. Rather, it is because the self, by its very nature, demands that one reckon with the sprawling web of the unconscious that one is mired in—that is the only way to unlock the self's power. Only then is a greater personality achieved (ibid., par. 136). Hence individuation is often equated with "becoming oneself" or realizing who one truly is (Samuels, 1985, p. 103). Now this 'greater personality' does not deify man nor dethrone God, but nevertheless it *is* the God within us (CW.

7, 1916/1966, pars. 399–400). That is because *the realization of the self is the actualization of one's essence*, which is a very degree of God's power. In other words, the debate between psyche or essence as the middle third is no debate at all.

The Eternal Psyche

This answer demands elaboration. Can we really believe that the psyche, the constellation of our conscious and unconscious processes—and of which the self is both center and circumference—is one and the same with the Spinozist modular existence, which is an expression of a singular essence? Yet the equality between the attributes mandates that this distinction is merely one of reason. Remember that a concept and its object are the same thing (E IIP7, CWS I, pp. 451–452). What Jung's psychology essentially does is synthesize common notions purely within the attribute of thought: that is, the study of symbols and archetypal images and their impact upon the human psyche is nothing other than the archaeology of how things are ordered and connected purely within the attribute of thought, and Jung's diligence in largely restricting his studies to a 'physics' of psyche and spirit, the concomitants of the ideal realm, is a credit to his Spinozism (see Ch. 4, pp. 132–135). Nonetheless, thought and extension share an identity because they explain the same thing. This principle can be used to clarify the identity of psyche and essence. Every archetype (like every other mode) is expressed in both thought and extension, or spirit and matter; its existence beyond this, or the psychoid, is the archetype's essence (see Ch. 5, pp. 164–169). This inevitably applies to the self as well: its ideal manifestations are found, for instance, in mandala imagery, because according to Jung such symbols manifest an "almost irresistible compulsion and urge to *become what one is*" (CW. 9i, 1950/1969b, par. 634). Yet also, surely, the ego itself is sort of an 'archetypal image', because it is the very personification of the unconscious of which the self is our principal basin of attraction (CW. 14, 1963/1970, par. 129). We should be able to describe the totality of the psyche purely in terms of ideal or 'spiritual' contents—because the psyche is expressed through spirit (see Ch. 1, pp. 37–41). Moreover, our ideas—indeed, our ego itself—are nothing more than our conception of our affections—*which always involve the body* (see Ch. 3, pp. 75–79, Ch. 5, pp. 157–159). Hence the unity of mind and body: the psyche and the body constitute the same singular essence. So really, Jung and Spinoza mean the same thing when they speak of a middle third. Jung simply is approaching the topic as a psychologist, and thus prioritizes what can be explained under the attribute of thought; whereas Spinoza approaches the issue as a meta-physician, and so he speaks of essence itself.

Does this identity of psyche and body apply to the self as well? Surely it must. After all, it is the return into the world, the plunging back into one's body and all the affectivity this entails, that is required for a glimpse into the *unus mundus*, where one realizes that there is no distinction between ideal and physical, that matter itself is alive (CW. 14, 1963/1970, par. 770). Matheron proposes a similar line of thought through Spinoza, noting that we could somehow "come to know our essence *in its singularity*," that we could organize our affections "according to an order that fully conforms to our essence" so that "our body succeeded in being truly *itself*, if it became entirely the master of itself by means of something like a kind of yoga," we would then know what it would be to have an eternal body. But, Matheron admits, we are a far way off from this—and so was Spinoza (2020, p. 79). It is a different case though, in terms of the mind.

The idea we have of ourselves while we exist may, by default, be woe-fully incomplete; nevertheless, there exists in God's Infinite Intellect an *eternal* idea of every one of us; this must be the case, because God has an idea of everything he can and must create (E VP22, CWS I, p. 607). This is the idea of our eternal essence; it is an idea we come to have when we act from adequate ideas; that is to say, from our own essence. This way of conceiving things does not rely on the context of durational existence, but rather the eye of eternity: for example, the third kind of knowledge, the intellectual intuition, where we perceive the essence of things and our-selves (E VP29S, CWS I, pp. 609–610). Now Spinoza explicitly says that this part of the mind cannot be destroyed with the body upon our death in this existence, but rather it remains and must be eternal; it exists under the eye of eternity (E VP23S, CWS I, pp. 607–608). Is Spinoza just speaking of a sort of impersonal 'formula' that constitutes the individual, a mathem-atical equation that constitutes their 'ratio of relations' in existence? This is what Leibniz, perhaps insincerely, accused Spinoza of really saying. If that were the case, what is the point of existence to begin with (Leibniz, 1855; Deleuze, 1968/1990, p. 317)? But Spinoza is saying quite a bit more than this. What is this eternity? Eternity is itself a kind of existence, but as opposed to durational existence, which is predicated upon our passage from one affect to the next, eternal existence merely refers to what can be explained without affection or duration, that is, God's absolute power (E ID8, CWS I, p. 409). Now the power of God is always filled with active affects, since nothing else can affect God (there is nothing outside of him!). And so when we act from our essence, and necessarily create active joys, these are affects that do not rely wholly on the body, but rather are caused by the eternal part of the mind (E VP31, CWS I, pp. 610–611). Active joys that come from our 'eternal mind' remain after the body is destroyed (E VP40C, CWS I, p. 615). Thus, the active joys we accrue in our durational existence survive after our death.

The final section of the *Ethics*, wherein Spinoza reveals that he believes something remains after we die, has long perplexed Spinoza scholars. Some, such as Nadler, prefer to try and minimize what Spinoza indicates here, by suggesting that Spinoza is merely suggesting that eternal truths about ourselves, such as the fact we are made of carbon atoms, persist after our death, but nothing more (Nadler, Ch. 9. 2006). Others, like Deleuze, recognize that such a secular interpretation does no justice to what Spinoza has in mind when it comes to the power of essence and active joys, and instead asks us to picture our death as "a subtraction, a cutting-back." We lose all the external parts that fulfilled our ratio of relations, and therefore we lose any affections that were predicated upon the utilization of those external parts. Therefore we can no longer experience passive affects; "*all that remains, indeed, is our power of understanding or action*" (Deleuze, 1968/1990, p. 315). This is why Spinoza states that memory, at least as we ordinarily think of it, is destroyed with the body, since memory is part of the imagination, which relies on the passage of affects; imagination is destroyed with the body (E VP21, CWS I, p. 607). Yet all those kernels of truth that our imagination groped at, and which we were able to explicate, survive; any understanding derived from our own essence *survives*. Hence the one who lives a life of virtue thinks little of death, has nothing to fear of it; whereas the person consumed by their passions meditates on nothing but death, and has everything to lose from it: if one's existence is actualized mostly through passive affects, then death will deprive them of everything; but the more they seek active joys, the less consequence death will have for them (E IVP67, CWS I, p. 584; VP38, pp. 613–614). Existence is not a moral test, Deleuze muses, but rather a chemical one, where the quality of some material—the material of our very life, and the consequences of our own choices—is assessed (1968/1990, pp. 317–319).

Now Jung certainly seems to share *something* like this latter interpretation of Spinoza's afterlife. During his near-death experience following a heart attack in 1944, Jung describes a vision of a black monolith of a temple floating over the earth; as he approached it, he had the sensation that "everything was being sloughed away" and that his entire earthly existence was being stripped from him; nevertheless, "something remained": a sort of eternal awareness of "everything I had ever experienced and done" that let him perceive, clearly, the context of his own existence, as if he was distilled down to the clearest understanding of who he was. Before Jung could contemplate this eternity further, he began to recover and thus he 'pulled out of it' and was brought back to his current life, a development that he at first rued greatly. "Now I must go back to this drab world," he complained, after experiencing something far more profound (1963/1989, pp. 289–292). It is as if Jung saw his brush with death as another experience of the inner world, which made him look at his outward life with disdain and contempt. Nevertheless, Jung later on came to see things a bit differently: in a later dream he stumbled upon a yogi meditating within a chapel; upon closer inspection, he realized the yogi was *him*. "He is the one who is meditating me," Jung concluded. When the yogi someday awakened from his meditation, Jung believed that was when he, Jung, would die. In other words, the yogi is a symbol of the self, and Jung's temporal existence is what allowed the yogi to learn, to be realized; in other words, souls or essences *need* existence (1963/1989, pp. 323–324). This very much aligns with Jung's statement that "It is not I who create myself. Rather I happen to myself" (CW. 11, 1954/1969d, pars. 390–391). Our life is the manifestation of our essence. Jung echoes a similar story in a dream he had not long before his mother's death, where his father appeared to him and immediately asked for the latest developments in the field of marital psychology—as if Jung's father realized he would soon need to recommence his marriage. It is as if the dead, with no sense of duration or passive affect, require the living to further understand things for themselves (1963/1989, pp. 315–316).

What Jung comes to realize is that *existence* is needed for the expression of *eternity*. It is perhaps not a coincidence that it was directly after the near-death experience in 1944 that Jung began a very "fruitful period of work" (ibid., p. 297); indeed, it was only after this that he formally distinguished the spirit from psyche, that he accorded outbound connections their proper respect, and he adopted a Spinozist position to express his metaphysics (see

Ch. 4, pp. 132–135). Perhaps it was this revelation, more than any other, that compelled Jung's move toward Spinoza: just as one cannot understand the Divine without understanding oneself, one cannot understand one's own nature without knowing something of God (CW. 11, 1952/1969d, par. 746).

The Meaning of Passage (or Life)

What does it mean to *pass* through a 'Blessed Self'? Passage is our procession from one affect to the next. It is our duration; it is, in a sense, our life (E IIIP8, CWS I, p. 499). So long as we are enthralled to the passions, a passage of volatility and misfortune is all we will ever know. But if we resolve to learn the intrinsic causes of things that affect us, if we attend to the symbols that implicate the archetypal core at the heart of those complexes that possess us, if we are willing to jettison the short-lived benefits of passive joys and the false sense of security that projections and reifications give us; if we are keen to make sense of other modes that compound us, archetypal or otherwise, so that we may understand their essence as well as our own, not through the incomprehensible deluge of durational existence, but through the eye of eternity—we will then know what it is to act from our own essence, and we will rejoice, because such action engenders a joy that can never be taken away from us (E VP37, CWS I, p. 613). And it is through the affects of our essence that we come to see and know things as they are eternally in the Infinite Intellect—or, we realize our unity with an *unus mundus*, and therefore we receive a holy love—or Blessedness, or collective meaning (Ch. 4, pp. 118–121). From the middle third, we at last arrive at the fourth.

The psyche is a microcosm of the *unus mundus* in the same way that our essence is a unique expression of divinity. This is not realized through hermitage or retreat; rather, someone who experiments in their time in this existence, who dares to see how they can act and be acted upon, will therefore have a body capable of a great many things, and therefore possess a psyche "whose greatest part is eternal." Spinoza rejects any attempt to project the human essence into the cosmos; nevertheless, he understands that humans are "capable of a great many things" compared with other modes in our part of the universe. It is true, a spider that weaves its web is demonstrating its active affectivity—but *we* alone are capable of *deliberately* organizing our affections to such a sophisticated degree that we can consciously seek the adequate in what is inadequate, can find joy in suffering, can achieve freedom from our own bondage (E VP39S, CWS I, pp. 614–615).

And so we discover what Jung means by stating that *we* are the 'second creators' of existence: *we are all alchemists*. We all can transform the passions around us into actions, for the benefit of ourselves and others. The alternative is to redouble our sorrows, to cause more and more anguish for all humankind. Passions beget more passions, forging compounds of misery that like a noxious gloom fulminates and multiplies within us and amongst us—and so that very quickly people who decry a lack of freedom therein happily raise their arms toward the state so that they may be enchained (TP, CWS II). "Immense power of destruction" lies in all of our hands, warns Jung (CW. 11, 1952/1969d, par. 745). Hence the psyche *is* indeed the world's pivot: an understanding of our unconscious, of our subliminal affections, and ultimately *our* self lets us disavow the passions in favor of seeking out joyful encounters. Only other finite modes can trigger the existence of other finite modes. This dawning responsibility upon us, that we can conjure the actualization of affections that *agree* with us and others, and thus foster compositions of solidarity that *increase* our happiness and vanquish the passions, is the final piece to the panentheism that Jung and Spinoza share: substance is more than us, and we move within that transcendental immanence—yet also, we in no small part help determine what comes to pass in our immediate lives (see Ch. 2, pp. 57–63).

Essence is the mystery between mind and body, at the heart of all of our lives (Letters, Vol. 2, 1975, p. 581). Salvation is not a hope reserved for the hereafter. It is something that must be extracted now, before the passage of time becomes too much—indeed, before we experience the passage of ourselves (Ep. 28, CWS I, p. 396). Such is the privilege of existence. This should not be viewed as a burden, nor a task to win the favor of a transcendent deity, a phantom projected over a horizon that we will never cross. Rather it is the glory that comes from living a life of virtue, to act not from the defenses of the ego but from the valor of the self. If we afford ourselves this opportunity, we will not merely diminish the passions in our lifetime in favor of active affects, though this will indeed occur (E VP38S, CWS I, pp. 613–614). Nor will we only discover that "completist expression" of our individuality, though this too will happen (CW. 7, 1916/1966, par. 404). By acting from essence, we enter a passage of existence that can never be corroded, never subtracted, never destroyed. When we realize the self, we will know what it is to be eternal within our own time—and thus, for all time.

Notes

1   All references to 'CWS I' belong to Spinoza (1985) and all references to 'CWS II' belong to Spinoza (2016). These are the two editions edited by Curley.
2   Descartes gives this *a posteriori* proof in the third section of his *Meditation on First Philosophy*, and also provides an expanded demonstration in his second set of replies to objections toward the *Meditations*. For the *Meditations*, see 1911/1996, translated by Haldene. For the *Objections and Replies*, see 2017, edited by Bennett.
3   'PP' refers to *Descartes' Principles of Philosophy*, which is the title of Spinoza's commentary on Cartesian Philosophy.
4   'CM' stands for '*Metaphysical Thoughts*', an appendix to *Descartes' Principles of Philosophy*.
5   Chantal Jaquet notes that by making finite modes reliant on God for their existence, Spinoza authors the ability for eternity to be a communicable property between God and modes. Eternity becomes a common notion, a property equal in the part (finite modes) and the whole (God) (2023, pp. 85–89).

References

Adler, G. & Jaffe, A. (1975). *C.G. Jung Letters 2: 1951–1961*. Translated by R. Hull. Princeton: Princeton University Press.

Atmanspacher, H. & Fach, W. (2019). "Exceptional Experiences of Stable and Unstable Mental States, Understood from a Dual-Aspect Point of View." in *Philosophies*, 4(1), 7.

Atmanspacher, H. & Rickles, D. (2022). *Dual-Aspect Monism and the Deep Structure of Meaning*. London & New York: Routledge.

Deleuze, G. (1968/1990). *Expressionism in Philosophy: Spinoza*. Translated by M. Joughin. New York: Zone Books.

Della Rocca, M. (2008). *Spinoza*. London & New York: Routledge.

Descartes, R. (1911/1996). *Meditations on First Philosophy*. Translated by E. Haldane. https://yale.learningu.org/download/041e9642-df02–4eed-a895–70e472df2ca4/H2665_Descartes'%20Meditations.pdf (Accessed May 1, 2023).

Descartes, R. (2017). *Objections to the Meditations and Descartes's Replies*. Translated by J. Bennett. www.earlymoderntexts.com/assets/pdfs/descartes1642.pdf (Accessed May 1, 2023).

Deveaux, S. (2007). *The Role of God in Spinoza's Metaphysics*. London: Continuum.

Fordham, M. (1963). "The Empirical Foundation and Theories of the Self in Jung's Works," in *Analytical Psychology: A Modern Science*. Edited by M. Fordham, et al. London: Heinemann.

Gieser, S. (2005). *The Innermost Kernel: Depth Psychology and Quantum Physics. Wolfgang Pauli's Dialogue with C.G. Jung.* Berlin: Springer.

Huskinson, L. (2002). "The Self as Violent Other: The Problem of Defining the Self." *Journal of Analytical Psychology*, 47, 437–458.

Jaquet, C. (2023). *Time, Duration and Eternity in Spinoza.* Translated by E. Aldieri. Edinburgh: Edinburgh University Press.

Jung, C.G. (1916). *Two Essays on Analytical Psychology*, 2nd ed. Translated by R. Hull. Collected Works of C.G. Jung, Vol. 7. Princeton: Princeton University Press, 1966.

Jung, C.G. (1939). "Conscious, Unconscious, and Individuation," in *The Archetypes and the Collective Unconscious*, 2nd ed. Translated by R. Hull. Collected Works of C.G. Jung, Vol. 9i. Princeton: Princeton University Press, 1969b.

Jung, C.G. (1940). "The Psychology of the Child Archetype," in *The Archetypes and the Collective Unconscious*, 2nd ed. Translated by R. Hull. Collected Works of C.G. Jung, Vol. 9i. Princeton: Princeton University Press, 1969b.

Jung, C.G. (1946). "On the Nature of the Psyche," in *The Structure and Dynamics of the Psyche*, 2nd ed. Translated by R. Hull. Collected Works of C.G. Jung, Vol. 8. Princeton: Princeton University Press, 1969a.

Jung, C.G. (1948). "The Phenomenology of the Spirit in Fairytales," in *The Archetypes and the Collective Unconscious*, 2nd ed. Translated by R. Hull. Collected Works of C.G. Jung, Vol. 9i. Princeton: Princeton University Press, 1969b.

Jung, C.G. (1950). "Concerning Mandala Symbolism," in *Archetypes and the Collective Unconscious*, 2nd ed. Translated by R. Hull. Collected Works of C.G. Jung, Vol. 9i. Princeton: Princeton University Press, 1969b.

Jung, C.G. (1952). "Answer to Job," in *Psychology and Religion: East and West*, 2nd ed. Translated by R. Hull. Collected Works of C.G. Jung, Vol. 11. Princeton: Princeton University Press, 1969d.

Jung, C.G. (1953). "Individual Dream Symbolism in Relation to Alchemy," in *Psychology and Alchemy*, 2nd ed. Translated by R. Hull. Collected Works of C.G. Jung, Vol. 12. Princeton: Princeton University Press, 1968.

Jung, C.G. (1954). "Transformation Symbolism in the Mass," in *Psychology and Religion: east and West*, 2nd ed. Translated by R. Hull. Collected Works of C.G. Jung, Vol. 11. Princeton: Princeton University Press, 1969d.

Jung, C.G. (1959). *Aion: Researches into the Phenomenology of the Self.* 2nd ed. Translated by R. Hull. Collected Works of C.G. Jung, Vol. 9ii. Princeton: Princeton University Press, 1969c.

Jung, C.G. (1963). *Mysterium Coniunctionis*, 2nd ed. Translated by R. Hull. Collected Works of C.G. Jung, Vol. 14. Princeton: Princeton University Press, 1970.

Jung, C.G. (1963/1989). *Memories. Dreams, Reflections.* Edited by A. Jaffe, Translated by R. Winston and C. Winston. New York: Vintage Books.

Knox, J. (2003). *Archetype, Attachment, Analysis: Jungian Psychology and the Emergent Mind.* London & New York: Routledge.

Lammers, A.C. and Cunningham, A. (eds.) (2007). *The Jung-White Letters*. London: Routledge.

Leibniz, G. (1855). *A Refutation Recently Discovered of Spinoza by Leibniz*. Translated and Edited by Comte Louis Alexandre Foucher de Careil. Translated by Octavius Freire Owen. www.google.com/books/edition/A_Refutation_Rece ntly_Discovered_of_Spin/7cwYAAAAIAAJ?hl=en&gbpv=0 (Accessed May 20, 2023).

Matheron, A. (2020). *Politics, Ontology, and Knowledge in Spinoza*. Translated by D. Maruzzella & G. Morejon. Edinburgh: Edinburgh University Press.

Meier, C.A. (ed.) (2001). *Atom and Archetype: The Pauli/Jung Letters 1932–1958*. London: Routledge.

Nadler, S. (2006). *Spinoza's 'Ethics': An Introduction*. Cambridge: Cambridge University Press.

Roesler, C. (2022). *C.G. Jung's Archetype Concept: Theory, Research, and Applications*. Translated by A. Ulyet & C. Roesler. London & New York: Routledge.

Saban, M. (2019). *'Two Souls Alas': Jung's Two Personalities and the Making of Analytical Psychology*. The Zurich Lecture Series: Volume 2. Asheville, NC: Chiron Publications.

Sampson, C. (2019). *Roaring Back: The Fall and Rise of Tiger Woods*. New York: Diversion Books.

Samuels, A. (1985). *Jung and the Post-Jungians*. London & New York: Routledge.

Spinoza, B. (1985). *The Collected Works of Spinoza*, Vol. I, Edited and translated by Edwin Curley. Princeton: Princeton University Press.

Spinoza, B. (2016). *The Collected Works of Spinoza*, Vol. II, Edited and translated by Edwin Curley. Princeton: Princeton University Press.

What It Takes (2021). 'Best of–George Lucas: The Force Will Be With You'. https://open.spotify.com/episode/5eNQZwi4D0ARDj4CbCbKwt?si=2e20b 6c68f414de0 (Accessed May 15, 2023).

Witt, P., Peakall, D. & Gause, R. (1977). "Spider Web-Building in Outer Space: Evaluation of Records from the Sky Lab Experiment." *Journal of Arachnology*, 4, 115–124.

Conclusion

In the final analysis, this text accomplishes two tasks: it addresses an outstanding question within the Jungian literature, and it also offers a conceptual solution to a persistent problem within Jungian theory itself. The question in the literature concerns Jung's connection to Spinoza, as well as Jung's strange attitude toward the Dutch philosopher. Chapters 2, 3, and 4 found that Jung's 'Spinoza complex' comes from Jung's fear of his own Spinozist tendencies—a sort of ontological claustrophobia. Jung nevertheless accepts those tendencies so that he may 'open' up his psychology. This brings us to the theoretical dilemma that casting Jung as a Spinozist attempts to solve.

In *Integration and Difference*, Grant Maxwell readily lists Jung alongside giants in the history of modern philosophy (2022). It is the canard that Jung is a mystic, Maxwell insists, that has prevented Jung from taking his rightful place in the intellectual pantheon (Acid Horizon, 2023). At a bare minimum, this text has demonstrated that Jung's thinking does indeed possess the rigor required to meet the ideas of a philosopher notorious for uncompromising complexity and precision. Yet at the same time, it was not possible to illustrate the tripartite monism that Jung and Spinoza share, as seen in chapters 1, 5, and 6, without also confronting the issues in Jung's thought that seriously hinder his ability to speak on metaphysics. Without addressing the primacy of the interior and the danger of anti-realism, how can one begin to work with Jung's monism in earnest? Furthermore, how does one handle these issues without effectively killing Jung's metaphysics altogether? No doubt Mark Saban is correct when he states that the "one-sidedness" of Jungian thought, the fact that Jung's introverted bias has been upheld by many Jungians to this day, is untenable (2019, pp. 234–235). But

DOI: 10.4324/9781003516996-8

if the archetypal remains tethered to the inner world, and if we then take the solution chosen by some Jungian scholars and simply diminish the inner world to balance the scales between it and the outer 'banal' world (see Ch. 4, p. 131), then what are we left with besides a Jung who is (rightfully) chastised for his introverted bias, yet who then is no longer in possession of what makes his psychology special? Why then even bother with Jung?

The two branches of this book are inseparable, because only together can they address the problem initially formulated in the introduction and touched upon again in Chapter 4: *how does one abolish the primacy of the interior yet maintain the implicit metaphysics essential to Jung's thought?* While chapters 5 and 6 convey how key Jungian concepts are conceived under a Spinozist lens and how this approach avoids certain philosophical problems encountered under a conventional dual-aspect framework, this metaphysical exercise is moreover meant to demonstrate that we can dispense with Jung's introverted bias while also preserving what Roderick Main calls the 'enchanting/reenchanting' aspects of Jung's psychology (2022). Recall that the introduction listed three general ideas that recur throughout this book. The first idea was *transcendental immanence*, which is characterized by the tripartite monism of matter, psyche, and spirit, and the realization that we move within the Divine. It is the distinction between psyche and spirit that lets Jung free the archetypal from the intrapsychic— in turn, this distinction is what allows us to work with Jung's metaphysics while also being free from a hermetically sealed interiority. Jung's move toward Spinoza is what enables this—Spinoza offers Jung an invitation to come out of the lonely tower that Hans Schmid Guisan lamented he had confined himself to (Beebe & Falzeder, 2013, p. 154). This invitation, however, does not diminish Jung's metaphysics—instead, it bolsters and makes explicit what Jung too often leaves hidden and implied. If I may interject at this point, this book, beyond being an investigation of Jung's reading of Spinoza or the interpretation of Jung as a Spinozist, is an attempt to rethink Jung while allowing Jung to still be *Jung*.

To be sure, this project began very much as 'just' a study of Jung and Spinoza. It is only with the benefit of hindsight that I can see I was wrestling with this deeper question of how to free Jung's metaphysics from the prism of inner versus outer. Perhaps fittingly, within the main argument, this task is first articulated in Chapter 4, in the very heart of the work—to cite

Deleuze, it was only then that I knew I had 'correctly posed the problem' (1966/1988, pp. 29–30). That it took a decade for me to reach that moment is no one's fault but my own.

I was, perhaps, overly optimistic about the amount of ground I was going to be able to cover in this book. There were inevitably topics that I chose to curtail or abandon in favor of heeding pacing and obeying allotted word limits. I could only introduce certain topics as a way to bridge one point of the argument to the next, and I believe some of those issues deserve fuller discussion than I was able to afford here. For instance, the 'problem of evil' was glossed over when discussing the issue of opposites in Chapter 4 (pp. 115–118). A whole chapter could have been dedicated to how Jung and Spinoza both grant evil an existence that is *immanent* to nature—not to mention that they both engage in very frustrating discussions with religious correspondents who decry their opinions (Letters, Vol. 2, 1975, pp. 58–61; Ep. 18–25, 27, CWS I, pp. 354–395)![1] Such a tangent is related to a broader issue that the two principal thinkers of this project treat intensely, and which was the second of the three notions I sketched in the introduction: *affectivity*. The 'affective turn' has become a prevalent trend in the social sciences, humanities, and even the 'hard' sciences.[2] The way Jung handles affectivity, how it necessarily ties the body and the world into his theory of the psyche, is a path worthy of further investigation. I contend that the Spinozist lens helps clarify Jung's potential contributions to this field. Among important insights that Jung and Spinoza can offer is the notion that affectivity is not simply a dichotomy between a negative and positive affect, or sorrow and joy; instead, there are also higher and lower kinds of joy, and ultimately a deeper division between passions and actions (see Ch. 3, 4). Spinoza may even clarify the way in which affects are related to moments of enantiodromia during psychic development. Chantal Jaquet outlines how passive affects can trigger a 'corrective gap' in a person—essentially, by touching the stove and feeling pain, one is impelled to pursue opposite affects that might give them joy, and thus become closer to their essence (2023, pp. 159–167). No doubt there may be utility in applying a 'cartography' of affects to clinical practice. The work of analyst Giles Clark, who recognized the value of a neo-Spinozan approach within the therapy room—may point the way forward on this (2006). And surely a study of affects, both in individuals and in compound modes, in people and whole societies, has something to offer a political theory. How does a Jung that embraces 'outbound connections' change our view of his political writings?

I would be remiss if I did not revisit the work of Harald Atmanspacher. Atmanspacher's articulation of the Pauli–Jung conjecture is indispensable for an understanding of Jung's metaphysics, and his work goes far beyond the critique I raised in chapters 5 and 6. My aim here was merely to treat specific philosophical concerns that have gone unexamined with the dual-aspect monism that Atmanspacher presents. These problems result almost entirely from the conflation of psyche and spirit, and the confusion between the mind and other ideas that ensues. Hence the necessity of my analysis. Beyond this conceptual discussion, Atmanspacher and his colleague Wolfgang Fach have collected a wide array of quantitative research, most notably concerning how different 'exceptional' experiences can be interpreted in a dual-aspect framework (Atmanspacher & Fach, 2013; Atmanspacher & Rickles, 2022, Ch. 3). One thought would be to try and interpret this data via the tripartite monism of spirit, psyche, and matter. How would this approach differ from the conclusions that Atmanspacher and Fach reach from their studies? Could this approach help explain why certain individuals, that is, particular psychological makeups, trend toward different kinds of exceptional experiences? My supposition is that accounting for the middle third, that is, the psyche, could offer what would hopefully be complementary data to both the theoretical and experimental work that Atmanspacher has already established.

In Chapter 4, I made the case that there is a Jung to be found in Spinoza, not just a Spinoza in Jung. To be more specific, I believe Jungian theory can offer something vitally important for Spinoza studies. In Chapter 6, I juxtaposed Spinoza's notions of active joys and blessedness alongside the Jungian theory of individuation and the self, hence the Blessed Self. I believe there is much more to say here that might offer insight into just how we are to pursue active joys and the higher kinds of knowledge. After all, what exactly is an *active joy*? Steven Nadler's secular explanation for what Spinoza has in mind—that, for instance, we know we are made of carbon atoms, and those atoms will still exist after we die—is almost certainly insufficient (see Ch. 6, pp. 193–197). Yet how does one begin to do this enigmatic subject justice without falling back on metaphysical jargon that inevitably becomes too abstract or too 'heady'? It is one thing

to have an intellectual understanding of Spinozism, to rationally apprehend that we move within a transcendental immanence. It is quite another
to *feel* it, and this is absolutely what Jung demands for any metaphysical
project (see Ch. 2, 3). Can one even 'open up' in the way I have chastised
Jung for being so loath to do without also seeking the visceral kind of
knowledge that Jung himself prioritizes? Of course, Spinoza also prioritizes affective knowledge. But it is Jung's work as a psychotherapist that
stresses the importance of the individual's *life* in their search for active
affects. The vignettes of Tiger Woods and George Lucas used in Chapter 6
display *narratives* in the pursuit of active joys and the realization of the
self. A study of Spinoza's theory of affects and knowledge under the lens
of Jungian individuation could do justice to the excellence Spinoza asks
us to seek.

Active joys, visceral knowledge, the self: it all comes back to how
affective knowledge cuts through the madness of the passions so that we
may better understand ourselves. In 'Psychology of the Transference', Jung
writes:

> We are so accustomed to hear that everybody has his "difficulties and
> problems" that we simply accept it as a banal fact, without considering
> what these difficulties and problems really mean. Why is one never satis-
> fied with oneself? Why is one unreasonable? Why is one not always good
> and why must one ever leave a cranny for evil? Why does one some-
> times say too much and sometimes too little? Why does one do foolish
> things which could easily be avoided with a little forethought? What is it
> that is always frustrating us and thwarting our best intentions? Why are
> there people who never notice these things and cannot even admit their
> existence? And finally, why do people in the mass beget the historical
> lunacy of the last thirty years? Why couldn't Pythagoras, twenty-four
> hundred years ago, have established the rule of wisdom once and for all,
> or Christianity have set up the Kingdom of Heaven upon earth?
>
> (CW. 16, 1946/1967, par. 387)

In his final work, the unfinished *Political Treatise*, Spinoza summarizes
how his philosophy deals with the folly of man by saying: "I took great
pains not to laugh at human actions, or mourn them, or curse them, but only
to understand them" (I4, CWS II, p. 505).

These two passages, perhaps more than any other, speak to the alliance of Jung and Spinoza in a way that even their shared vision of God, of eternity and our being within that divinity, cannot. After all, one cannot become aware of transcendental immanence without first understanding oneself. What Jung and Spinoza offer is far more practical than a mighty 'theory of everything' could ever be. They give us a method to refrain from succumbing to those toxins of resentment and bitterness toward those who let us down (including ourselves), a pledge to instead understand the workings of the soul, so that we may tease out from ourselves that which is indeed divine.

The last of the three general concepts I gave in the introduction was *destiny*: to act from our affective power is to act from our very soul. Jung's move toward Spinoza is enabled by his distinction of psyche and spirit. But as the last chapter demonstrates, what this distinction rests upon is an understanding that the sacred part of oneself—whether one calls it essence, the self, or even the soul—is not identical to the mind, but rather is the middle third between mind and body, the eternal essence expressed by both thought and extension, or the psyche that sits between spirit and matter. Now Jung does refer to the psyche as being part of spirit—and this is true insofar as we speak of the language of psychology, that is, the symbolic and the archetypal images. In the Spinozist framework even one's personal psyche should be considered under the attribute of thought, since it is nothing other than the idea one has of oneself (E IIP13S, CWS I, pp. 457–458). And even the true idea we can achieve of our essence—or the self—is, by nature of being an idea, within the realm of thought or spirit (see Ch. 6, pp. 193–197). But this 'Blessed Self' is what sits between our mind and body, and this is why Jung can also speak of the psyche as being a microcosm of the Divine— and Spinoza readily agrees with this, since our singular essence is a part of the absolutely infinite power. It is in this way that the psyche can be conceived both as spirit and as neutral essence (and, really, as body as well— consider Matheron's argument cited in the previous chapter, p. 194). And so in this sense, the original German word that Jung used interchangeably with psyche, *Seele*, becomes quite pertinent again. *Seele* encompasses what we traditionally think of as the 'mind', as well as the soul (CW. 12, 1953, par. 9, footnote). Small wonder then that Jung believed his psychiatric investigations led him to discover things that have very little to do with 'psychology' as it is typically conceived (CW. 8, 1946/1969, pars. 421, 439, 440).

Deleuze states that every great philosopher has a "scream." By scream, Deleuze means that some philosophers create a concept out of sheer exasperation, an urgent need to say something that had yet to be thought through. The scream is expressed and pervades the rest of that thinker's work (1980). Jung may not have considered himself a philosopher, yet his psychology may nonetheless possess a 'scream' of his own. One might ask if it is one of his great theories: the archetypes and the collective unconscious, his work on unconscious complexes, his de-sexualization of libido, the symbol as meaning, or even his monism that this project labored to reconstruct. Yet the one idea of Jung's from which all his other concepts are derived, the one key point that defines his psychology both as an ontology and as a method, is that the psyche is that through which all our experience passes. Everything that Jung conceives begins with his conviction that 'psychic truths' are primary. The urgency to give the psyche its due, to deny anyone who would reduce it to a bundle of nerves or attach it to metaphysical scaffolding, is evident in his thinking from as early on as the talks he gave to his fraternity in his university days, the Zofingia Lectures, and acts as a throughline in his entire body of work. Concepts like psyche, spirit, and psychoid gradually germinated and differentiated from one another throughout his writing, to culminate in his mature thought. All of this, however, rests on the stance that the psyche is both metaphysically irreducible and epistemologically primary (Addison, 2009; Grivet-Shillito, 1999; CW Supplementary Vol. A, 1983).

Meanwhile, Deleuze believes that Spinoza's 'scream' is his conviction that no one has determined in its entirety what the body can do, much less than what the mind can do—in other words, what a thing can do is much more important than stating what something is (E IIIP2S, CWS I, pp. 494–497; 1970/1988, pp. 17–18). What we are left with then is Jung, on the one hand, claiming that the experience of the psyche is irreducible, and Spinoza, on the other, telling us that experimentation is what defines what a thing is. On their own, we may perceive this once more as Jung favoring an introverted perspective, while Spinoza takes the extraverted approach. I submit that this work, if nothing else, blends these two 'screams' into one. The experiencing psyche is primary—but also, these experiences can only be defined by our outbound relations and how those relations affect us. Individuation then becomes, as Saban puts it, an "interminable engagement with the other" (2019, p. 234). But this 'other' is, in fact, the infinity of other things that we encounter during existence, at scales both wildly smaller and vastly greater than we can comprehend. Who can blame Jung for finding that realization horrifying, that we are the eye that does not realize it is bound to nerve and skull, or the worm in blood that is ignorant of the larger organism? We are enmeshed within a sea of endless composition and decomposition. Yet our affective power is uniquely our own and can transcend the assemblage we find ourselves in, and this power can only be discovered through our very navigation of that assemblage. Essence is always found within existence; the second conjunction must occur. What Jung and Spinoza jointly champion is the individual's right to make this passage, to not be consumed by a greater whole nor reduced to bare parts, but to instead see oneself, immutable and unbroken, through the eye of eternity.

Notes

1 All references to 'CWS I' belong to Spinoza (1985) and all references to 'CWS II' belong to Spinoza (2016). These are the two editions edited by Curley.
2 For instance, see Clough and Haley (2007).

References

Acid Horizon. (2023). "The Jung/Deleuze Connection with Acid Horizon, Grant Maxwell, and Friends." www.youtube.com/watch?v=uD_8qbqsl8k (Accessed September 2023).

Addison, A. (2009). "Jung, Vitalism, and 'the Psychoid': A Historical Reconstruction." *Journal of Analytical Psychology*, 54, 123–142.

Adler, G. & Jaffe, A. (1975). *C.G. Jung Letters 2: 1951–1961*. Translated by R. Hull. Princeton: Princeton University Press.

Atmanspacher, H. & Fach, W. (2013). "A Structural–Phenomenological Typology of Mind–Matter Correlations." *Journal of Analytical Psychology*, 58, 219–244.

Atmanspacher, H. & Rickles, D. (2022). *Dual-Aspect Monism and the Deep Structure of Meaning*. London & New York: Routledge.

Beebe, J. & Falzeder, E. (2013). *The Question of Psychological Types: The Correspondence of C.G. Jung and Hans Schmid Guisan, 1915–1916*. Princeton: Princeton University Press.

Clark, G. (2006). "A Spinozan Lens onto the Confusions of Borderline Relations." *Journal of Analytical Psychology*, 51, 67–86.

Clough, P. & Haley, J. (eds.) (2007). *The Affective Turn: Theorizing the Social*. Durham, NC: Duke University Press.

Deleuze, G. (1966/1988). *Bergsonism*. Translated by H. Tomlinson & B. Habberjam. New York: Zone Books.

Deleuze, G. (1980). "Leibniz: Philosophy and the Creation of Concepts," in *The Deleuze Seminars*. Translated and edited by Purdue University. https://deleuze.cla.purdue.edu/seminars/leibniz-philosophy-and-creation-concepts/lecture-01 (Accessed July 2022).

Grivet-Shillito, M. (1999). "Carl Gustav before He Became Jung." Translated by Joseph-David Shesko. *Journal of Analytical Psychology*, 44, 87–100.

Jaquet, C. (2023). *Time, Duration and Eternity in Spinoza*. Translated by E. Aldieri. Edinburgh: Edinburgh University Press.

Jung, C.G. (1946). "On the Nature of the Psyche," in *The Structure and Dynamics of the Psyche*, 2nd ed. Translated by R. Hull. Collected Works of C.G. Jung, Vol. 8. Princeton: Princeton University Press, 1969.

Jung, C.G. (1946). "Psychology of the Transference," in *The Practice of Psychotherapy*, 2nd ed. Translated by R. Hull. Collected Works of C.G. Jung, Vol. 16. Princeton: Princeton University Press, 1967.

Jung, C.G. (1953). "Individual Dream Symbolism in Relation to Alchemy," in *Psychology and Alchemy*, 2nd ed. Translated by R. Hull. Collected Works of C.G. Jung, Vol. 12. Princeton: Princeton University Press, 1968.

Jung, C.G. (1983). *The Zofingia Lectures*. Translated by J. Heurck. Collected Works of C.G. Jung, Supplementary Vol. A. Princeton: Princeton University Press, 1983.

Main, R. (2022). *Breaking the Spell of Disenchantment: Mystery, Meaning, and Metaphysics in the Work of C.G. Jung*. The Zurich Lecture Series: Volume 8. Asheville, NC: Chiron Publications.

Maxwell, G. (2022). *Integration and Difference: Constructing a Mythical Dialectic*. London & New York: Routledge.

Saban, M. (2019). *'Two Souls Alas': Jung's Two Personalities and the Making of Analytical Psychology*. The Zurich Lecture Series: Volume 2. Asheville, NC: Chiron Publications.

Spinoza, B. (1985). *The Collected Works of Spinoza*, Vol. I, Edited and translated by Edwin Curley. Princeton: Princeton University Press.

Spinoza, B. (2016). *The Collected Works of Spinoza*, Vol. II, Edited and translated by Edwin Curley. Princeton: Princeton University Press.

Index

For Product Safety Concerns and Information please contact our EU
representative GPSR@taylorandfrancis.com
Taylor & Francis Verlag GmbH, Kaufingerstraße 24, 80331 München, Germany

www.ingramcontent.com/pod-product-compliance
Lightning Source LLC
Chambersburg PA
CBHW070324270326
41926CB00017B/3752